M359 Block 3
UNDERGRADUATE COMPUTING
Relational databases: theory and practice

The database language SQL

This publication forms part of an Open University course M359 *Relational databases: theory and practice*. Details of this and other Open University courses can be obtained from the Student Registration and Enquiry Service, The Open University, PO Box 197, Milton Keynes MK7 6BJ, United Kingdom: tel. +44 (0)845 300 60 90, email general-enquiries@open.ac.uk

Alternatively, you may visit the Open University website at http://www.open.ac.uk where you can learn more about the wide range of courses and packs offered at all levels by The Open University.

To purchase a selection of Open University course materials visit http://www.ouw.co.uk, or contact Open University Worldwide, Michael Young Building, Walton Hall, Milton Keynes MK7 6AA, United Kingdom for a brochure: tel. +44 (0)1908 858793; fax +44 (0)1908 858787; email ouw-customer-services@open.ac.uk

Sybase, iAnywhere and SQL Anywhere are trademarks of Sybase, Inc.; Java is a trademark of Sun Microsystems, Inc. Other product and company names may appear in the M359 course material. Rather than use a trademark symbol with every occurrence of a trademarked name, we use the names only in an editorial fashion and to the benefit of the trademark owner, with no intention of infringement of the trademark.

The Open University
Walton Hall, Milton Keynes
MK7 6AA

First published 2007

Copyright © 2007 The Open University

All rights reserved. No part of this publication may be reproduced, stored in a retrieval system, transmitted or utilised in any form or by any means, electronic, mechanical, photocopying, recording or otherwise, without written permission from the publisher or a licence from the Copyright Licensing Agency Ltd. Details of such licences (for reprographic reproduction) may be obtained from the Copyright Licensing Agency Ltd, Saffron House, 6–10 Kirby Street, London EC1N 8TS; website http://www.cla.co.uk.

Open University course materials may also be made available in electronic formats for use by students of the University. All rights, including copyright and related rights and database rights, in electronic course materials and their contents are owned by or licensed to The Open University, or otherwise used by The Open University as permitted by applicable law.

In using electronic course materials and their contents you agree that your use will be solely for the purposes of following an Open University course of study or otherwise as licensed by The Open University or its assigns.

Except as permitted above you undertake not to copy, store in any medium (including electronic storage or use in a website), distribute, transmit or retransmit, broadcast, modify or show in public such electronic materials in whole or in part without the prior written consent of The Open University or in accordance with the Copyright, Designs and Patents Act 1988.

Edited and designed by The Open University.

Typeset by S&P Enterprises (rfod) Limited, Glos.

Printed and bound in the United Kingdom by Martins the Printers, Berwick-upon-Tweed.

ISBN 978 0 7492 1575 0

CONTENTS

1	Introduction	6
	1.1 A brief history of SQL	6
	1.2 Outline of this block	9
2	Retrieval using simple queries	10
	2.1 Basic queries: `SELECT` and `FROM`	11
	2.2 Data types	17
	2.3 The `WHERE` clause	28
	2.4 Using joins	35
	2.5 The `GROUP BY` clause	44
	2.6 The `HAVING` clause	49
	2.7 The `ORDER BY` clause	52
	2.8 Constructing SQL queries	54
	2.9 Summary	58
3	Retrieval using composite queries	60
	3.1 The UNION operator	60
	3.2 Subqueries	65
	3.3 Outer references and correlated subqueries	67
	3.4 Quantifiers	69
	3.5 Subqueries versus joins	74
	3.6 Subqueries in the `FROM` clause	75
	3.7 Summary	80
4	Use of NULL	82
	4.1 Basic queries involving NULL	82
	4.2 Conditions involving NULL	86
	4.3 Outer joins	89
	4.4 NULL and referential integrity	91
	4.5 NULL and default values	93
	4.6 Summary	93
5	Database definition and population	95
	5.1 An extension to the University model	95
	5.2 Table definition and deletion	96
	5.3 Inserting and updating data	100
	5.4 Defining constraints	109
	5.5 Use of domains in SQL	119

5.6	Modifying tables	121
5.7	Constraint evaluation	126
5.8	Defining and using indexes	128
5.9	Summary	130

6 Database management and administration — 132

6.1	Views	132
6.2	Sharing data	143
6.3	Table definition	145
6.4	Access control	148
6.5	Using views to limit access	154
6.6	Summary	158

7 SQL control statements — 160

7.1	SQL routines	160
7.2	Temporary tables	170
7.3	Cursors for row-by-row processing	171
7.4	Triggers	178
7.5	Transaction management	183
7.6	Summary	192

Block summary	193
Solutions to Exercises	194
Index	221

M359 COURSE TEAM

This course was produced by the following team (affiliated to The Open University, unless otherwise stated):

Course team

Kevin Waugh   Course Team Chair and Author
Ian Cooke   Author
Mike Newton   Author
Judith Segal   Author
Steven Self   Author
Alistair Willis   Author
Kay Bromley   Academic Editor
Ralph Greenwell   Course Manager and Accessibility Consultant

External assessor

Barry Lowden   University of Essex

Critical readers

Sue Barrass
Peter Blachford
Terry Burbidge
Pauline Butcher
Pauline Curtis
Hugh Darwen
Ivan Dunn
Gillian Mills
Ron Rogerson

LTS Media team

Andrew Seddon   Media Project Manager
Steve Rycroft   Editor
Andrew Whitehead   Designer and Graphic Artist
Phillip Howe   Compositor
Kamy Yazdanjoo   Software Developer
Sue Stavert   Technical Testing Team

Thanks are due to the Desktop Publishing Unit of the Faculty of Mathematics and Computing.

1 Introduction

In *Block 1*, you were introduced to various concepts associated with database management. In particular, in *Block 1*, Section 3 we described a processing architecture that distinguishes tasks associated with database management (defining the structure of the data and controlling access to it) from tasks associated with user processes (retrieving and updating the data). The processing architecture uses a data definition language (DDL) to define the database schema and implement controls on the access to a database for retrieval or updating. The architecture also uses a data manipulation language (DML) to retrieve and update data. The DML and/or the DDL may be embedded in an application process to allow an application to access particular data in a database, or to be used interactively so that a user writes DML statements at a terminal for immediate execution.

SQL (Structured Query Language) is a language that is designed to carry out these tasks for relational databases; it has become the standard relational database language. SQL has DDL and DML components, and so provides a single interface to the database. It can be used both as an embedded language for application processes and interactively as a query language. It is also intended to be relatively easy to learn and use.

In this block, we will introduce you to SQL, and demonstrate how SQL is used to carry out data management tasks. We will show you how to write simple queries, and how to build up complex queries with control flow tools. We will also illustrate the tools within SQL that allow SQL queries to be embedded in other application processes. For the rest of this section, we will examine some of the background to the development of SQL so that you can appreciate its role in database management and, in particular, the SQL Anywhere DBMS that you will use for the practical activities.

1.1 A brief history of SQL

SQL originated in the mid-1970s as part of a research project of the computer company, IBM. The purpose of this project was to investigate the feasibility of the relational ideas of Edgar (Ted) Codd, an employee of IBM at that time. A database management system called System R was developed to organise and control the relational database. SQL was developed as a database language both for embedding in application programs and for use as an interactive query language. The name first given to the language was Structured English Query Language (because the syntax was intended to be more readable than that of relational languages such as the relational calculus or relational algebras used at the time), and this was abbreviated to SEQUEL. The name was later changed to Structured Query Language, and it is now referred to by just the initials SQL. 'SQL' is therefore usually pronounced as 'ess-cue-el', but because of the history of the language, many practitioners refer to it as 'sequel'.

After the success of this research project, IBM and many other companies developed DBMSs based on the use of SQL. We refer to such a DBMS as an **SQL implementation**. There are now many SQL implementations available (just as there are many C++ compilers, for example); **SQL Anywhere**, the DBMS provided for your computing activities, is only one such implementation.

1 Introduction

SQL is a growing language, with new features being added as requirements evolve. IBM's work dominated the early developments, to the extent that each company developing an SQL implementation would ensure that their DBMS was similar in many respects to IBM's version. But different companies had different ideas on what was important to users, so each DBMS and the SQL it supported differed in some way. However, many customers wanted a version of SQL that was the same for different DBMSs, and so an International Standard for SQL was developed by the International Organization for Standardization (ISO) in conjunction with the American National Standards Institute.

The first International Standard for SQL was published in 1987. It is referred to as **SQL:1987**. The main aim in developing this initial standard was to ensure application program portability, so that a program written in, for example, C++, which used standard embedded SQL for use with one SQL implementation should work in exactly the same way when used with another SQL implementation. The resulting specification of SQL included a DDL and a DML for a basic core of SQL, which was common to many SQL implementations at that time. There are many DBMSs available which conform to most of the 1987 Standard; for these DBMSs, any SQL statement that is part of the standard also behaves in the way that the standard specifies.

As a result of including only the common core of existing implementations in the SQL:1987 Standard, there were many DBMS capabilities that were not included. In particular, it lacked some of the features of the relational model, especially primary key and foreign key constraints. To rectify this specific deficiency, a revision of the SQL Standard was published in 1989, entitled *Database Language SQL with Integrity Enhancement*. This version, referred to as **SQL:1989**, specified the constraint definitions that could be used, but otherwise it does not provide any additional capabilities for defining or accessing data. Although the approach to developing SQL:1987 ensured that there were many implementations conforming to the SQL Standard, the constraints specified in SQL:1989 were a new development not based on the SQL implementations available at that time. Most SQL implementations now support these constraints to some extent.

The introduction of constraints in 1989 still left many deficiencies in the SQL Standard, including another basic feature of the relational model – domains. Further development of SQL by ISO and ANSI resulted in domains and many other new capabilities being specified in another International Standard, which was published in 1992 and referred to as **SQL:1992**; it is also known as **SQL2** and was published by **ISO** as ISO 9075:1992.

A further SQL Standard was released in 1999 (known as **SQL:1999**) adding triggers, which allow procedures to be executed when tables are updated. The most recent release, **SQL:2003**, was produced in late 2003 and introduces many XML-related features.

We will introduce you to many of these features in this block. As you can see, many aspects of the current SQL Standard have evolved and have been introduced over time, rather than from the outset.

SQL dialects

Although features like triggers were not introduced to the SQL Standard until 1999, they had previously been incorporated into many SQL implementations. Each SQL implementation contains features that the vendor provides in addition to the SQL Standard, called **extensions**. Each implementation of SQL is called a **dialect**. As database vendors introduce new functionality to their SQL implementations, the dialects are moving further apart. However, the central core of the SQL language is becoming more standardised. Since 1992, subsets of the SQL Standard have been identified as the core of the language which is implemented by majority of vendors. A subset of SQL:1992 is classified as Entry level. **Entry level SQL** is essentially the same as SQL:1989, ensuring that the previous versions of SQL remain compatible with the new one. Most implementations provide Entry level SQL2 compatibility and many features of SQL2 onwards.

So there are many dialects in each of the several SQL Standards, and each SQL implementation may support all or part of the various SQL Standards. In this course, we consider the general principles of SQL that you should be able to use with most implementations, and we base our teaching on the current International Standard. SQL:2003 defines a set of features called **Core SQL** that a vendor must implement to claim **conformance** with the SQL:2003 Standard. The SQL Anywhere DBMS provided for your practical activities conforms very closely to the SQL:2003 Standard; that is, SQL Anywhere implements almost all Core SQL and processes most SQL statements in the same way as other SQL implementations.

Caveat: As with all implementations of SQL, the behaviour of SQL Anywhere occasionally differs from the Standard. This is in order to maintain **backward compatibility** with previous implementations of SQL Anywhere. Where the SQL Anywhere implementation differs from the Standard, we will make this explicit in the notes.

EXERCISE 1.1

(a) Identify the different SQL Standards.

(b) Name at least one SQL implementation.

Non-SQL DBMS functions

As well as differences arising from the evolution of SQL, a second reason for the differences between SQL implementations is that SQL is not intended to support all the functions of a DBMS. Those functions of a DBMS that are not specified by an SQL Standard may be implemented in a DBMS as its implementor chooses. For example, there is no storage DDL (as described in *Block 1*) specified in any SQL Standard, so a variety of file storage and access methods can be found in different implementations. Another example of implementation dependence concerns the use of interactive SQL, where although the effect of any SQL statement may be defined by an SQL Standard, both the way a statement may be input and the formatting and control of output are generally different for each implementation.

In line with our aim of focusing on the general principles of SQL supported by many implementations, we shall not examine such non-SQL functions in detail. While you obviously have to know how to use such features of SQL Anywhere to do your practical work, that is not considered an essential part of the teaching of this course and we shall always point out any aspect of your work with SQL Anywhere which is an implementation feature rather than being based on an SQL Standard.

SQL and the relational model

As we have mentioned, the original development of SQL was based upon the concepts of relational theory described in *Block 2*. Although many of the relational concepts are represented in SQL in some way, SQL does not adhere strictly to the relational model described in *Block 2*. In particular, SQL uses different terminology. For example, a 'relation' and an 'attribute' are known as a '**table**' and a '**column**' respectively in SQL, while the relational 'tuples' are known as '**rows**' in SQL. Tables are defined in a logical schema and can be simply manipulated directly (there is no external schema); a table that has stored data is known as a **base table** and a table that is derived from base tables is known as a **view**.

Since there are some variations in the concepts and the terminology between SQL and relational models, our approach in this block is to present SQL in an independent way. We will refer to the relational theory only when it may help understanding or prevent misunderstanding.

1.2 Outline of this block

This block is devoted to various aspects of SQL. Section 2 is a practical introduction to the basics of the SQL language. It deals with the processes of retrieving data from a database. In this section you will learn about SQL queries: how they are specified in formal syntax and how they are logically processed to produce their final result. It begins with a consideration of what we term **simple queries**. Section 3 extends the ideas to **composite queries** involving unions and subqueries.

Section 4 discusses NULL – a method of dealing with cases where the data for a column might be unavailable or inappropriate.

Section 5 discusses how to define database tables and populate them with data using SQL. It examines the specification and definition of data to be stored in the database, the construction of constraints to maintain database integrity, and the SQL environment in general. Section 6 discusses administrative issues such as restricting access to data and the roles of different users of the DBMS.

Finally, Section 7 introduces more complex control in SQL. We discuss how SQL can be used within application programs and how to construct routines for storage and execution by a DBMS. Transactions are also considered in this section.

The study of SQL in this block is almost entirely based on the Core SQL, as implemented by the SQL Anywhere DBMS you use for the practical activities. However, our coverage should not be considered comprehensive, even of this subset of the Standard. The SQL Standard is very large and cannot be covered in a single block. In this course we shall rather concentrate upon the main principles.

You have already been introduced to some of the elements of SQL in *Block 1*. In this block we shall use two databases, called University and Hospital. These are implementations of the tables in the University and Hospital databases which are shown on the *Database Cards*.

As we introduce SQL statements, we shall give an outline of the syntax needed to do the activities and answer the exercises. However, the statements often have a richer syntax than we use in the course: the SQL Anywhere online documentation contains the complete description of this implementation of SQL. You should also refer to the online documentation in the first instance if you are unclear about the behaviour of the SQL we discuss in this block. However, you will not be assessed beyond what appears in this block.

After completing your study of this block, you should be able to do the following.

1   Use SQL to retrieve data from a database.
2   Update a database.
3   Describe the processing model for a given SQL statement.
4   Create, modify and remove base tables and views.
5   Apply constraints to data in a database.
6   Describe the main implementation issues for a DBMS.

2 Retrieval using simple queries

In this section and Section 3, you will learn about using the DML component of SQL to retrieve data from a database. Data is retrieved using a type of SQL statement known as a **query statement** which, for simplicity, we shall refer to as a **query**. Queries, and other kinds of SQL statements, use a basic building block referred to as a **query specification**. A query specification consists of (at most) the following five **clauses**:

```
SELECT <select list>
FROM <table list>
WHERE <search condition>
GROUP BY <grouping column list>
HAVING <search condition>
```

> `SELECT`, `FROM`, `WHERE`, `GROUP BY` and `HAVING` are five of the many **keywords** used by SQL. Keywords appear capitalised in this text.
>
> Throughout this block, angled brackets are used to indicate points at which appropriate identifiers or expressions should be inserted.
>
> Note that we use 'statement' or 'query' to refer to a piece of executable SQL; the individual parts are *clauses*.

For some queries, a single query specification is the complete query statement. In this course, such queries using no more than these five clauses are referred to as **simple queries**, as opposed to **composite queries** which will be dealt with in Section 3. In this section, our main aim is to teach you how to write and run simple queries.

Some notes on the activities

In order to enable you to carry out the exercises and activities in this section, we have provided you with two databases: one contains the University data and the other the Hospital data. When carrying out exercises or activities, you will need to apply queries to the appropriate database. The exercises and activities state which database you should use, although it will generally be clear from the tables that you are querying. The *Software Guide* explains how to switch between the various databases.

Generally in activities, we will give you an SQL query to execute. We then either discuss the results of that query or ask you to determine what the query is intended to mean. For example, in Activity 2.1 we ask you to execute the following query in the Hospital database.

```
SELECT *
FROM patient
```
patient_data

So that we can refer back to the query for discussion, most queries in the text are labelled: in this case, the query is called **patient_data**. We have also provided a file of statements that you can use, so that you will not need to type in each statement; the *Software Guide* describes how to use the filed statements. However, you will probably find that with short queries like the one above, you can type in the statement directly quite quickly.

The activities will progressively introduce you to the retrieval facilities offered by SQL. When you have seen several examples of SQL queries in action, we will ask you to carry out exercises in which you will be required to formulate your own SQL queries.

2 Retrieval using simple queries

Naming conventions: SQL table names and relational headings

The University and Hospital databases that you will use in this block implement the same data that you used in *Block 2* while studying relational concepts. In the SQL implementations, however, a different naming convention is used for table and column names. The relational headings capitalise each word, to give table names such as **ConsistsOf** and column names such as **StaffNo** and **TeamCode**. The SQL uses a convention whereby all the words are presented in lower case and separated by underscores. Therefore, the **ConsistsOf** relation, which has relational headings **StaffNo** and **TeamCode**, is implemented in the Hospital database by a table called `consists_of`, which has columns named `staff_no` and `team_code`.

2.1 Basic queries: SELECT and FROM

Every query for retrieving data from a database must contain at least a `SELECT` clause and a `FROM` clause. The first activity in this block is an example containing only these two clauses.

ACTIVITY 2.1

Using the Hospital database, run the following query.

```
SELECT *
FROM treatment
```
treatment_data

Remember that a semicolon is required by SQL Anywhere to terminate statements.

You should find that this produces a table which contains all the data from the `treatment` table as shown on the *Hospital Database Card* (we will look at the processing of this query in more detail shortly). So we can express this query in English as follows:

> List all the data about all the treatments represented in the `treatment` table.

This English expression of the query explicitly mentions the particular table that contains the information that we are interested in (`treatment`).

For all the queries in this block, we will show the SQL keywords in upper case, and table and column names in lower case. This is only a convention; SQL is not case sensitive for keywords and table names. There are some additional considerations for matching strings, which we will look at later in this section.

When querying a database, we normally wish to find out something about the *world*, or more precisely, the **domain of discourse**. This is independent of how the database (which *represents* the world) is structured. We call this a **request**, or **problem statement**. A problem statement should contain no information about how the database is structured. A problem statement for the query **treatment_data** might be as follows:

Recall the discussion of *meaning* in *Block 1*, Section 1.9.

> Which patients have been given treatments, and what are the staff number of the administering doctor, the starting date and the reason for each of those treatments?

The problem statement does not make any mention of how the data in the specific database has been structured, and so does not refer to the columns or tables in the database.

Here, there are three different concepts, which you should be able to distinguish.

1 A *query*, which is written in SQL and can be executed to produce a table.
2 The *query expressed in English*, which is written in English and describes which tables (and possibly which columns) should be used to obtain the result of the query.
3 A *request* or *problem statement*, which is written in English and does not make reference to specific tables or columns in a database.

In this discussion, we have started from a query and derived a problem statement from it. When using databases, it is more usual to start with a request and then formulate a query to produce a table, which can then be used to answer that request. We say that *a query answers a request* if the SQL query generates a table that contains precisely the information that the user needs to answer his or her request.

In the activities and exercises in this section and Section 3, you will use mainly English expressions of queries so that you can become comfortable with interpreting and writing SQL queries. In Section 2.8, we will look at techniques to help translate a problem statement into a query.

EXERCISE 2.1

Is the following a query, a query expressed in English, or a request/problem statement?

> List the name of every patient represented in the **patient** table whose height is greater than 170.0 cm.

Justify your answer.

> Rerun the query **treatment_data**.

There are a number of points regarding the query **treatment_data** that you should note.

▶ Perhaps the most important thing that the example illustrates is that *the result of the query is a table*. This is true for all SQL queries: no matter how many clauses they contain or how complicated they are, they always result in a table. A result consisting of only one data value is still a table, with one row and one column. If there are no rows that satisfy the given request, the result is an empty table with no rows.

▶ The asterisk, *, in the **SELECT** clause is a shorthand way of referring to all the columns in the table. You can check what the columns are from the *Hospital Database Card*, and see that **treatment_data** is therefore equivalent to:

```
SELECT staff_no, patient_id, start_date, reason
FROM treatment
```

2 Retrieval using simple queries

If you try to run this query, you should receive the following table (although the rows may appear in a different order):

staff_no	patient_id	start_date	reason
131	p07	2007-02-09	marrow infection
462	p08	2007-02-03	high temperature
156	p09	2007-01-01	low temperature
156	p15	2007-02-05	low temperature
389	p31	2007-01-09	pain relief
517	p37	2006-12-05	pain relief
462	p38	2006-12-27	inflamed joints
603	p38	2007-01-01	low temperature
603	p38	2007-02-01	pain relief
200	p39	2006-03-11	septicaemia
603	p39	2007-01-01	high grade fever
110	p68	2007-01-11	vomiting
603	p88	2006-12-29	high grade fever
178	p89	2006-12-23	pain relief
389	p98	2007-02-05	inflamed joints

Note that in general, SQL does not display a table with the rows in any particular order. In this case, we have shown the rows in ascending order of **patient_id**, but when you run the query, the order of rows may be different. We will see how to display the rows in a particular order in Section 2.7.

Often we do not want to see all the columns in a table. We can use the **SELECT** clause to show only the columns in which we are interested.

➢ Run the following query.

    SELECT staff_no, patient_id
    FROM treatment

treatment_columns

The displayed table contains only two of the four columns in the **treatment** table, namely, **staff_no** and **patient_id**. Notice that these columns are shown in the order as specified in the query, rather than in the order in which they appear when the whole **treatment** table is displayed (when using the asterisk, columns are shown in the order in which they are defined for the table). Therefore, the query can be expressed in English as:

> List the staff number and patient identifier of each administered treatment represented in the **treatment** table.

The **treatment_columns** query shows that we can use the **SELECT** clause to specify the names of the columns we want in the final table and the order in which we want them to be displayed. In comparing the effect of the **SELECT** clause of **treatment_columns** with that of **treatment_data**, we can see that the logical processing of the **treatment_columns** query's `SELECT` clause results in a selection, or a vertical slicing, of the columns of the intermediate table *and* a reordering of the columns into the specified sequence to give the final table.

➢ Now run the following query.

```
SELECT patient_id
FROM treatment
```

patient_id

This will result in a table containing only the `patient_id` column from the `treatment` table. The query can be expressed in English as:

List the patient identifier of every patient represented in the `treatment` table.

The result of this query answers the request:

What are the patient identifiers of all the patients currently in the hospital?

You should see that the displayed table contains duplicate rows because some patients (for example, the patient whose identifier is p38) have received multiple treatments.

➢ Now run the following query.

```
SELECT DISTINCT patient_id
FROM treatment
```

distinct_patient_id

The final table resulting from running **distinct_patient_id** contains the same patient identifiers as that of the **patient_id** query but with no duplicates. This demonstrates the use of the `DISTINCT` operator in a `SELECT` clause; in general, its purpose is to prevent any duplicate rows occurring in the final table.

The `SELECT` (`DISTINCT`) and `FROM` clauses are comparable with the *project* operator in the relational algebra.

Recall from Block 2, Section 2.1 that relations do not contain duplicate rows. While the relational operator *project* always returns a relation, the table returned by `SELECT` in SQL can contain duplicate rows, unless `DISTINCT` is used.

The logical processing model

An SQL query aims to express what data is required, without considering how the DBMS may actually retrieve the data from the particular file structures it uses to store the data. However, in examining the role of the different clauses of an SQL statement, a processing *model* can help you understand the effect of different forms of SQL statement. The purpose of such a model is to provide you with a simple way to work out the result of any statement, without having to be concerned with details of how it could be executed in practice. This result will be the same as that produced by a DBMS, which has to take account of how a statement can be processed in a real computer system. So the output of the processing model is logically equivalent to processing by a DBMS, and so we refer to this kind of model as a **logical processing model**.

The logical processing of a query statement always begins with the `FROM` clause. The logical processing ignores details of how to retrieve any stored data required by the query and simply assumes that the table named in the `FROM` clause is available. The model defines a clause by clause process for obtaining the final table returned by the query.

We will build up the processing model over the course of this block, as you learn more SQL constructions. To start, we consider the logical processing of the query **treatment_data**. The `treatment` table given in the `FROM` clause is the **initial table**, and is processed first: it is treated as the input to the processing carried out by the `FROM` clause. The output of this step is an **intermediate table**, which is a copy of the whole `treatment` table. We call this output an intermediate table because it forms the input to the next clause.

In this case, the intermediate table forms the input to the only other clause in this query, the SELECT clause. In processing the SELECT clause, the columns specified in that clause (for this query, the asterisk means all columns of the treatment table) are all simply copied to a further table, which is the **final table**, giving the result of the SQL query.

We summarise the logical processing model for the SELECT and FROM clauses in Figure 2.1.

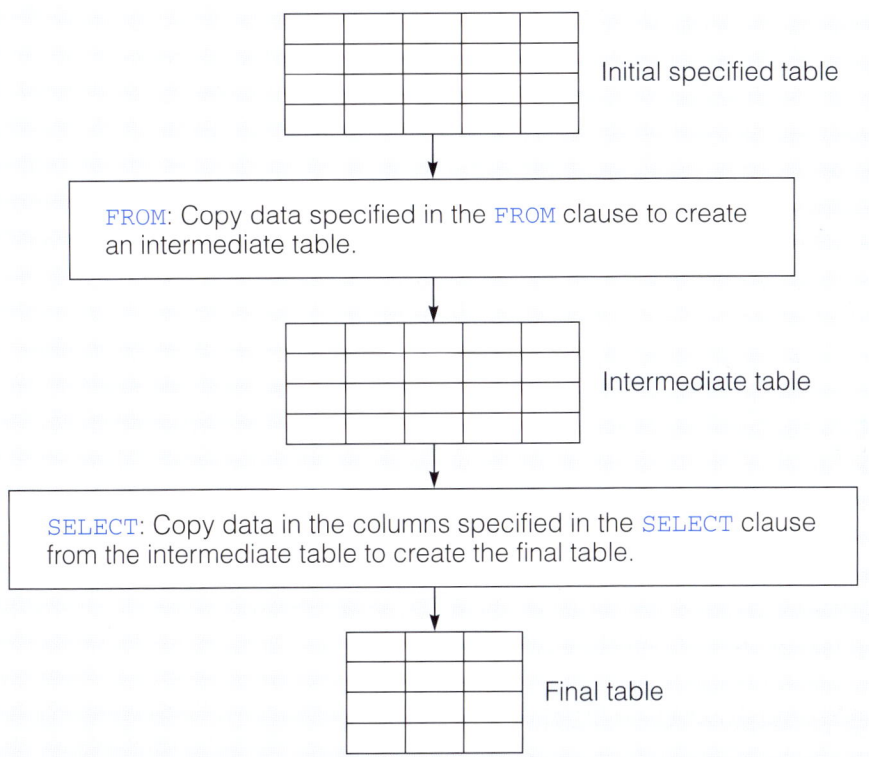

Figure 2.1   Logical processing model for elementary SELECT and FROM clauses

We can use the logical processing model illustrated in Figure 2.1 to understand the logical processing of **treatment_data**.

▶ First, the FROM clause takes the initial specified table (treatment in the case of **treatment_data**) and produces an intermediate table, which in this case is a copy of the whole treatment table.

▶ Second, processing the SELECT clause takes the intermediate table as input and copies the specified columns (in this case, all the columns, as defined by SELECT *) into a final table.

For **treatment_data**, the final table will of course have the same number of columns as the intermediate table because we have used SELECT *, but for queries in general the output from the SELECT clause will have fewer columns than its input.

We can extend the processing model described in Figure 2.1 to take into account the possible use of DISTINCT. The processing model for queries using DISTINCT in the SELECT clause is illustrated in Figure 2.2.

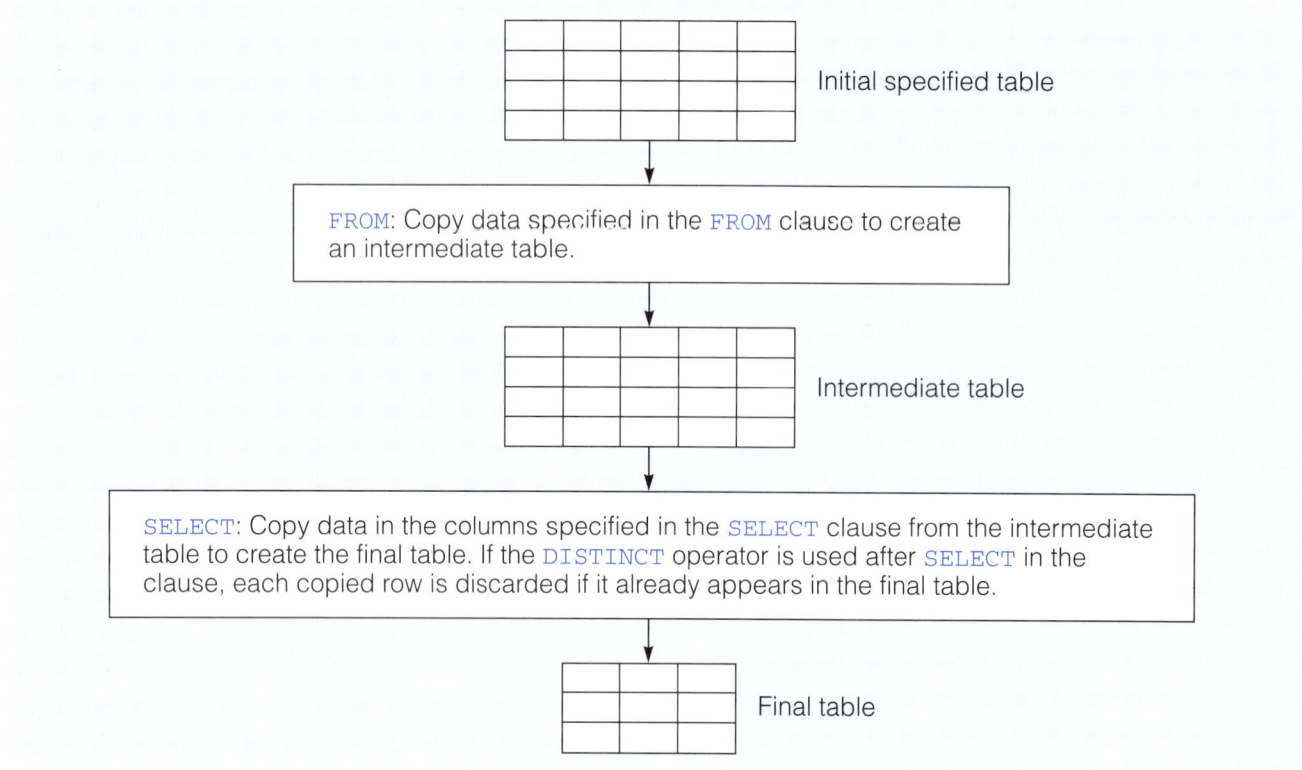

Figure 2.2 Logical processing model for elementary SELECT and FROM clauses with DISTINCT

We can examine the logical processing of **distinct_patient_id** using the model shown in Figure 2.2.

▶ First, processing the FROM clause results in an intermediate table which is a copy of the whole treatment table, as for **treatment_data**.

▶ Second, processing the SELECT clause takes the intermediate table as input and copies the specified columns (in this case, just patient_id) into the final table, omitting any repeated values.

Unlike the final table in Figure 2.1, the final table in Figure 2.2 contains fewer rows than the intermediate table, illustrating that including DISTINCT within a SELECT clause will generally result in a smaller table. Of course, if the intermediate table contained no duplicates, then the final table would contain the same number of rows as the intermediate table.

You may be wondering why the FROM clause is necessary if it simply creates an intermediate table that is identical to its input table. This processing of the FROM clause will become clear in Section 2.4, when we discuss queries that use more than one input table.

EXERCISE 2.2

Given base tables as shown on the *University Database Card*, write and run queries that may be expressed in English as:

(a) Display the whole of the **staff** table.

(b) List the name and staff number of every member of staff represented in the **staff** table.

When formulating these queries be careful to use an underscore character, not a hyphen, in column names like **staff_number**.

2 Retrieval using simple queries

(c) List, without duplication, the staff numbers of every staff member who tutors some students as represented in the `tutors` table, together with the student identifier of each student they tutor.

Describe the logical processing, clause by clause, of the query given in the solution to part (c), and explain your `SELECT` clause.

This logical processing sequence is an example of the use of the logical processing model for SQL, and it provides a way in which an SQL statement may be analysed and understood. Note that it is only a *logical* processing model: a particular DBMS will not process an SQL statement in exactly the way described by the model. Also note that the order in which clauses are logically processed (`FROM` followed by `SELECT`) is different from the order in which they are written (`SELECT` followed by `FROM`).

While these examples may seem simplistic, the benefit of thinking of SQL statements in this way will become apparent as queries become more complex. As you learn more about SQL, we shall extend this logical processing model to take account of more features. A full account of the SQL logical processing model is beyond the scope of this course, but we shall extend the model to cover those aspects of SQL that we deal with in this block.

2.2 Data types

Every entry within a column must have the same **data type**; a data type is a set of possible values that an entry may take. For example, in the `ward` table in the Hospital database, all the entries in the `number_of_beds` column should be whole numbers. SQL allows **predefined data types** (that is, built into SQL) and **user-defined data types**. In Section 5, you will see how to define your own data types, but for now we will consider the SQL predefined data types; user-defined data types are defined in terms of the SQL predefined types.

Compare with relational *domains*, which you met in Block 2, Section 2.2.

Some of the SQL predefined data types are given in Figure 2.3. You will be given the types of data in the tables when you need them. Several of the data types have minimum or maximum values, or a parameter defining precision: we will discuss these more fully in Section 5 of this block.

Data type	Description
Character string types	
`CHARACTER(len)` (or `CHAR(len)`)	Fixed-length character strings of length `len`
`VARCHAR(max_length)`	Variable-length character strings, up to length `max_length`
Numeric data types	
`INTEGER` (or `INT`)	Integer numbers
`SMALLINT`	Small integer numbers
`BIGINT`	Big integer numbers
`DECIMAL(p, s)` (or `DEC(p, s)`)	Decimal numbers containing at least `p` digits altogether, with `s` digits after the decimal point

`NUMERIC(p, s)`	Decimal numbers containing exactly **p** digits altogether, with **s** digits after the decimal point
`FLOAT`	Single precision floating-point number
`REAL`	Single precision floating-point number
`DOUBLE PRECISION`	Double precision floating-point number
Bit string types	
`BIT(len)`	Fixed-length bit string of length **len**
`BIT VARYING(len)`	Variable-length bit string up to length **len**
Date–time types	
`DATE`	Calendar date
`TIME(p)`	Clock time of precision **p**
`TIMESTAMP(p)`	Date and time of precision **p**
`INTERVAL`	Time interval
Large object string types (but see note below for SQL Anywhere)	
`CHARACTER LARGE OBJECT(size)` (or `CLOB(size)`)	Character data of size up to **size**
`BINARY LARGE OBJECT(size)` (or `BLOB(size)`)	Binary data of size up to **size**

Figure 2.3   The SQL predefined data types

> SQL Anywhere implements all the data types defined by the SQL Standard. However, there is a small syntactic difference for large object string types. In SQL Anywhere, you should use
>
> `LONG VARCHAR` and `LONG BINARY`
>
> rather than `CHARACTER LARGE OBJECT` and `BINARY LARGE OBJECT`. In addition, SQL Anywhere does not require the maximum size of the object to be made explicit in the declaration; an object of type long varchar or long binary can be of arbitrary length up to the SQL Anywhere upper limit of 2 GB.

The maximum size of the large object string types is implementation specific, but in general, the maximum size is very large compared to the other data types. The given size can be appended with **K**, **M** or **G** to indicate that the size is in kilobytes, megabytes or gigabytes, respectively. For example, if the database were to contain an image of each staff member requiring up to 100 kilobytes, those objects would have type `BINARY LARGE OBJECT(100K)` (or `BLOB(100K)`).

For the `TIME` and `TIMESTAMP` data types, the precision **p** is the number of digits in the fraction of a second. If **p** is not specified, the default is zero.

Some of the implementation details for the other data types in SQL Anywhere are given in Figure 2.4.

> A value of type `CHAR` is treated as `VARCHAR`, so spaces are not added.
>
> A character string may be up to 32 767 characters in length.
>
> A `SMALLINT` uses 2 bytes of storage, giving values of -2^{15} to $2^{15}-1$, or $-32\,768$ to $+32\,767$.
>
> An `INTEGER` uses 4 bytes of storage, giving values of -2^{31} to $2^{31}-1$, or $-2\,147\,483\,648$ to $+2\,147\,483\,647$.
>
> A `BIGINT` uses 8 bytes of storage, giving values of -2^{63} to $2^{63}-1$, or $-9\,223\,372\,036\,854\,775\,808$ to $+9\,223\,372\,036\,854\,775\,807$.
>
> A `REAL` uses 4 bytes of storage, giving values of -3.402823×10^{38} to 3.402823×10^{38}. Values may be subject to rounding-off errors beyond the sixth significant figure.
>
> A `DOUBLE PRECISION` uses 8 bytes of storage, giving values of $2.22507385850721 \times 10^{-308}$ to $1.79769313486231 \times 10^{308}$. Values may be subject to rounding-off errors beyond the fifteenth significant figure.
>
> `NUMERIC` and `DECIMAL` are the same, and have default precision `p` of 30, and a default `s` of 6.
>
> The precision parameter `p` is omitted for values of types `TIME` and `TIMESTAMP`, which both use a precision of 6.
>
> The data type `INTERVAL` is not supported.

Figure 2.4 Implementation of data types for SQL Anywhere

Value expressions

So far each example query has a `SELECT` clause that specifies columns to appear in the final table. This corresponds to the way you can manipulate relations using the relational model and effectively copies data from the columns of the table named in the query to the columns of the final table (i.e. individual values are unchanged). However, SQL is capable of specifying more general forms of result. Instead of just copying all the entries in a column, SQL can instruct the DBMS to process the data in a column (or columns) before producing the final output. To carry out this task, we include in the `SELECT` clause a **value expression** consisting of operators and functions involving column names. The operators include the numeric operators (`+`, `-`, `*`, `/`) and the string concatenation operator (`||`).

A value expression is an expression that involves operations on the data that is contained in a column or columns. Generally speaking, a value expression involves some operation or function that is applied to the values in the required columns of each row to produce the final column of results.

In some of the simplest cases, a value expression might just involve a single column. For example, when executed in the Hospital database, the following query displays the information in the `drug` table, but with an extra 0.05 added to the value in the `price` column (representing an additional 5 pence per dose).

```
SELECT price + 0.05
FROM drug
```

increased_price

If you execute the query **increased_price**, you will see that the column is headed '`price + .05`'. We can give this column a more meaningful name by using the `AS` keyword. The column containing the expression `price + 0.05` can be renamed to `increased_price` by writing:

```
SELECT price + 0.05 AS increased_price
FROM drug
```

rename_increased_price

As well as improving the legibility of the final table, this use of `AS` to name columns will be necessary when we come to look at nested queries and subqueries. Columns must be given unique names so that other queries can refer to them; you will see why this is necessary when subqueries are discussed in Section 3. For now, we will simply ensure that all columns are given a unique name within the table.

A value expression can involve any number of constants and columns. SQL applies the specified operation to each row of the intermediate table which is the input to `SELECT` and places the result in the table which is the output of `SELECT`.

In the following examples, **expression1** produces a table of the height-to-weight ratios of patients in the `patient` table in centimetres per kilogram by using the height and weight columns. Then **expression2** returns a table of the height-to-weight ratios in inches per pound by using an additional constant to convert the values.

> Multiplying by 0.179 converts centimetres per kilogram into inches per pound.

```
SELECT height/weight AS hw_ratio
FROM patient
```

expression1

```
SELECT (height/weight)*0.179 AS hw_ratio_in_per_lb
FROM patient
```

expression2

Value expressions may involve operators such as addition or division, as you have just seen, and also built-in functions. These operators and functions are discussed below.

Numeric and string operators

A numeric operator is one of the arithmetic operators `+`, `-`, `*`, `/`. The columns used in a numeric expression are from the table specified in the `FROM` clause of a query, and must be of numeric data type. An example of such an expression is `(height/weight)*0.179`. Note that a numeric column by itself (e.g. `height`) and numeric constants (e.g. `0.179`) are special cases of numeric expressions.

The main string operation is concatenation, symbolised by `||`. String operations involve columns of data type character string (i.e. `CHAR` or `VARCHAR`), and may include constant character strings (enclosed in single quotes) with a character string operator.

In the next activity, we shall look at how expressions can be used. You should note that the units for most of the columns in the tables are given in the relational representations. For example, the headings of the columns of the tables on the *Hospital Database Card* do not indicate the units for the values in those columns, but these can be obtained from the Hospital relational representation. For example, the relational representation tells us that the values in the `height` column in the `patient` table are in centimetres, which means that the patient named Bell is 171.3 cm tall.

ACTIVITY 2.2

Using the Hospital database, run the following filed statement.

```
SELECT patient_id, patient_name,
       (height/weight)*0.179 AS hw_ratio_in_per_lb
FROM patient
```

hw_ratio_conversion

2 Retrieval using simple queries

The query called **hw_ratio_conversion** can be represented in English as follows:

> For each patient represented in the `patient` table, give that patient's identifier, name and height-to-weight ratio in inches per pound.

There are several points to note about the query **hw_ratio_conversion**.

▶ The `SELECT` clause of the query uses three types of expression: two column expressions, `patient_id` and `patient_name`, which are character strings, and a numeric expression, `(height/weight)*0.179`, to specify the columns that are to be produced in the final table. Notice that the numeric expression contains the column names `height` and `weight` from the `patient` table and a numeric constant, 0.179.

▶ The column produced by the `(height/weight)*0.179` expression is displayed under the heading `hw_ratio_in_per_lb`. The columns `height` and `weight` are not displayed.

▶ The brackets, `()`, in the expression are not essential, because multiplication and division are evaluated left to right. The expression without the brackets would give the same value, but we include them to make our intention explicit. The brackets are necessary for some expressions; an expression to divide a column `x` by the product of two columns `y` and `z` would have to be written as `x/(y*z)`.

▶ The numeric expression in the `SELECT` clause causes a column of values to be calculated according to the given formula. This column exists only in the *displayed* table, and ceases to exist once you remove the display.

The logical processing of **hw_ratio_conversion** may be described as follows.

1   First, the intermediate table, which is produced by processing the `FROM` clause, is the whole of the `patient` table.

2   Second, processing the `SELECT` clause requires two steps.

   (a) The first step processes the numeric expression `(height/weight)*0.179` by producing a new column. The expression is evaluated for each row of this column according to the given formula by using the values in the specified columns of the intermediate table.

   (b) In the second step, the columns specified in the `SELECT` clause, which include the new column, are used to produce the final table.

EXERCISE 2.3

Using the `patient` table in the Hospital database, write a query that lists the identifiers of all patients, their height in inches (1 in = 2.54 cm), and their weight in stones (1 stone = 6.35 kg). Make sure that your query returns a table that has columns with unique and meaningful names.

Occasionally, it is useful to be able to evaluate an expression without making reference to any of the tables in the database at all. Consider the query:

```
SELECT 5+8 AS thirteen
FROM patient
```

no_table_expression

If you execute **no_table_expression** using the Hospital database, you should receive a table that contains a single column named `thirteen`, which has several rows, each containing the single value 13 (the value returned by evaluating the expression in the

SELECT clause). The table resulting from this query contains one row for each row in `patient`. Apart from the number of rows, the actual contents of `patient` are not used at all in this query; if we only wanted to know what the expression evaluated to, any table could be used. However, Standard SQL does not allow a query without a `FROM` clause, and so to evaluate an expression independently of the specific data in the database, we need to use an arbitrary table.

SQL Anywhere provides a special table called `SYS.DUMMY`, which contains a single row, and is useful in situations when a user wishes to know the value of an expression independently of any of the specific tables in the database. So if you run the query

```
SELECT 5+8 AS thirteen
FROM SYS.DUMMY
```

dummy_no_table_expression

you will find that a table is returned which contains a single column named `thirteen`, with one row containing the value 13. `SYS.DUMMY` is an example of a system table, which we discussed briefly in *Block 1*, Section 3.4. Because `SYS.DUMMY` is always available in SQL Anywhere, it can be used whenever a function needs to be evaluated independently of any of the tables in the database.

Functions

SQL provides a number of **built-in functions**; a function takes a number of input values, known as its **arguments**, and returns a single value. In SQL, the simplest functions operate on each value in a column to generate a new column of values.

ACTIVITY 2.3

Using the Hospital database, run the following filed statement.

```
SELECT patient_name, LENGTH(patient_name) AS name_length
FROM patient
```

length

The query returns a table with two columns; the second column contains the length of the patient name which is given in the first column.

In the query **length**, the function `LENGTH` gives you the number of characters in each value of the column `patient_name`. So one value, a character string, is the argument for this function, and one value, an integer, is the result. Another example is the string operation function `SUBSTR`, which extracts part of a string.

```
SELECT patient_name, SUBSTR(patient_name, 1, 3) AS substring
FROM patient
```

substring

> The first character in an SQL string is at position 1, unlike, for example, C and Java, which both start from position 0.

The `SUBSTR` function has a character string argument followed by two integer arguments. The function results in the part of the string argument that starts at the position in the string specified by the first number and has a length specified by the second number. So the above query gives the string 'Rub' for 'Rubinstein'.

The built-in functions that are available are dependent on the particular implementation of DBMS. However, the table in Figure 2.5 summarises a number of functions that are part of the SQL Standard.

Function	Result
`BIT_LENGTH(string)`	Number of bits in bit string
`CAST(value AS data_type)`	Value converted to data type
`CHAR_LENGTH(string)`	Length of character string
`CURRENT_DATE`	Current date
`CURRENT_TIME(p)`	Current time to precision `p`
`CURRENT_TIMESTAMP(p)`	Current date and time to precision `p`
`EXTRACT(part FROM source)`	Specified `part` (`DAY`, `HOUR`, and so on) from `source` date or time value
`LOWER(string)`	`string` converted to lower case
`SUBSTRING(source FROM n FOR l)`	Substring of `source` starting at position `n` of length `l`
`UPPER(string)`	`string` converted to upper case

Figure 2.5 Some Standard SQL built-in functions

There are some slight syntactic differences from the Standard in the way that SQL Anywhere implements some of the functions in Figure 2.5. The function `EXTRACT` is not implemented, and the `SUBSTRING`, `CURRENT_DATE` and `CURRENT_TIME` functions have a slightly different syntax, as shown in Figure 2.6.

Function	Result
`SUBSTRING(source n,l)`	Substring of `source` starting at position `n` of length `l`
`CURRENT DATE` (note: no underscore)	Current date
`CURRENT TIME` (note: no underscore)	Current time
`DAY(date)`	The day of `date`, where `date` is a date data type
`MONTH(date)`	The month of `date`, where `date` is a date data type
`YEAR(date)`	The year of `date`, where `date` is a date data type
`SECOND(time)`	The second of `time`, where `time` is a time data type
`MINUTE(time)`	The minute of `time`, where `time` is a time data type
`HOUR(time)`	The hour of `time`, where `time` is a time data type

Figure 2.6 SQL Anywhere variations on Standard SQL functions

Casts

When using functions, it is often useful to be able to convert the data type of one of the function's arguments. SQL provides a capability known as a **cast**, which converts data from one data type to another.

ACTIVITY 2.4

Using the Hospital database, run the following filed statement.

```
SELECT CAST(staff_no AS INT)*2 AS twice_staff_no
FROM nurse
```

cast1

This query shows the `CAST` function being used to convert a value of one data type to another. The result of this example will give the number which is used as a character for `staff_no` converted to an integer and multiplied by 2. (This multiplication is to show you that an integer has been produced; otherwise there would be no indication on screen that the conversion had taken place.)

➢ Now execute the following statement.

```
SELECT drug_code, 'GBP'|| CAST(price AS CHAR(4)) AS new_price
FROM drug
```

cast2

This query shows the `CAST` function being used to convert objects of `DECIMAL` type into a character string. In this example, the result is obtained by converting the decimal values in the `price` column of the `drug` table to a string. To show it is a string, it is concatenated with another string (`'GBP'`: strings must always be expressed in single quotes) using the `||` operator, to give a column representing the price in pounds sterling (GBP).

We will not give a complete account of casts in this course, but the following rules cover the most widely used conversions between the predefined data types.

1. Any numerical value, date–time value or bit string value can be converted into a character string value. If the character string is too short to hold the converted value, then the value will be truncated. So the result of the expression `CAST(4.9938 AS CHAR(4))` is '4.99'.

2. Any numerical value can be converted to any other numerical value. If the value being converted does not fit into the new data type (such as trying to cast a `FLOAT` of value 4 000 000 into a `SMALLINT`), then an error is generated. If you try to convert a numerical value to a type with less fractional precision, then the value will be truncated. So the result of the expression `CAST(4.9 AS INTEGER)` is 4.

3. Any character string can be converted to any other data type, as long as the content of the string makes sense for the target type. For example, the string '23.45' can be cast into a `FLOAT` or a `DECIMAL(5, 3)`, but not into a `DATE`. The string '2005-03-02' can be cast into a `DATE`, but not a `FLOAT` or an `INTEGER`.

These rules apply only to the predefined data types; we discuss user-defined data types in Section 5, and will extend the discussion of casts there.

Aggregate functions

An **aggregate function** is another kind of built-in function. Unlike the functions we have already seen, aggregate functions produce tables that consist of only a single row of data. This is illustrated in Activity 2.5 involving the aggregate function `AVG`.

2 Retrieval using simple queries

ACTIVITY 2.5

Using the Hospital database, run the following query.

```
SELECT AVG(number_of_beds) AS average_beds
FROM ward
```
avg_beds

The result of this query is just a single value, but it should still be considered a table; it has one column, named `average_beds` in the display, and one row. The result is obtained by averaging the collection of values in the `number_of_beds` column of the `ward` table. The query can be expressed in English as follows:

Find the average number of beds of all wards represented in the `ward` table.

➢ Now run the following filed query.

```
SELECT AVG(height) AS average_height
FROM patient
```
avg_height

When the processing of **avg_height** is complete and the result is displayed, it appears similar to the result of **avg_beds**, and so the query can be expressed in English as:

Find the average height of all the patients represented in the `patient` table.

The logical processing of **avg_height** may be explained as follows. First, processing the `FROM` clause produces an intermediate table identical to `patient`. Second, processing the `SELECT` clause uses just the column referred to in the aggregate function (i.e. `height`) to calculate the average of the collection of values for that column to give a final table which has one column and one row.

We need to update our processing model to include value expressions as shown in Figure 2.7 (overleaf).

When used in the above kinds of query, aggregate functions always result in a single value or row, whereas other kinds of value expression result in as many rows as there are in the original table. Including both kinds of value expression in a `SELECT` clause would generally cause a conflict in the number of rows in the result. To prevent this, aggregate functions (like `AVG`) cannot be used in a `SELECT` clause alongside other kinds of expression. This rule ensures that all the value expressions in a `SELECT` clause always result in the same number of rows. For example, the following query is invalid.

```
SELECT AVG(height) AS average_height, weight
FROM patient
```
invalid_aggregate

However, it is possible to include more than one aggregate function in a `SELECT` clause, since they both result in a single row. For example, the following query is valid and gives the average of both height and weight for each patient represented in the `patient` table.

```
SELECT AVG(height) AS average_height,
       AVG(weight) AS average_weight
FROM patient
```
multiple_aggregates

So far, the examples have used `AVG` with a single column name as an argument. But an aggregate function may also have a more complex expression as an argument, as the following query shows.

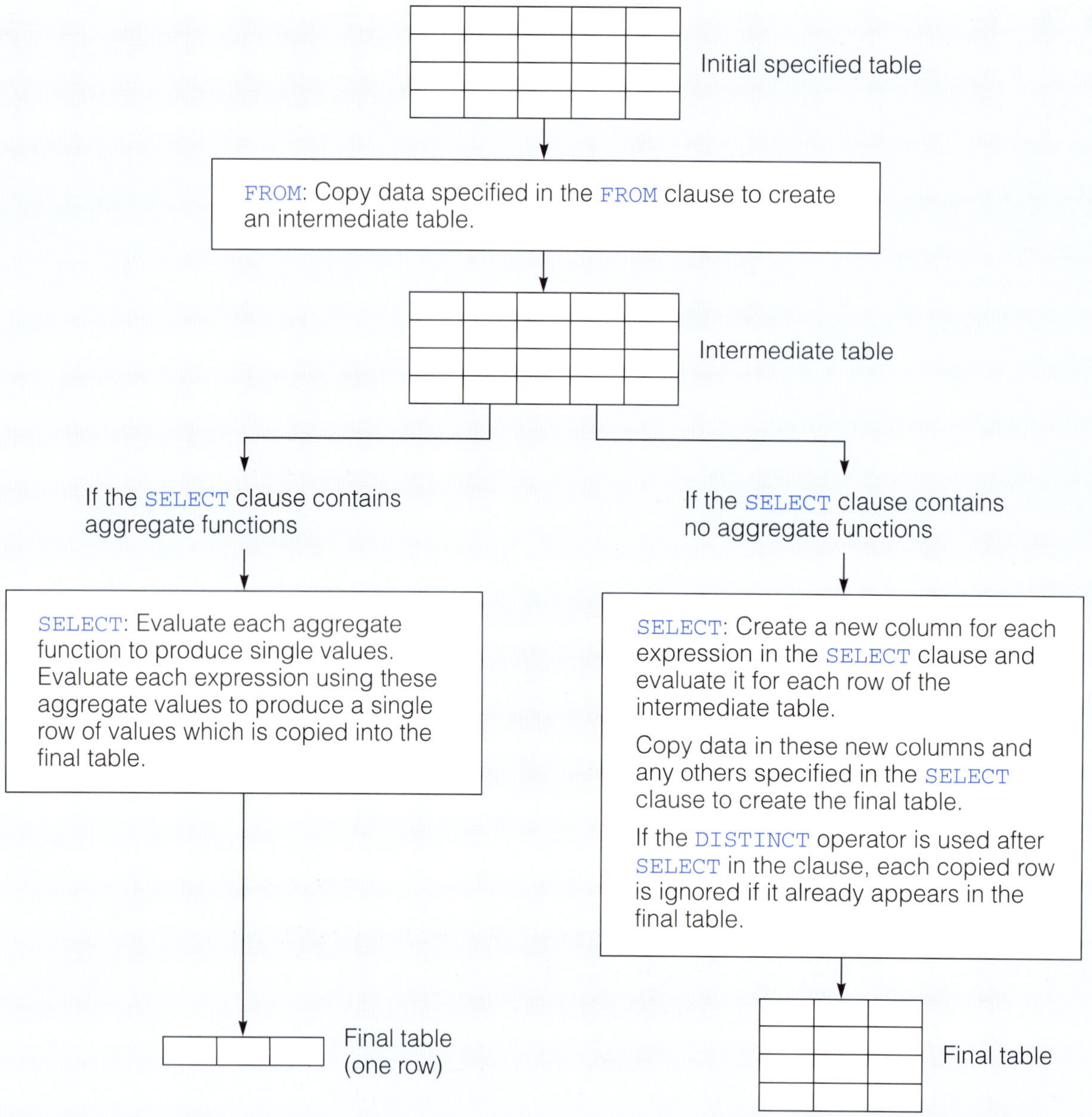

Figure 2.7 Logical processing model for elementary SELECT and FROM clauses with value expressions

➤ Run the following query.

```
SELECT AVG((height/weight)*0.179) AS avg_hw_ratio_in_per_lb
FROM patient
```

avg_ratio

Again, this results in a final table containing one column and one row.

EXERCISE 2.4

Express the query **avg_ratio** in English (recall the significance of the conversion factor 0.179 from the expression in Activity 2.2).

Another form of argument for an aggregate function is to include DISTINCT before the column expression: this results in all duplicates being ignored. Exercise 2.5 demonstrates this, but first we can summarise the definition of AVG as follows.

AVG: The argument for the aggregate function **AVG** is a collection of values defined by an expression which returns a value of numeric data type. **AVG** returns the average of the values in the collection. If **DISTINCT** is included in the argument, all duplicate values are ignored in the calculation.

A fuller definition, which covers NULL, is given in Section 4.

EXERCISE 2.5

(a) Explain why the following two queries give different results when they are run in the Hospital database.

```
SELECT AVG(number_of_beds) AS average_beds
FROM ward
```
avg_beds

```
SELECT AVG(DISTINCT number_of_beds) AS average_beds
FROM ward
```
avg_beds2

(b) Without running the following query, explain what is wrong with it.

```
SELECT type, AVG(price) AS average_price
FROM drug
```
avg_drug_type_price

The next aggregate function we shall look at is **COUNT**. It provides a useful way of finding either the number of rows in a table or the number of values in a column.

➤ Using the Hospital database, run the following query.

```
SELECT COUNT(*) AS num_nurses
FROM nurse
```
count_nurse

This results in a final table having one column, named **num_nurses** as specified in the **SELECT** clause, and one row. The query is expressed in English as:

How many rows are there in the **nurse** table?

In general, the **COUNT** function with an asterisk results in the number of rows in a table. The aggregate function **COUNT** can also be used to count the number of values in a particular column, in which case the argument is a column name. As with other aggregate functions, such as **AVG**, if **DISTINCT** is included then duplicates are ignored. The definition of **COUNT** with a column-name argument is as follows.

COUNT: The argument for the aggregate function **COUNT** is a collection of values defined by a column name of any data type. **COUNT** returns the number of values in the collection. If **DISTINCT** is included in the argument, all duplicate values are ignored in the calculation. If the collection is empty, then the function results in zero.

See Section 4 for a full version covering NULL.

EXERCISE 2.6

Explain why the following two queries give different results when they are run in the Hospital database.

```
SELECT COUNT(patient_name) AS num_patient_names
FROM patient
```
count_name

```
SELECT COUNT(DISTINCT patient_name) AS num_distinct_names
FROM patient
```
count_dist_name

See Section 4 for full versions covering NULL.

There are three other SQL aggregate functions: **SUM**, **MAX** and **MIN**. Their usage follows that of **AVG** and **COUNT** quite closely. They are defined as shown below and you will see examples of their use later in this section.

SUM: When applied to a collection of values defined by an expression of numeric data type, **SUM** results in the sum of all values in the collection. If **DISTINCT** is included in the argument, all duplicate values are ignored in the calculation.

MAX: When applied to a collection of values defined by an expression of any data type, **MAX** results in the maximum value in the collection. In the case of character string data types, the maximum value results in the last entry that would be found in a dictionary. **DISTINCT** can be included in the argument, but it does not have any effect.

MIN: This aggregate function operates in exactly the same way as **MAX**, except that it selects the minimum value in the collection.

EXERCISE 2.7

(a) Use the *Hospital Database Card* to determine what table the following query would produce.

```
SELECT MAX(price)
FROM drug
```

(b) If the function used were **MIN**, what would the result be?

EXERCISE 2.8

What is the difference between aggregate functions and the other built-in functions?

In this subsection, we have seen how value expressions can be used in a **SELECT** clause and result in columns in the final table of a query. But remember that there is one proviso: all the value expressions in a **SELECT** clause must result in the same number of values.

2.3 The WHERE clause

Compare with the *where* condition of the relational algebra that you saw in Block 2.

So far we have considered only queries in which all the rows from the table specified in the **FROM** clause of a query are required in the result. We now move on to learn about queries in which only some of the rows are required. Such queries include not only a **SELECT** clause and a **FROM** clause but also a **WHERE** clause which specifies a **search condition**. Only those rows which satisfy the condition given in the **WHERE** clause of a query contribute to its result.

ACTIVITY 2.6

Using the University database, run the following query.

```
SELECT staff_number
FROM staff
WHERE name = 'Jennings'
```

where_Jennings

This query answers the following request:

What are the staff numbers of all staff members who are called Jennings?

In fact, there is only one such staff member, who has staff number 3158.

2 Retrieval using simple queries

The following points should be noted about the query **where_Jennings**.

▶ The search condition of the `WHERE` clause contains just a single condition, `name = 'Jennings'`, that must be the case for all the rows in the resulting table. The conditions in the `WHERE` clause are **conditional expressions** that evaluate to either TRUE or FALSE. There are several types of expression that can be used in `WHERE` clauses, which will be introduced in the following pages.

The SQL **comparison operators** are `=`, `<`, `>`, `<=`, `>=` and `<>` (not equal to).

▶ The `name` column referenced in the search condition of the `WHERE` clause is not required in the final table but could be included if you particularly wanted to check that the condition is satisfied.

▶ The `WHERE` clause uses the condition `name = 'Jennings'`, where the string `'Jennings'` is a mixture of upper and lower case. The database that we have provided in this course is case insensitive, and so the condition could equally well have been `name = 'jennings'` or `NAME = 'JENNINGS'`.

Although SQL is not sensitive to the case of keywords or table names (as we noted in Activity 2.1), the database administrator decides whether SQL should be case sensitive for conditions involving strings. This decision is made when the database is created. The databases that you are using for M359 are defined to be case insensitive.

Conditional expressions can also evaluate to UNKNOWN, as we will see in Section 4.

The logical processing of the **where_Jennings** query may be described as follows.

▶ First, processing the `FROM` clause produces an intermediate table, which is the whole of the `staff` table.

▶ Second, the `WHERE` clause is processed, taking the rows satisfying the specified condition from this initial intermediate table, that is, a horizontal slicing, to give a second intermediate table. Each row is checked, and if the search condition evaluates to TRUE for that row (in this case, those rows where the column `name` has the value 'Jennings'), then the row is copied to the second intermediate table.

▶ Finally, processing the `SELECT` clause takes the specified column, `staff_number`, from the second intermediate table to produce the final table.

We are now in a position to extend our general logical processing model again, by inserting the step for the `WHERE` clause, as shown in Figure 2.8 (overleaf).

EXERCISE 2.9

Explain why it is necessary for the logical processing of the `WHERE` clause in the **where_Jennings** query to be before the `SELECT` clause.

ACTIVITY 2.7

Using the Hospital database, run the following query.

```
SELECT patient_id, (height/weight)*0.179 AS hw_ratio
FROM patient
WHERE (height/weight)*0.179 < 0.45
```

where_expression

This query can be represented in English as:

List the patient identifier and height-to-weight ratio (in in/lb) of every patient represented in the `patient` table who has a height-to-weight ratio of less than 0.45 in/lb.

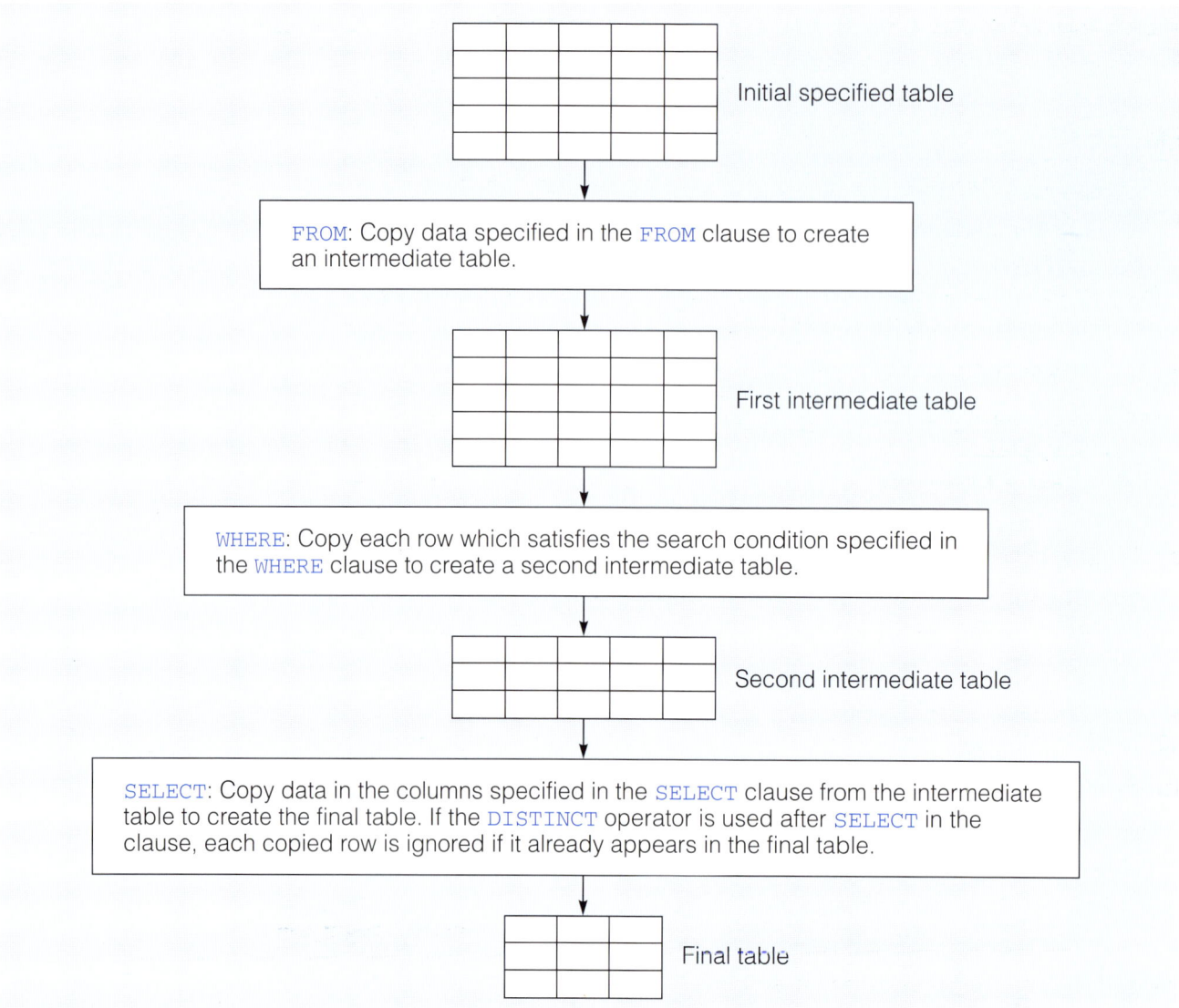

Figure 2.8 Logical processing model for elementary SELECT, FROM and WHERE clauses

Note that the condition in the WHERE clause in the query **where_expression** is a fairly complex expression. This illustrates that value expressions can be used in the condition of a WHERE clause.

The logical processing of the query **where_expression** can be described as follows.

▶ First, processing the FROM clause produces an intermediate table, which is the same as the **patient** table.

▶ Second, processing the WHERE clause evaluates the condition for each row of this intermediate table and produces a second intermediate table containing only those rows for which the condition evaluates to TRUE.

▶ Finally, processing the SELECT clause creates a new column for the expression, evaluates it for each row of the second intermediate table and then selects the required columns, including the new one, to give the final table.

The above example of a logical processing model illustrates the general situation for this kind of query. Conditions can contain comparisons between two expressions of the same data type. For example, character strings are ordered alphabetically, so the condition **patient_name > 'Ming'** could be used to find patients whose surname comes after 'Ming' in alphabetical order. Notice that checking that the condition is true for each row can involve only values in that row. Aggregate functions are therefore not allowed in the conditions of a **WHERE** clause.

EXERCISE 2.10

An SQL query is required for the University database that can be expressed in English as:

> List the student identifier, course code and mark for each assignment submission in the **assignment** table, where the mark awarded is greater than the average mark for all assignment submissions.

(a) Explain why the following query does not answer this.

```
SELECT student_id, course_code, mark
FROM assignment
WHERE mark > AVG(mark)
```
above_avg

(b) Describe how you could get around the problem that you identified in part (a).

(Hint: you do not yet have sufficient knowledge of SQL to formulate a single query to answer this request.)

ACTIVITY 2.8

Using the Hospital database, run the following query.

```
SELECT AVG(price) AS average_price
FROM drug
WHERE type = 'Painkiller'
```
where_aggregate

The query **where_aggregate** can be expressed in English as:

> What is the average price of the drugs in the **drug** table that have the type 'Painkiller'?

To understand the logical processing of this query, consider the processing models illustrated in Figures 2.7 and 2.8. Rather than evaluating the aggregate function in the **SELECT** clause on the first intermediate table created by the **FROM** clause, as shown in Figure 2.7, the aggregate function is applied to the second intermediate table that is created by processing the **WHERE** clause (Figure 2.8).

EXERCISE 2.11

Write and run a query to answer the following request in the Hospital database:

> What is the average height-to-weight ratio (in cm/kg) of the male patients in the hospital?

The **AND**, **OR** and **NOT** operators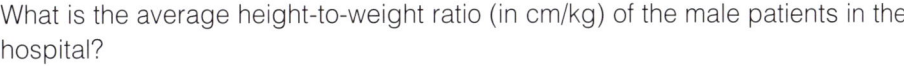

The search conditions in the **WHERE** clauses that you have seen so far have used a single comparison operator. The query in Activity 2.9 shows how the **logical operators** **AND**, **OR** and **NOT** can be used to combine logical expressions into more complex search conditions.

ACTIVITY 2.9

Using the Hospital database, run the following query. (The different parts of the condition in the `WHERE` clause are numbered; these are not part of the SQL, but are to aid the discussion.)

```
SELECT patient_id, patient_name
FROM patient
WHERE gender = 'F'                          (1)
   AND (height < 160 OR weight > 60)        (2)
   AND NOT patient_name = 'Maher'           (3)
```

and_or_not

This query can be expressed in English as follows:

> List the patient identifier and name of every female patient represented in the `patient` table who has either height less than 160 cm or weight more than 60 kg, except for the patient whose name is 'Maher'.

In accordance with the rules of classical logic, when `AND` is used to conjoin two conditions, both must evaluate to TRUE for the combined condition to evaluate to TRUE. On the other hand, when `OR` is used, at least one of the conditions must evaluate to TRUE for the combined condition to evaluate to TRUE. `OR` is considered **inclusive**, that is, the `OR` condition evaluates to TRUE if either one of the conjoined conditions evaluates to TRUE, or if both of them evaluate to TRUE. `NOT` reverses the truth value of the condition to which it applies, so that TRUE becomes FALSE and FALSE becomes TRUE. So in the case of **and_or_not**, the patient named Rubinstein has both height under 160 cm and weight over 60 kg, so the `OR` condition evaluates to TRUE.

Given these definitions, you should be able to work out why the rows that are shown in the final table have been chosen: they are the only ones for which the whole search condition evaluates to TRUE.

As an illustration of the detailed logical processing of **and_or_not**, we shall consider how two of the rows in the `patient` table are processed for the `WHERE` clause. First notice that the search condition contains three separate conditions, which are combined using the `AND` operator. This means that each one must evaluate to TRUE for the whole search condition to be satisfied and the row to be chosen. We shall look at the patients with identifiers p01 and p07.

p01: Condition (1) is TRUE because `gender` is equal to 'F'.

> Condition (2) is TRUE because although `height` is not less than 160, `weight` is greater than 60.
>
> Condition (3) is TRUE because the value of `patient_name` is not 'Maher'.
>
> So the whole search condition evaluates to TRUE, and the row containing the patient with patient identifier p01 is included in the intermediate table which results from processing the `WHERE` clause.

p07: Condition (1) is FALSE because `gender` is not equal to 'F'.

> So without even checking the other conditions, we know that the search condition evaluates to FALSE and the row containing the patient with identifier p07 does not appear in the intermediate table that results from processing the `WHERE` clause.

EXERCISE 2.12

In the same style that we have used for patients p01 and p07, use the *Hospital Database Card* to check whether the data for the patient with patient identifier p89 should be included in the final table produced by **and_or_not**.

EXERCISE 2.13

Using the University database, give SQL queries that can be expressed in English as follows.

(a) Give the details from the **student** table, except student identification numbers, of all the students named Ellis or Reeves.

(b) From the table **assignment**, list the student identification numbers of all the students who have been awarded a mark of 70 or over on any assignment for a course that does not have course code c4, together with the course codes of the courses on which they obtained these marks.

The use of logical operators and comparison operators allows complex conditions to be expressed in a **WHERE** clause. However, as conditions become increasingly complex, it can become harder to ensure that the query will correctly answer the original request.

The BETWEEN and IN operators

The comparison operators that you have looked at so far are essentially the same as those used in high-level programming languages such as Java. SQL also provides the **BETWEEN** and **IN** operators.

➢ Using the Hospital database, run the following query.

```
SELECT prescription_no, quantity
FROM prescription
WHERE quantity BETWEEN 50 AND 100
```
between_query

This query can be expressed in English as:

List the prescription number and the quantity of the prescription, as represented in the **prescription** table, for which the quantity in the prescription falls within the range 50 to 100 (in the units of the table).

Note that the **BETWEEN** operator is inclusive, so the prescription with number P0101 and the quantity of 100 is included in the result of the query. The expression **quantity BETWEEN 50 AND 100** means that any value for **quantity** equal to or between 50 and 100 satisfies the condition.

➢ Now run the following query.

```
SELECT patient_id, patient_name
FROM patient
WHERE patient_id IN ('p37', 'p78', 'p87')
```
in_query

This query can be expressed in English as:

List the patient identifiers and names of all the patients represented in the **patient** table whose patient identifiers are p37, p78 or p87.

In this example, the expression involving **IN** is satisfied when a value in the column being compared is equal to one of the values given in the list.

Both `BETWEEN` and `IN` can be used with `NOT`, as the following examples illustrate.

```
WHERE a NOT BETWEEN b AND c
WHERE NOT (a BETWEEN b AND c)
WHERE credit NOT IN (30, 60)
```

The expressions in the first two examples both represent the condition that `a` must lie outside the range from b to c, that is, that we must have either $a < b$ or $a > c$, for the expression to evaluate to TRUE. The expression in the third example represents the condition that a credit value must not be 30 or 60, that is, that `credit` <> 30 and `credit` <> 60, for the expression to evaluate to TRUE.

EXERCISE 2.14

(a) Formulate the search condition in the `WHERE` clause of **between_query** in a way that does not use `BETWEEN`.

(b) Formulate a query to find from the `nurse` table the staff numbers and names of all the nurses whose names lie alphabetically between 'Descartes' and 'Sesonske' inclusive.

(c) Rewrite the `WHERE` clause in the query **in_query** so that the query provides the results for all the patients in the `patient` table *except* those whose patient identifiers are p37, p78 or p87.

(d) Using the University database, write a query that uses the `IN` operator to find the student identification numbers and course codes of all those students who sat the examinations in Bedford, Taunton or Bath, according to the `examination_administration` table.

(e) Rewrite the `WHERE` clause of your solution to part (d) so that the query does not use the `IN` operator.

The `LIKE` operator

Another kind of SQL operator commonly used in search conditions is `LIKE`, which is used to match a value from a column (of some string type) with a known string or part of a string.

➤ Using the Hospital database, run the following query.

```
SELECT drug_code, drug_name
FROM drug
WHERE drug_name LIKE 'c%i_'
```

like

The condition in the query **like** is an example of SQL's string matching capability. The `LIKE` keyword is used in a situation where you wish to compare character string values in a column with a **pattern** in the form of a character string. The string can represent a *set* of strings that it is allowed to match in the database. To do this, the underscore character, _, stands for any single character, while the percentage symbol, %, stands for any sequence of zero or more characters. With this interpretation, the pattern 'c%i_' can be matched as follows. The `c` at the beginning means that the string being matched must begin with a 'c'. The % sign followed by `i` means that any sequence of zero or more characters can then follow as long as they are followed by an 'i'. The final underscore means that the 'i' must be followed by one more character.

So the query **like** can be represented in English as:

> List all the drug names in the **drug** table which begin with a 'c' and have 'i' as the second-to-last letter.

In general, conditions using `LIKE` can be used to match any column of data type character string with any constant string (enclosed in quotes). `NOT` can also be used, as `NOT LIKE`.

As with tests for equality of strings (such as the query **where_Jennings**), the behaviour of `LIKE` depends on whether the database has been defined as case sensitive or case insensitive. As the database provided for the course is case insensitive, when the query **like** is executed, the initial 'c' of 'c%i_' matches with the 'C' of 'Capillucanis', even though the cases do not match. For all the exercises in this block, assume that the database is case insensitive.

EXERCISE 2.15

(a) Use the *Hospital Database Card* to work out which entries for `patient_name` in the `patient` table would satisfy the clause `WHERE patient_name LIKE 'm%r%'`.

(b) What is the difference between the set of character strings that satisfy the condition `BETWEEN 's' AND 't'` and the set of character strings satisfying `LIKE 's%'`?

EXERCISE 2.16

(a) Notice that all painkillers in the `drug` table have a code beginning with a 'P'. Write a query to list the names of all the drugs in the `drug` table that are painkillers, by using a `LIKE` query to find values in the `drug_code` column which begin with 'P'.

(b) Write and run a query that finds the ward number and ward name of every ward in the `ward` table whose name includes the letter 'a'.

2.4 Using joins

Up until now our queries have contained `FROM` clauses which refer to only one table. However, more than one table can be referenced in the `FROM` clause, and this is the basis of multiple-table query processing in SQL.

In this subsection, we shall examine the formation of *joins* and *Cartesian products* in SQL. In SQL, the general form of the join is a refinement of a general combination of data from two tables known as a **Cartesian product**. The Cartesian product of two tables is another table, which consists of all possible pairs of rows from the two tables. The Cartesian product here behaves in the same way as that described for the relational algebra in *Block 2*, Section 3.5.

The process of forming pairs of rows by matching the contents of two related columns, taking data from each of the original tables, is called a **join** of the tables. (In this section, we shall use the term 'join' to refer to the most common form of join known, more accurately, as an **inner join**. We shall consider an alternative called an **outer join** in Section 4.)

To illustrate how joins and Cartesian products can be expressed in, and processed as, SQL queries, we shall use the two small tables shown in Figure 2.9, which are based on the `ward` and `occupied_by` tables in the Hospital database.

*Joining tables in SQL parallels the joining of relations using the **join** operator of the relational algebra in Block 2.*

small_occupied_by

patient_id	ward_no
p07	w3
p37	w3
p80	w2

small_ward

ward_no	ward_name	no_beds
w2	Wessex	8
w3	Anglia	8

Figure 2.9 Two small tables in the Hospital database

ACTIVITY 2.10

Using the Hospital database, run the following query.

`SELECT *`
`FROM small_occupied_by, small_ward`

cartesian_product

The query **cartesian_product** results in the table shown in Figure 2.10.

patient_id	small_occupied_by.ward_no	small_ward.ward_no	ward_name	no_beds
p07	w3	w2	Wessex	8
p37	w3	w2	Wessex	8
p80	w2	w2	Wessex	8
p07	w3	w3	Anglia	8
p37	w3	w3	Anglia	8
p80	w2	w3	Anglia	8

Figure 2.10 Result of the query **cartesian_product**

The table in Figure 2.10 represents the Cartesian product of the two tables specified in the **FROM** clause. It has the columns of both the tables referred to in the **FROM** clause, and every row of the second table has been appended to each row of the first. Consequently, the number of columns in the final table is equal to the sum of the numbers of columns in the tables in the **FROM** clause (2 + 3 = 5, in this case), and the number of rows in the final table is the product of the numbers of rows in the tables in the **FROM** clause (3 × 2 = 6, in this case).

The **cartesian_product** query has no **WHERE** clause to restrict rows, and the use of the asterisk in the **SELECT** clause means that all columns are displayed. So the final table includes all the rows and all the columns from the intermediate table that results from the **FROM** clause. The logical processing of this query can be described as follows.

▶ First, processing the **FROM** clause constructs an intermediate table in which each column relates to one of the columns of the specified tables. The rows of this intermediate table are formed from all possible combinations of a row from the first table and a row from the second table. That is, the intermediate table is the Cartesian product of the tables in the **FROM** clause.

2 Retrieval using simple queries

▶ Second, processing the `SELECT` clause uses all the columns in this intermediate table to produce the final table which, in this case, is the same as the Cartesian product in the intermediate table.

Notice that the two tables in Figure 2.9 both have a column called `ward_no`. Now that we know how to refer to more than one table in the `FROM` clause, we need a way to specify exactly which of the two `ward_no` columns we mean. For example, if we wanted to add a condition such as `ward_no = 'w3'` in a `WHERE` clause, it would be ambiguous. To reference a column unambiguously you must qualify a column name with the name of the table in the `FROM` clause to which it relates, using a dot notation similar to the one that is used for relations in *Block 2*. Therefore, for reference purposes, the fully **qualified names** of the columns in the **cartesian_product** query would be `small_occupied_by.patient_id`, `small_occupied_by.ward_no`, `small_ward.ward_no`, `small_ward.ward_name` and `small_ward.no_beds`. If there is no ambiguity, the column name need not be qualified. So the above condition would have to be expressed as `small_ward.ward_no = 'w3'`, but `ward_name = 'Wessex'`, for example, could be written without qualifying the column name.

The Cartesian product of two tables is usually too general to be useful in itself. However, some of the columns drawn from the two tables may have identical entries. This indicates a potential relationship between the two tables. In our example, for instance, the ward numbers in the `small_ward` table are also numbers of wards ('w2' and 'w3') in the `small_occupied_by` table.

To produce a joined table based on such a relationship, we can use the Cartesian product of the two tables and impose a condition (called a **join condition**) that the two corresponding columns must be equal. This condition is specified in the `WHERE` clause of a query, and is treated no differently from any other conditions that may be included in the query.

EXERCISE 2.17

Using the Cartesian product resulting from the **cartesian_product** query as a mental aid:

(a) Identify the columns that indicate a relationship between the two tables `small_ward` and `small_occupied_by`.
(b) Write a join condition that relates the values in these columns.
(c) Modify the **cartesian_product** query so that the result lists the patient identifier of every patient in `small_occupied_by` together with the number of the ward that he or she occupies and the name of that ward from `small_ward`.

For ease of reference, we reproduce here the query as proposed in the solution to Exercise 2.17(c).

```
SELECT patient_id, small_ward.ward_no, ward_name
FROM small_occupied_by, small_ward
WHERE small_occupied_by.ward_no = small_ward.ward_no
```
join1

The relation of this query's final table to the Cartesian product derived from the tables specified in its `FROM` clause is illustrated in Figure 2.11. This shows the rows of the Cartesian product that satisfy the `WHERE` condition.

patient_id	small_occupied_by.ward_no	small_ward.ward_no	ward_name	no_beds
p80	w2	w2	Wessex	8
p07	w3	w3	Anglia	8
p37	w3	w3	Anglia	8

Figure 2.11 Rows of Cartesian product which satisfy the **WHERE** condition of **join1**

The logical processing of the **join1** query may be described as follows.

▸ First, processing the **FROM** clause produces an intermediate table, which is the Cartesian product of **small_occupied_by** and **small_ward**, that is, the whole of the table as shown in Figure 2.10.

▸ Second, processing the **WHERE** clause applies the join condition to the rows of this Cartesian product and so chooses those rows which represent the relationship between the two tables, that is, **small_ward.ward_no = small_occupied_by.ward_no**, which is satisfied by the third, fourth and fifth rows of the table in Figure 2.10. These rows form the second intermediate table, shown in Figure 2.11.

▸ Finally, the **SELECT** clause is processed and the specified columns are given in the final table. So the final table contains the columns named **patient_id**, **small_ward.ward_no** and **ward_name** from the table shown in Figure 2.11.

In general, any number of tables may be specified in the **FROM** clause, and the first intermediate table is then the Cartesian product of all of them. This extension of the **FROM** clause to allow more than one table name means that we can update our logical processing model again, as shown in Figure 2.12.

EXERCISE 2.18

(a) Using the University database, write a query that uses the **tutors** table to list the identification number of each student who is tutored by a member of staff whose staff number is either 3158 or 8431, together with the code of the course for which they are tutored.

(Hint: this part does not involve a join. Remember also that staff numbers are of type **STRING**.)

(b) Modify your answer to part (a), using a join, so that the final result also includes the names of the students. Identify the join condition.

In the proposed solution to Exercise 2.18(b), there is another condition in the **WHERE** clause apart from the join condition, i.e. **staff_number IN ('3158', '8431')**. This serves to restrict further the rows in the intermediate table produced by the **WHERE** clause, but it is only the join condition that is relevant to the relationship between the tables participating in the join. It is often helpful to put any join conditions first in the **WHERE** clause, so that their roles may be distinguished.

EXERCISE 2.19

(a) If a **FROM** clause refers to two tables, one consisting of 10 rows and the other 20 rows, how many rows will be contained in the intermediate table resulting from the logical processing of this clause?

(b) What does a join condition do?

2 Retrieval using simple queries

```
                    ┌─ Initial specified tables
                    ▼
┌─────────────────────────────────────────────────────────────┐
│ FROM: Create an intermediate table from all the tables       │
│ specified in the FROM clause by forming all possible         │
│ combinations of choosing one row from each table.            │
└─────────────────────────────────────────────────────────────┘
                    │
                    ▼
                    ┌─ First intermediate table
                    ▼
┌─────────────────────────────────────────────────────────────┐
│ WHERE: Copy each row which satisfies the search condition    │
│ specified in the WHERE clause to create a second             │
│ intermediate table.                                          │
└─────────────────────────────────────────────────────────────┘
                    │
                    ▼
                    ┌─ Second intermediate table
                    ▼
┌─────────────────────────────────────────────────────────────┐
│ SELECT: Process each value expression specified in the       │
│ SELECT clause from the second intermediate table to create   │
│ new columns.                                                 │
│ Copy data in these new columns and any other columns         │
│ specified in the SELECT clause to create the final table.    │
│ If the DISTINCT operator is used in the SELECT clause, each  │
│ copied row is ignored if it already appears in the final     │
│ table.                                                       │
└─────────────────────────────────────────────────────────────┘
                    │
                    ▼
                    ─ Final table
```

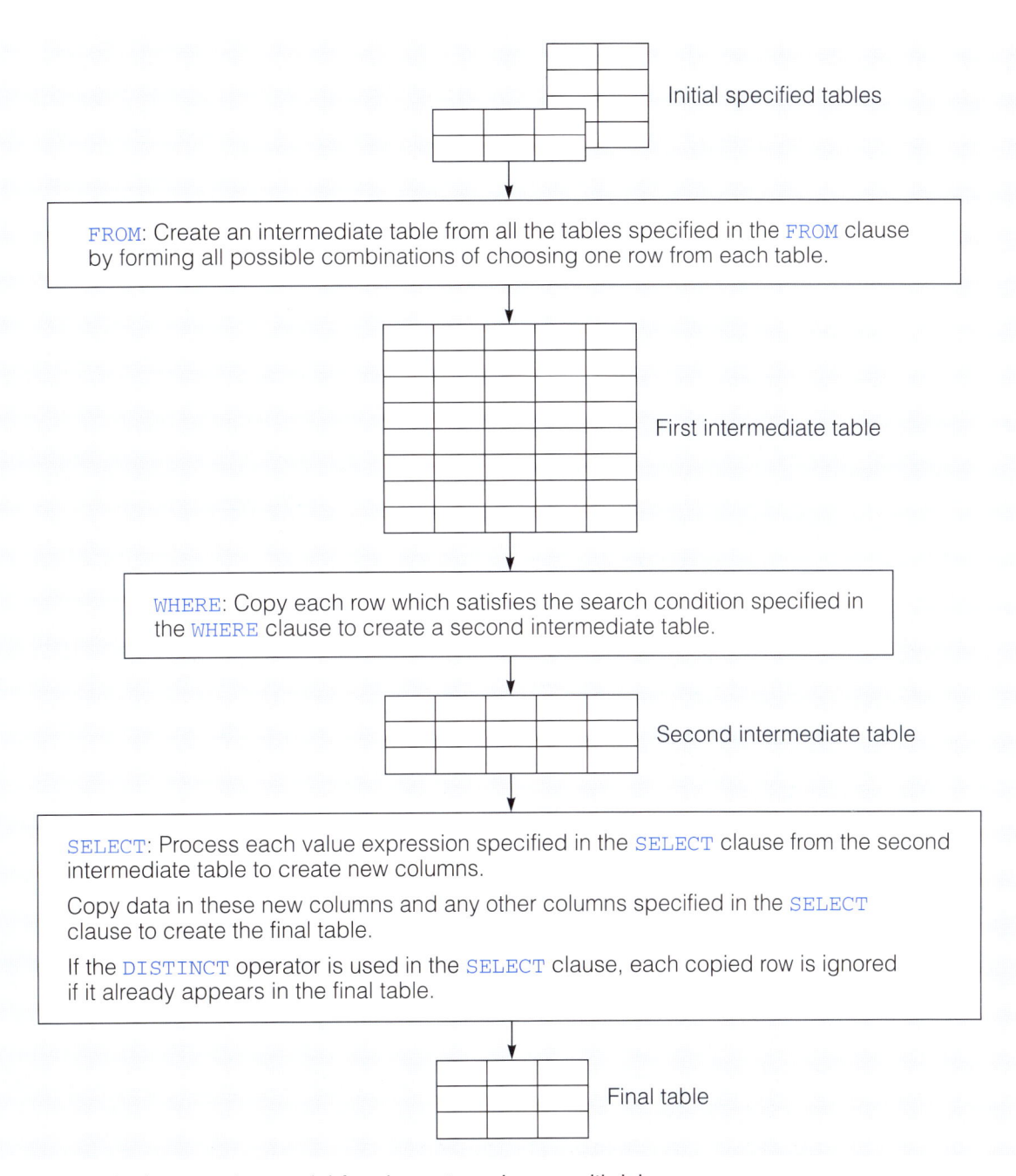

Figure 2.12 Logical processing model for elementary clauses with joins

The examples so far have shown a relationship between two tables represented by the equality of values in one column in each table, but it is also possible that a relationship might be represented by the equality of two or more columns in each table. For example, the table **enrolment** is related to the table **assignment** by the columns **student_id** and **course_code** in each table. In this case, the join condition is expressed by the two equalities

```
enrolment.student_id = assignment.student_id
   AND enrolment.course_code = assignment.course_code
```

More generally, any number of tables can be specified in the FROM clause of a query, and the WHERE clause can include any number of conditions; therefore, many joins may be specified in one statement.

Aliases and self joins

SQL aliases parallel the relational algebra aliases described in *Block 2*, Section 3.2. SQL allows you to provide an alternative name for each reference to a particular table in a query. This alternative name is called a table **alias**. There are two advantages of using aliases.

▶ First, some queries can be made more readable by renaming the tables in the `FROM` clause with an alias.

▶ Second, queries which involve joining a table to itself (called **self joins**) are only possible with the use of aliases.

Consider again the query **join1** which uses two tables, `small_occupied_by` and `small_ward`. We can simplify the query by introducing a short, one-letter alias for each of these two tables. This is achieved by following each table name in the `FROM` clause with its alias. Then each reference to the table elsewhere in the query can just refer to the alias. Using the alias `a` for `small_occupied_by`, and `b` for `small_ward`, we can rewrite **join1** as follows:

```
SELECT patient_id, a.ward_no, ward_name
FROM small_occupied_by a, small_ward b
WHERE a.ward_no = b.ward_no
```

aliases

EXERCISE 2.20

(a) Using the University database, write and run a query that does *not* use aliases to list the name and address for each student and their tutor.

(b) Write and run a second query which does use aliases which gives the same result as your solution to part (a).

EXERCISE 2.21

Suppose that we wish to use the Hospital database to answer the following, seemingly simple, request:

List the staff numbers and names of all the nurses who have the same name as another nurse.

(a) Based on the **nurse** table on the *Hospital Database Card*, what answer would you give to this request?

(b) Briefly describe how you obtained this answer.

Before trying to use SQL for this query, we should consider how we may expect an SQL logical process to answer this request. The important point is that the SQL logical processing model allows the comparison of values only in the same row of a table, and not on different rows as you did in scanning the *Hospital Database Card*. In order to compare one row of the staff table with another row of the staff table, we can think of it in terms of two copies of the same table. If these two copies are joined, the Cartesian product combines each row with every other row, and we can use the join condition that the value of the name from each of the tables must be equal. However, the table resulting from this simple join will also include rows in which each member of staff is related to themselves; these rows need to be eliminated. This elimination can be done using the staff numbers.

Activity 2.11 shows how we can formulate this query, using aliases to avoid the problem of having two references to the same table.

ACTIVITY 2.11

Using the Hospital database, run the following filed statement.

```
SELECT p.staff_no, p.nurse_name, q.staff_no
FROM nurse p, nurse q
WHERE p.nurse_name = q.nurse_name
  AND p.staff_no < q.staff_no
```
self_join

This query results in a final table containing just one row, in which two staff numbers are associated with the name 'Cooke'. As an aside, note that we have used the comparison operator < rather than 'not equal to' (<>), which might at first be thought appropriate for restricting the rows to those where staff numbers are different. The reason for using 'less than' is that the relationship is symmetric (i.e. if the person with staff number 153 has the same name as 424, then 424 has the same name as 153), and therefore each pair with the same name would have been represented twice if we had used <>.

However, what is of most interest to us in this query is the way in which the columns of the one table, **nurse**, have been referenced by two aliases, **p** and **q**. These aliases are forms of label which are specified in the **FROM** clause of the query. Each alias follows a specification of the table for which it is an alias, that is, **nurse** is specified twice – once for **p** and once for **q** – emphasising that the query requires the use of two copies of the **nurse** table.

The above simple example was helpful in introducing the need for aliases, and demonstrating the use of two copies of a table as a processing model for joining a table to itself (remember that this is not how a DBMS would do it in practice). However, a common practical reason for joining a table to itself occurs in the case of a recursive relationship.

EXERCISE 2.22

A supermarket database contains a table called **floor_staff** with columns **staff_no**, **name** and **supervisor_no** (all character strings). Formulate a query to find the name of the supervisor of the member of the floor staff who has staff number 345.

You can see that the use of aliases is necessary to join a table with itself, and in Section 3 you will find that there are other situations where aliases are essential, but they can also be used in any query. In particular, they can be helpful when qualified column references are required because a brief alias can make typing easier and the resulting query may be clearer. However, an alias can be as long as any other name, and you need to balance brevity with clarity.

Note that when an alias is defined in a **FROM** clause, the original table name cannot be used in the rest of the statement unless it is separately specified as part of the **FROM** clause. For example, in **self_join**, **nurse** cannot be used in the **WHERE** or **SELECT** clauses, but if the **FROM** clause were changed to

```
FROM nurse, nurse q
```

(i.e. without the alias **p**), then **nurse** would refer to the first table, and **q** to the second. So only one alias is strictly essential in such cases, but two are often used to distinguish clearly between the two references.

In SQL, an alias is usable only within the query specification in which it is defined. This behaviour is different from that of aliases in the relational algebra, in which an alias can be used across a sequence of expressions.

Inner joins

The SQL join operation combines rows from two tables by taking related pairs of rows, one from each table. The rows that make up the joined table are those where the data in the matching columns in each of the two tables satisfies the join condition.

The type of join we have considered so far is known as an **inner join**. SQL has an alternative syntax for inner joins that makes this explicit using the keywords `INNER JOIN` and `ON` as part of the `FROM` clause. In this syntax there is no `WHERE` clause. For example, under the alternative syntax, the earlier query **join1** becomes:

```
SELECT patient_id, small_occupied_by.ward_no, ward_name
FROM small_occupied_by INNER JOIN small_ward
  ON small_ward.ward_no = small_occupied_by.ward_no
```

inner_join

EXERCISE 2.23

Rewrite the solution to Exercise 2.22 using the `INNER JOIN` syntax.

Why are there two ways of writing inner joins? The use of the 'comma' syntax exists to maintain compatibility with SQL:1989. The `INNER JOIN` syntax exists to parallel the syntax for outer joins, which we will study in Section 4.

Natural joins

So far, we have seen how inner joins and self joins can be represented in the SQL syntax. In *Block 2*, you used the **natural join** as the method of joining relations. SQL also provides the syntax for natural joins on tables.

ACTIVITY 2.12

Using the University database, run the following filed statement.

```
SELECT *
FROM course c, quota q
WHERE c.course_code = q.course_code
```

course_quotas

The table returned by **course_quotas** lists, for each course, the course code, title, credit and quota of students allowed on that course, along with the review date for that quota. Notice that the matching columns have the same name, which is `course_code`.

This situation, where a join is required on tables by making identical column names equal, is very common. SQL allows the use of the keyword `NATURAL JOIN` to provide a shorthand under such circumstances. Instead of having to give a join condition, `NATURAL JOIN` allows you to specify just the tables involved in the join. The expression using a natural join that is equivalent to **course_quotas** is:

```
SELECT *
FROM course c NATURAL JOIN quota q
```

natural_join

2 Retrieval using simple queries

The query **natural_join** results in the following table.

course_code	title	credit	limit	date_reviewed
c2	Syntax	30	3000	2007-01-10
c4	Semantics	60	250	2007-01-10
c5	Logic	60	250	2007-04-23

Note that, unlike with an inner join, columns that occur in both joined tables appear only once in the resulting table. In the case of the query **natural_join**, the resulting table contains only one column named course_code. So to select the column course_code, we can use the following query, **natural_join_select**, in which the selected column (course_code) is not connected with either of the joined columns.

```
SELECT course_code
FROM course c NATURAL JOIN quota q
```
natural_join_select

> The implementation of SQL Anywhere differs from the Standard, in that the columns that appear in both the joined tables appear twice. Executing the query **natural_join** within the SQL Anywhere environment results in the following table.
>
> | c.course_code | title | credit | q.course_code | limit | date_reviewed |
> |:---:|:---:|:---:|:---:|:---:|:---:|
> | c2 | Syntax | 30 | c2 | 3000 | 2007-01-10 |
> | c4 | Semantics | 60 | c4 | 250 | 2007-01-10 |
> | c5 | Logic | 60 | c5 | 250 | 2007-04-23 |
>
> Therefore, when using **SELECT** with **NATURAL JOIN** in SQL Anywhere, you will need to use a correlating column name, for example:
>
> ```
> SELECT t.staff_number
> FROM telephone_tutored_by t NATURAL JOIN contracts_with c
> ```
> *natural_join_select_SQLAnywhere*

Note that, although in **natural_join** there is only one column name shared by the two tables, a natural join will match any number of columns (see Exercise 2.24). Care must therefore be taken to ensure that only the intended columns have the same names (in this case, just course_code) otherwise the match would require equality on columns other than those where you really wanted it.

EXERCISE 2.24

We wish to know which prescription numbers were used to treat the relevant symptoms. Using the Hospital database, write a query using **NATURAL JOIN** which gives, for each prescription number in the **prescription** table, the reasons for a particular prescription to be made.

Caveat: Although natural joins are supported by SQL, it is often not advisable to use them in writing SQL for non-trivial database projects. To understand a natural join, you need to understand the structure of the database because the key information about the join (i.e. the columns used in the join condition) is not explicit; this is precisely the information that a natural join hides. If the database is restructured (as any large database system will be), it may not be possible to determine which columns were matched by the natural join, and therefore what the join was supposed to do in the first place!

Databases often have a very long lifespan, and so any technique that reduces the maintainability of the database should be avoided. For this reason, we will avoid using natural joins in the remainder of this block. However, in *Block 4*, we will look at these issues in more depth.

2.5 The GROUP BY clause

The next clause in a query specification that is to be considered is the GROUP BY clause. We shall introduce this clause by using an example that illustrates one of the problems it solves.

EXERCISE 2.25

Using the SQL query facilities you have learnt so far, describe how you would find out how many students are registered in each region from the University database. (Hint: you will need more than one query.)

Exercise 2.25 is an example of a particular kind of requirement based on the need to group rows of data together so that each group can be processed in a similar way. In the exercise, you had to do this grouping by producing a separate query for each group. The GROUP BY clause allows you to do this with a single query.

ACTIVITY 2.13

Using the University database, run the following query.

```
SELECT region_number, COUNT(*) AS number_of_students
FROM student
GROUP BY region_number
```

group_by_region

This results in a final table which gives the information that is required to answer Exercise 2.25. However, you will notice that there are no rows corresponding to region 12 because there are no students registered in this region. Grouping the rows in the **student** table by **region_number** does not give any results for region 12, and so this region does not appear in the final table. We will look at ways to address this in Sections 3 and 4.

The best way to understand how the query **group_by_region** does the work of five queries is to analyse the logical processing of the query. First, processing the FROM clause gives an intermediate table, which is the whole of the **student** table. Second, the GROUP BY clause is processed: this groups together the rows of the intermediate table so that all the rows in each group have the same value in the column specified in the GROUP BY clause – in this case, **region_number**. The intermediate table produced by processing the GROUP BY clause is shown in Figure 2.13. (For clarity, only the **student_id** and **region_number** columns are shown; in fact, the intermediate table contains all the columns from the **student** table.)

2 Retrieval using simple queries

student_id	...	region_number
s22	...	1
s38	...	1
s42	...	2
s46	...	2
s01	...	3
s07	...	3
s02	...	4
s05	...	4
s09	...	4
s10	...	4
s57	...	4

Figure 2.13 The intermediate table after processing the **GROUP BY** clause

Note that the rows of the table have been grouped into four distinct groups, based on the common values in the `region_number` column.

This brings us to the processing of the **SELECT** clause. This clause behaves differently when there is a **GROUP BY** clause in the statement, and this difference is important to understanding the effect of **GROUP BY**. In the final table, we replace each set of rows in a group with a single row by applying the value expressions in the **SELECT** clause. In this case, there are two terms in the **SELECT** clause: the grouped column `region_number`, and the aggregate function **COUNT(*)** (which the **AS** keyword renames to `number_of_students`). So for each set of rows in a group we discard columns other than `region_number` and count the number of rows in the group. The resulting table is given in Figure 2.14.

Remember that the rows of the table may be displayed in any order.

region_number	number_of_students
1	2
2	2
3	2
4	5

Figure 2.14 The final table after processing the **SELECT** clause

The purpose of this kind of query is for each group of rows to be represented by just a single row in the final table. Therefore, the columns that appear in a **SELECT** clause in such a query must be:

either

(a) a grouping column – that is, a column specified in the **GROUP BY** clause with the same value in every row of each group (e.g. `region_number` in the query **group_by_region**),

or

(b) a column contained within an aggregate function, which results in one value for every group.

The processing therefore uses the grouped intermediate table and, for each group, produces a single row of the final table according to the specification of the `SELECT` clause, based on the descriptions in (a) and (b) above. The query **group_by_region** produces a final table which shows each region and the number of students associated with it.

We show how our logical processing model is updated for grouped queries in Figure 2.15.

Initial specified tables

`FROM`: Create an intermediate table from all the tables specified in the `FROM` clause by forming all possible combinations of choosing one row from each table.

First intermediate table (Cartesian product)

`WHERE`: Copy each row which satisfies the search condition specified in the `WHERE` clause to create a second intermediate table.

Second intermediate table

`GROUP BY`: Copy each of the rows in the second intermediate table into a third intermediate table, grouping them according to the values in the columns specified in the `GROUP BY` clause.

Third intermediate table

`SELECT`: Replace each set of rows in the same group with a single row by applying the value expressions in the `SELECT` clause to each group (value expressions may only contain the `GROUP BY` columns or aggregate functions).

Final table

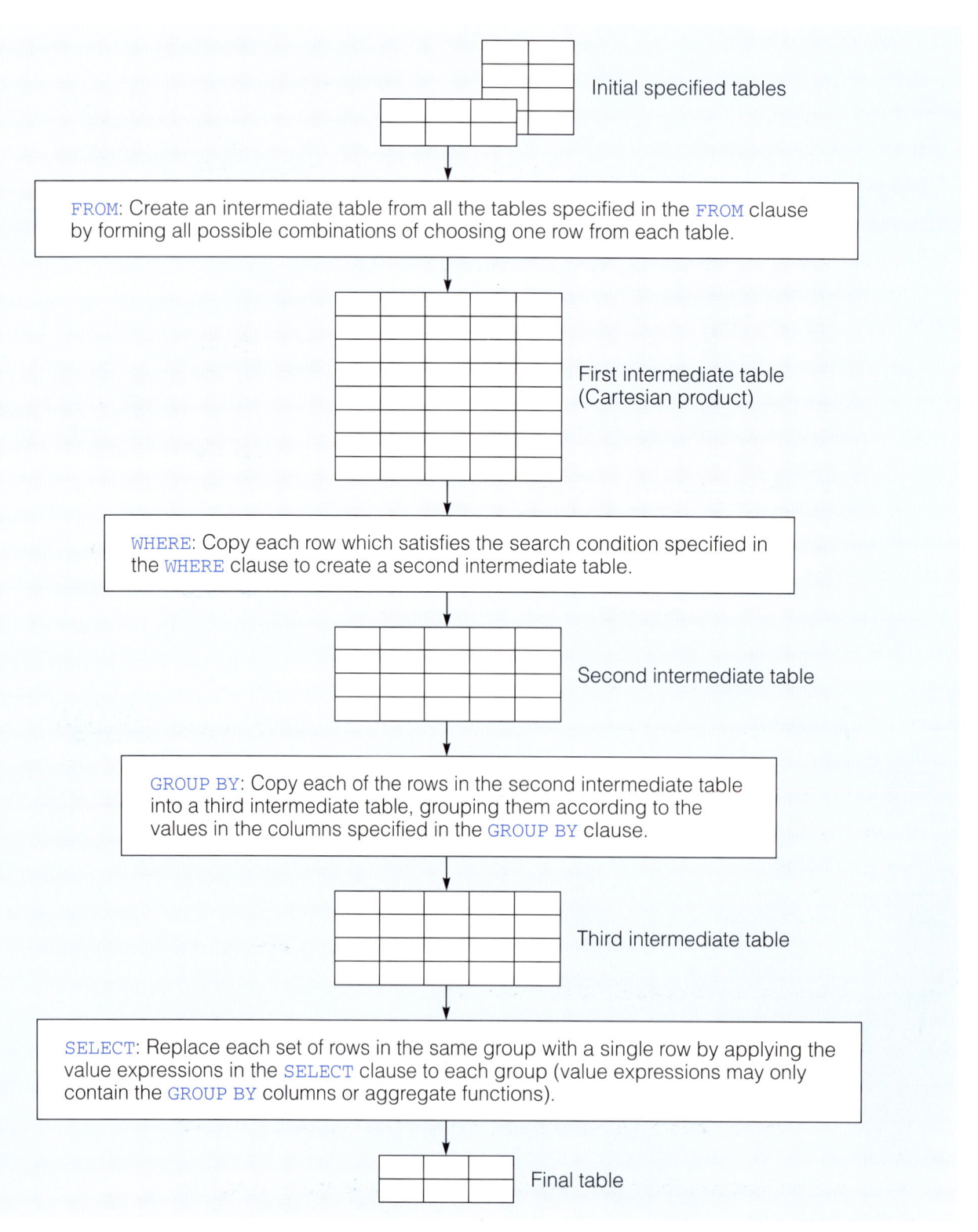

Figure 2.15 Logical processing model for grouped queries

When you have written a query containing a **GROUP BY** clause, you should apply the following simple check on each column referenced in the **SELECT** clause. Is the column either a grouping column or a column contained in an aggregate function? If a referenced column is neither of these then the query needs to be reformulated.

The next exercise asks you to identify whether some proposed SQL queries are well formed. We say a query is **well formed** if it is syntactically correct SQL (that is, it returns a table without generating an error). Note that a query can be well formed without answering the request for which it was intended; well-formedness is concerned only with syntactic correctness.

EXERCISE 2.26

Are the following three queries well formed? If not, why not? After you have written down your answers, try running the three queries using the Hospital database. (Note that the **start_date** column in the **treatment** table has the **DATE** data type. **DATE**s in SQL are ordered, and from a set of dates, **MIN** will choose the earliest.)

(a) SELECT patient_id, MIN(start_date) AS first_start_date
     FROM treatment
     GROUP BY patient_id

group1

(b) SELECT drug_name, MAX(price) AS max_price
     FROM drug
     GROUP BY type

group2

(c) SELECT type, MAX(price) AS max_price,
            COUNT(drug_code) AS num_of_type
     FROM drug
     GROUP BY type

group3

ACTIVITY 2.14

The following query illustrates the effect of grouping when there is also a **WHERE** clause in the statement.

Using the University database, run the following filed statement.

    SELECT course_code, COUNT(student_id) AS number
    FROM enrolment
    WHERE course_code IN ('c2', 'c4')
    GROUP BY course_code

group_code

The **group_code** query can be expressed in English as:

> For the courses with codes c2 and c4, list the course code and the number of students enrolled on that course according to the **enrolment** table.

To understand how **group_code** produces its result, consider how it would be logically processed.

▶ First, processing the **FROM** clause produces an intermediate table, that is, a copy of the **enrolment** table.

▶ Second, processing the **WHERE** clause produces a further intermediate table containing only rows having c2 or c4 in the **course_code** column.

- Third, processing the GROUP BY clause divides this intermediate table into two groups, one based on c2 and the other on c4, and copies them into a third intermediate table. (Note that this matches Figure 2.15, the general processing model that includes a GROUP BY clause.)
- Finally, processing the SELECT clause produces the required table by replacing each group with a single row, and reducing the specified columns to a single value for each group. It can do this because course_code is a grouping column and student_id has an aggregate function, COUNT, applied to it.

It is possible to specify more than one grouping column in the GROUP BY clause. In this case, SQL treats each pair, triple, and so on, of grouping column values as a single entry to be grouped. Note that as before all the columns in the SELECT clause must appear in the grouping clause (but not necessarily the other way around).

The following query illustrates a two-column grouping.

> Using the University database, run the following query.

```
SELECT student_id, course_code, COUNT(*) AS number
FROM assignment
GROUP BY student_id, course_code
```
two_groups

In **group_by_region** the aggregate function COUNT(*) was used to count each occurrence of a different value of region_number in student. In **two_groups**, COUNT(*) is used to count each occurrence of a different combination of student_id and course_code in assignment.

EXERCISE 2.27

Complete the following table by showing the order, as written and as logically processed, of the four clauses of the query specification we have dealt with so far: SELECT, WHERE, GROUP BY and FROM.

Sequence of clauses as written:	Sequence of clauses as logically processed:
1 ...	1 ...
2 ...	2 ...
3 ...	3 ...
4 ...	4 ...

EXERCISE 2.28

(a) Use the *Hospital Database Card* to work out the final table that the following query returns. Then run the query in the Hospital database to check your answer.

```
SELECT type, COUNT(drug_code) AS number,
       SUM(price) AS total_price
FROM drug
WHERE type IN ('Painkiller', 'Antibiotic')
GROUP BY type
```
group_prod

(b) Use the Hospital database to write and run a query that uses the table patient to list, for each ward number except wards w5 and w7, the number of patients who occupy that ward.

2.6 The `HAVING` clause

The `HAVING` clause is to groups what the `WHERE` clause is to rows. Rather than applying to individual rows, `HAVING` operates on the results of aggregate functions. In the same way that rows have to satisfy the search condition in a `WHERE` clause, so whole groups must satisfy the search condition in a `HAVING` clause in order to be processed further.

ACTIVITY 2.15

Using the Hospital database, run the following query.

```
SELECT type, COUNT(drug_name) AS number,
       MIN(price) AS lowest_price
FROM drug
GROUP BY type
HAVING MIN(price) > 0.15
```
having_min

We can express the query **having_min** in English as follows:

> For each type of drug represented in the `drug` table, list the number of drugs of that type and the lowest price of any drug of that type, provided that the minimum price is at least 0.15.

Check the table that is generated by executing **having_min** against the English expression of the query.

To understand how the `HAVING` clause works, we will consider the logical processing of the **having_min** query.

▶ First, processing the `FROM` clause produces an intermediate table, which is the whole of the `drug` table.

▶ Second, since there is no `WHERE` clause to restrict the rows of this table, the next processing step is carried out for the `GROUP BY` clause that divides the table into groups of rows associated with each `type`.

▶ Third, processing the `HAVING` clause tests every group of rows in the intermediate table which is produced by the `GROUP BY` clause. The search condition in the `HAVING` clause is applied to each group, and the output includes only those groups which satisfy the condition. In the case of **having_min**, each group will therefore be tested against the condition that the minimum value in the `price` column must be greater than 0.15, and those that satisfy this condition (three groups in this case, with 3, 2 and 2 rows) will become part of the intermediate table produced by the `HAVING` clause.

▶ Finally, the `SELECT` clause is processed in the way described previously for queries containing the `GROUP BY` clause, to give the final table of 3 rows. Note that according to this model, the expression `MIN(price)` is calculated twice: once for the condition in the `HAVING` clause, and once in the `SELECT` clause. The result of the expression is not stored.

In practice, a DBMS might store and reuse the result, but this is not part of the processing model.

The role of the `HAVING` clause is to apply a search condition to each group of rows in the intermediate table that is produced by the `GROUP BY` clause. This means that the conditions which are contained in the search condition of a `HAVING` clause must satisfy similar restrictions to those laid down for the `SELECT` clause when a `GROUP BY` clause is present: they can only apply to values which are common to each group. In other words, any column referenced in an expression in the search condition of a `HAVING` clause must be a grouping column or must have an aggregate function applied to it.

The logical processing model to deal with group search conditions is given in Figure 2.16.

Initial specified tables

FROM: Create an intermediate table from all the tables specified in the FROM clause by forming all possible combinations of choosing one row from each table.

First intermediate table (Cartesian product)

WHERE: Copy each row which satisfies the search condition specified in the WHERE clause to create a second intermediate table.

Second intermediate table

GROUP BY: Copy each of the rows in the second intermediate table into a third intermediate table, grouping them according to the values in the columns specified in the GROUP BY clause.

Third intermediate table

HAVING: Copy each group of rows which satisfies the HAVING search condition into a fourth intermediate table.

Fourth intermediate table

SELECT: Replace each set of rows in the same group with a single row by applying the value expressions in the SELECT clause to each group (value expressions may only contain the GROUP BY columns or aggregate functions).

Final table

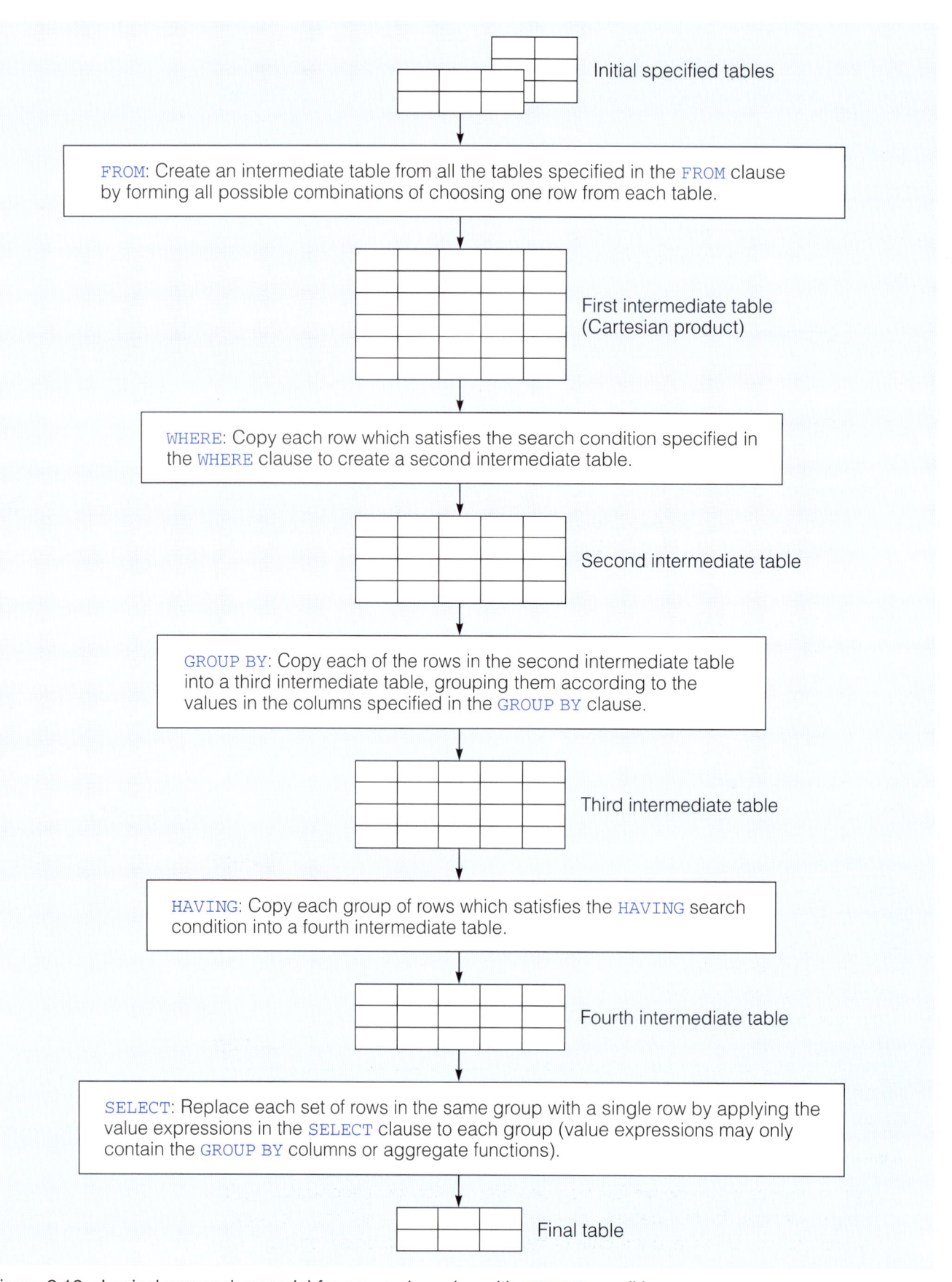

Figure 2.16   Logical processing model for grouped queries with HAVING conditions

2 Retrieval using simple queries

EXERCISE 2.29

The query **group_code** in Activity 2.14 can be used to answer the request:

How many students are enrolled for each of the courses c2 and c4?

Modify the query **group_code** by using a **HAVING** clause rather than a **WHERE** clause to answer the same request.

Exercise 2.29 and the query **group_code** show how, for certain requests, there is a choice of formulating a query so that a condition is expressed at either the row or the group level. Note that this is possible only when a condition in a **WHERE** clause is allowable in a **HAVING** clause. In this example, the condition in the **WHERE** clause uses **course_code**, which is a grouping column and therefore allowable in the **HAVING** clause as well.

EXERCISE 2.30

What are the restrictions placed on the search condition in a **HAVING** clause?

EXERCISE 2.31

Are the following three queries well formed? If not, why not? After you have written down your answers, try running the queries using the Hospital database.

(a) `SELECT type, COUNT(drug_name) AS number,`
        `MIN(price) AS lowest_price`
   `FROM drug`
   `GROUP BY type`
   `HAVING MIN(price) > 0.15`
     `AND drug_code NOT IN ('B23', 'B48')`

having1

(b) `SELECT type, COUNT(drug_code) AS number,`
        `AVG(price) AS average_price`
   `FROM drug`
   `WHERE MAX(drug_name) >= 'G'`
   `GROUP BY type`
   `HAVING AVG(price) >= 0.30`

having2

(c) `SELECT type, SUM(price) AS total_price`
   `FROM drug`
   `GROUP BY type`
   `WHERE drug_name >= 'G'`
   `HAVING SUM(price) > 1.00`
     `OR type IN ('Placebo', 'Painkiller')`

having3

EXERCISE 2.32

(a) Using the **prescription** table in the Hospital database, write and run a query that answers the following request:

For each patient for whom more than one prescription has been written, list the patient identifier for that patient, the number of prescriptions that have been written for him or her, and the date of the earliest of those prescriptions.

(You may find this difficult, but later we shall describe a systematic approach to constructing queries to find answers to this sort of request.)

(b) How would you modify the query you wrote in part (a) to exclude treatments administered by the member of staff whose staff number is 462?

(c) How would you modify the query of part (b) to exclude the patient whose patient identifier is p39?

2.7 The ORDER BY clause

So far, the rows in any table resulting from an SQL query have not been presented in any particular order. Queries, as we have been describing them, do not control the order of rows in any output table. Therefore, different queries that return the same table may not present those tables with the constituent rows in the same order.

In fact, the specific order of the rows in any output table is undefined and the final rows are in a sequence determined by the implementation (SQL Anywhere in our examples), often related to how the data is stored. Although the order of the rows in the output table is not relevant to the logical processing model of the DBMS, it is often useful for the user to have the rows presented in a particular order. To this end, a query can be augmented with an ORDER BY clause within a query statement to provide control over the sequencing of the rows in an output table.

Note that the ORDER BY clause is a different kind of clause from the other clauses that we have seen in this section because it has no effect whatever on the *contents* of the final table. It simply controls the *presentation* of that table. We shall explore this clause in Activity 2.16.

ACTIVITY 2.16

Using the University database, run the following query.

```
SELECT *
FROM staff
```
staff

Note the order in which the values in the **name** column appear in the final table: the order is not defined, and so the values may not appear in the same order as those on the *University Database Card*.

➢ Now run the following query.

```
SELECT *
FROM staff
ORDER BY name
```
order_by

This results in a final table in which the rows of the table have been sorted in ascending order of values in the **name** column.

The query **order_by** can be expressed in English as:

List all the information in the **staff** table, ordered so that the values in the **name** column are sorted into alphabetical order.

By default, the ORDER BY clause assumes that the rows are to be sorted in ascending order. However, this could have been explicitly specified in the ORDER BY clause using the order parameter ASC as follows.

```
ORDER BY name ASC
```

2 Retrieval using simple queries

However, it is also possible to order the rows in descending order. To do this in the case of the **order_by** query we would use the following ORDER BY clause.

```
ORDER BY name DESC
```

> Change the **order_by** query to include ASC and DESC, in turn, and run the revised queries. Check that you get the expected results.

An ORDER BY clause may be included as the last clause in any kind of query statement that we have considered in this section. The clause is the last step in the logical processing of the query, taking the table resulting from the rest of the query and sorting it according to the column(s) and order as specified in the clause. Therefore, only one ORDER BY clause can be included.

To order the rows for queries which contain (non-trivial) value expressions in the SELECT clause, we must make use of AS to assign names to the results of the expressions. For example, suppose we wanted the result of the query

```
SELECT patient_id, height/weight
FROM patient
```

to have the rows sorted in ascending order of the column containing the result of the expression **height/weight**. We would need to use an alias as follows.

```
SELECT patient_id, height/weight AS hw_ratio
FROM patient
ORDER BY hw_ratio
```

order_by_AS

Of course, by now you should be in the habit of always using AS to name columns containing the results of value expressions.

> Using the Hospital database, run the **order_by_AS** query, and check that you have obtained the expected results.

The above examples specify just one column in the ORDER BY clause, but more than one column is allowed, and each column can have its own order parameter.

> Now run the following query.

```
SELECT *
FROM drug
WHERE type <> 'Placebo'
ORDER BY type, price DESC
```

multi_order_by

EXERCISE 2.33

Study the final table generated by the query **multi_order_by**. Express the query in English.

ASC is the default when the order is not specified. To order the rows according to descending values of both columns, we need to write DESC after type as well as after price.

The query **multi_order_by** accomplishes a two-stage ordering. First, the table is sorted in ascending order according to the first column specified in the ORDER BY clause which, in this case, is type. Then, wherever a number of adjacent rows have the same value for type, they are sorted in descending order according to the second specified column, that is, price.

EXERCISE 2.34

Would the final table resulting from **multi_order_by** have been changed if the last clause had been written as follows?

```
ORDER BY type, price DESC, drug_name
```

> A historical note: SQL:1992 only allowed rows to be ordered by columns or expressions named in the `SELECT` clause. This requirement was removed in SQL:1999, and the rows in tables can now be ordered by any expression in the `ORDER BY` clause; the columns do not have to appear in the query's `SELECT` clause.

2.8 Constructing SQL queries

All the remaining exercises in this section use the University database.

A request for information often appears difficult to unravel and formulate into an SQL query. This can be a particular problem where grouping of data is needed. In this subsection, we propose a clause-by-clause method that may help you to carry out this process. The method will be presented by means of a sequence of exercises that build up to an answer to the following request:

> For each course, except c4 and c7, list those students whose average mark for all assignments, not including assignment 3, is over 70. Also, list the average marks for these students.

We will begin with the `FROM` clause, and identify the table(s) that provide the input data that will be processed according to the query. In general, the data may come from several tables.

EXERCISE 2.35

(a) Write a `FROM` clause for this request.   *FROM assignment*

(b) What would be the intermediate table resulting from the processing of this clause?

Next consider the `WHERE` clause, identifying any rows of the base table that are explicitly required or can be omitted. Rows to be included might be indicated by phrases such as 'for (some value)' or 'for all (values)'. Rows to be omitted can be identified by looking for phrases such as 'except', 'greater than', 'unless', and so on, in the request. Avoid, however, search conditions that require input from more than one row at a time (which will need `GROUP BY` and `HAVING` clauses).

EXERCISE 2.36

Write a `WHERE` clause for the request.

It would be wrong to include in this `WHERE` clause the code `AVG(mark) > 70`. Remember that aggregate functions cannot be used in conditions applied to individual rows.

In developing a complex query, it is often useful to imagine how the intermediate tables of the logical processing model would look. Usually it is possible to write an SQL query

2 Retrieval using simple queries

that actually allows you to display a table that shows the values in a particular intermediate table.

EXERCISE 2.37

Write a query that would result in a table indicating what the intermediate table would look like after the logical processing of the **WHERE** clause.

We next consider the **GROUP BY** clause, examining the request for phrases like 'for each ... ', 'those ... ', and so on, that may indicate which columns (as opposed to aggregate functions of a column) are needed in the final table and so might identify the columns that are used to group data.

EXERCISE 2.38

(a) What needs to be done to the intermediate table resulting from the **WHERE** clause so that it accords with the words 'for each course' that begin the request?

(b) Write a **GROUP BY** clause that achieves the required grouping.

Exercise 2.38 requires grouping by course code as illustrated in Figure 2.17.

student_id	course_code	assignment_number	mark
s05	c2	1	78
s05	c2	2	63
s09	c2	1	92
s09	c2	2	76
s22	c2	1	74
s22	c2	2	68
s02	c5	1	70
s02	c5	2	65
s38	c5	1	51
s57	c5	1	74

Figure 2.17 The intermediate table after grouping according to course_code

EXERCISE 2.39

(a) Looking at each of the groups in Figure 2.17, how does each group need to be organised to accord with the words 'those students' in the request?

(b) Extend the **GROUP BY** clause developed in Exercise 2.38 to achieve the additional grouping you identified in part (a).

The **GROUP BY** clause developed in Exercise 2.39 can be interpreted as: 'within each course_code group, group the rows according to student_id'. This **GROUP BY** clause would produce the intermediate table shown in Figure 2.18.

student_id	course_code	assignment_number	mark
s02	c5	1	70
s02	c5	2	65
s05	c2	1	78
s05	c2	2	63
s09	c2	1	92
s09	c2	2	76
s22	c2	1	74
s22	c2	2	68
s38	c5	1	51
s57	c5	1	74

Figure 2.18 The intermediate table after grouping according to course_code and student_id

Next, we must consider the HAVING clause by examining the request for conditions involving aggregation, such as the words 'average', 'maximum', 'total', 'number of', and so on, as well as any conditions involving the columns contained in the GROUP BY clause.

EXERCISE 2.40

(a) Write a HAVING clause for the request.
(b) How will the incorporation of the HAVING clause into the query affect the intermediate table shown in Figure 2.18?

Figure 2.19 shows groups that have an average mark greater than 70.

student_id	course_code	assignment_number	mark
s05	c2	1	78
s05	c2	2	63
s09	c2	1	92
s09	c2	2	76
s22	c2	1	74
s22	c2	2	68
s57	c5	1	74

Figure 2.19 The intermediate table after eliminating average marks less than or equal to 70

Finally, the SELECT clause needs to be written to organise the data into appropriate columns to answer any remaining parts of the request.

EXERCISE 2.41

(a) Write a `SELECT` clause that will answer the remainder of the request, including the need to list the average marks.

(b) How will the processing of this `SELECT` clause affect the intermediate table in Figure 2.19?

Figure 2.20 shows the final table after the completion of Exercise 2.41.

course_code	student_id	avg_mark
c2	s05	70.5
c2	s09	84.0
c2	s22	71.0
c5	s57	74.0

Figure 2.20   The final table arrived at after processing the `SELECT` clause

It only remains to put the clauses in the correct order as required by an SQL query.

EXERCISE 2.42

Go back to the answers of the previous exercises and piece together the whole query which is required to answer the original request.

ACTIVITY 2.17

Run **construct** from Solution 2.42 and check that the final table that is produced matches Figure 2.20. Remember that the rows may be in a different order in the final table.

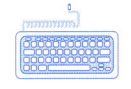

The step-by-step approach which was used to develop **construct** has demonstrated a method for developing queries based on the logical processing model. In general, the method is a three-stage process. The first stage is to build up a query according to the steps you think are necessary for the logical processing and to write an appropriate clause for each step. The second stage is to gather the clauses together into a correctly organised query; for some queries you may have to resolve naming ambiguities by means of qualified column names or aliases. The third stage is to run the query, if possible, testing the query by using data for which you know the result; if the test does not give you the results you expect, return to the first two stages.

In detail, the first stage may be tackled, clause by clause, as follows.

1 Write the `FROM` clause by deciding which table(s) the data will come from.

2 Write the `WHERE` clause, first by identifying any join conditions if there is more than one table in the `FROM` clause, and then by asking whether the rows should be restricted in any way. Terms like 'except', 'in', 'provided that', 'where', 'greater than', and so on, are pointers to possible conditions. Note that it can be helpful to test this clause (with the `FROM` clause) by adding `SELECT *` to give a query which you can run to check the results.

3 Write the `GROUP BY` clause by checking whether the data needs to be grouped in any way. The need for aggregate functions may be indicated by terms like 'total',

'average', 'number of', 'how many', 'maximum', and so on (though remember these terms may also be applied to the whole table without grouping), and then you need to find the grouping columns which may be indicated by terms like 'each', 'every', and so on.

4   Write the **HAVING** clause after checking whether the groups need restricting in any way. Conditions similar to those identified for the **WHERE** clause may occur, and may be used with either grouping columns or aggregate functions noted for the **GROUP BY** clause.

5   Write the **SELECT** clause by deciding what columns (names, functions, expressions) should appear in the final table.

EXERCISE 2.43

Write and run a query to answer the following request:

For the staff members whose identifiers are 5324 and 8431, list those courses for which they tutor more than one student, and give the number of students that they tutor on those courses.

2.9 Summary

In this section, we have dealt with the details of the query specification and have used it to formulate the query statements which we term simple queries. The clauses of simple queries are written in the following order:

```
SELECT ...
FROM ...
WHERE ...
GROUP BY ...
HAVING ...
```

We developed a logical processing model, which showed that the clauses of simple queries are logically processed in the following order:

```
FROM ...
WHERE ...
GROUP BY ...
HAVING ...
SELECT ...
```

The logical processing of a simple query begins with one or more tables. The logical processing of each clause in turn produces another table, which is called an intermediate table in all cases except for the **SELECT** clause. The intermediate table from each clause constitutes the input to be logically processed by the next clause. The final clause to be logically processed in a simple query is the **SELECT** clause, and the table produced by the **SELECT** clause is called the final table. The logical processing model led us to a three-stage method for developing simple queries from an informal request.

We saw that the effect of each of the five clauses was as follows.

FROM   This mandatory clause specifies the table(s) to be processed. If one table is specified, then the intermediate table resulting from the clause is simply the table itself. However, if more than one table is specified, the intermediate table is the Cartesian product of those tables. Tables can also be given a label in this clause by specifying an alias.

WHERE This optional clause has the effect of restricting the rows of the intermediate table it receives from the **FROM** clause by using an expression in a search condition, which is applied to each row. Individual conditions are represented by expressions which contain SQL's comparison operators, or the operators **BETWEEN**, **IN** and **LIKE**. Expressions can be combined using the logical operators **AND**, **OR** and **NOT**.

GROUP BY This optional clause is used to collect the rows of a table into groups, based on the values in one or more grouping columns. Aggregate functions in the **HAVING** and **SELECT** clauses are then applied to the column values in these groups rather than to the whole table.

HAVING This optional clause restricts the groups which have been formed by the **GROUP BY** clause. It does this on the basis that referenced columns in a search condition must be grouping columns or have aggregate functions applied to them.

SELECT This mandatory clause performs the task of producing the columns for the final table from the intermediate table it receives as input. The columns it has to produce are specified in terms of value expressions, which may include expressions or aggregate functions. **DISTINCT** may be included to prevent duplicate rows in the final table.

We have also seen how query specifications can be augmented by the **ORDER BY** clause to sort the rows in the final table according to the values in one or more columns. Columns resulting from value expressions must be assigned names using **AS** to be ordered in this way.

We saw that the aggregate functions – **AVG**, **COUNT**, **SUM**, **MAX** and **MIN** – when applied to an expression, return a single value. We also saw how duplicate values in a column can be ignored by using the **DISTINCT** operator. We saw how the data in two tables can be joined using the Cartesian product of the tables, together with an appropriate join condition, in a **WHERE** clause to eliminate unwanted rows.

LEARNING OUTCOMES

Having completed this section, you should now be able to do the following:
- Distinguish between a request, a query, and a query expressed in English.
- List the clauses that can occur in a query specification.
- Distinguish between an aggregate function and other functions.
- Describe the effect of using **DISTINCT** in a query.
- Construct the Cartesian product of two tables.
- Construct the table resulting from a join of two tables.
- Given a simple SQL query, or a query involving an **ORDER BY** clause, describe the purpose of each clause, provide a logical model of the processing of the query and write an informal request that is satisfied by the query.
- Given an informal request, write a simple SQL query or a query involving an **ORDER BY** clause that satisfies the request.

3 Retrieval using composite queries

This section continues to deal in a practical way with the SQL retrieval facilities. In Section 2, you learnt how to formulate and run queries containing just one query specification involving SELECT, FROM, WHERE, GROUP BY and HAVING clauses. However, a single query specification with these five clauses could not answer all requests. As you saw in Exercise 2.10, a single query specification does not allow you to compare each row of a table against the result of an aggregate function. In Exercise 2.10, you used one query to obtain the result of the aggregate function, and then used that result to build a second query to obtain the final answer.

In SQL, if the output from one query is needed to form a subsequent query, we use a **composite query**. In composite queries, a **query statement** is formed from more than one query specification. In this section, you will learn about the two ways of formulating composite queries: one using the UNION, EXCEPT and INTERSECT operators and the other using subqueries.

In this section, the distinction between a query statement and a query specification is important. A query specification is formed from at most one of each of the SELECT, FROM, WHERE, GROUP BY and HAVING clauses. A query statement is a combination of many clauses that can be processed, resulting in a single table. As we shall see, the FROM, WHERE and HAVING clauses of a query specification may themselves include further queries.

3.1 The UNION operator

The UNION operator of SQL essentially corresponds to the *union* operator of the relational algebra.

The UNION operator constitutes a way of combining the results of separate, compatible queries.

ACTIVITY 3.1

Consider the following request to retrieve information from the Hospital database:

> Provide a table which contains the staff number, name and position of each doctor and nurse working in the hospital. The table should represent a nurse's position as 'Nurse'.

The data needed for the comparison can be obtained by means of these two queries.

```
SELECT staff_no, doctor_name, position
FROM doctor
```
union1

```
SELECT staff_no, nurse_name, 'Nurse'
FROM nurse
```
union2

Examine both **union1** and **union2** carefully and predict how the final tables will look. Using the Hospital database, run the two queries to see if you were right.

Note that the third column of the table resulting from **union2** contains the constant 'Nurse'. This is simply a value expression (see Section 2.2) in the SELECT clause which gives a column having the value '**Nurse**' in every row of the column. It is a value expression that contains no column names or string operators, which yields the same constant value no matter what other values there might be in each row.

The effect of this use of the constant '**Nurse**' is to ensure that the results of the two queries **union1** and **union2** are **union compatible**. For tables to be union compatible in SQL, the values in each corresponding column must be of the same predefined data type (therefore the values in the first column of each table must be of the same data type, the values in the second column must be of the same data type, and so on). In this case, the **position** column in the **doctor** table is a string, and the constant '**Nurse**' is a string, and so the resulting tables are union compatible. When combining tables in this way, if the values on two corresponding columns are of different data types then a cast should be used to convert one column to the type of the other.

The results of the two queries can be combined into a single table using the following composite query:

```
SELECT staff_no, doctor_name AS staff_name, position
FROM doctor
UNION
SELECT staff_no, nurse_name, 'Nurse'
FROM nurse
```

union3

▶ Now run **union3** and check that the final table answers the retrieval request.

union3 is one query statement consisting of two query specifications.

The final table resulting from **union3** is the union of the final tables of the two individual queries, **union1** and **union2**. The columns are given in the sequence specified by each **SELECT** clause.

There are some points to note about tables that are returned by queries using **UNION**.

- **UNION** is unusual in SQL processing in that it automatically removes duplicate rows. Duplicate rows are removed whether the duplication originated within or between the two intermediate tables. Therefore, when using **UNION**, you do not need to specify **DISTINCT** to explicitly request that duplicate rows should be removed. If you particularly do not want duplicate rows to be removed, then you can use the operator **UNION ALL**.

- Each query specification is processed independently, so column names or aliases specified in one specification have no meaning in the other. For example, in **union3**, the column name **position** could not be used in the second query specification since there is no column named **position** in the **nurse** table.

- The final column names are defined by the first query of those composed with **UNION**. In the case of **union3**, the second and third columns of the final table are **staff_name** and **position**, which are the names set in the first query specification.

- Each query specification results in a final table. These tables must be union compatible, that is, they must have the same number of columns and corresponding columns must have the same data types. Exact matching of the parameters of the data type is not required, so that character strings, for example, may have different lengths.

The need for **UNION** may be recognised whenever a table whose rows may come from two or more other tables is required. More than two tables can be a source of such rows because in general, a single statement may include the union of a number of query specifications.

EXERCISE 3.1

We require a table that contains, in the first column, the name of each patient in the `patient` table and the name of each nurse in the `nurse` table, and in the second column, the height of each patient and the string '`Unknown`' for each nurse (as the database does not contain the nurses' heights).

The following query is intended to return the required table, but in fact generates an error.

```
SELECT patient_name, height
FROM patient
UNION
SELECT nurse_name, 'Unknown'
FROM nurse
```

union_fail

Given that `patient_name` and `nurse_name` are defined as `VARCHAR`s and `height` is defined as `DECIMAL(4, 1)`:

(a) Why does executing **union_fail** in the Hospital database generate an error?

(b) Rewrite the query so that it returns the required table.

Using `EXCEPT` and `INTERSECT`

As well as `UNION`, SQL provides two more operators for combining the results of union compatible queries. These are `INTERSECT` and `EXCEPT`.

`INTERSECT` and `EXCEPT` are similar to the *intersection* and *difference* operators of the relational algebra, respectively.

ACTIVITY 3.2

Using the University database, run the following two queries.

```
SELECT student_id, course_code
FROM enrolment
EXCEPT
SELECT student_id, course_code
FROM assignment
```

except1

```
SELECT student_id, course_code
FROM assignment
INTERSECT
SELECT student_id, course_code
FROM examination
```

intersect1

Use the *University Database Card* to determine requests that these two queries can be used to answer.

The query **except1** shows the `EXCEPT` operation, which lists the *difference* between two result sets. The table that results from executing **except1** is the table generated by the first query specification, *except* for any rows that are also generated by the second query specification. So **except1** can be used to answer the following request:

> What are the student identifier and course code of each enrolment that has been made, for which no assignment has been submitted?

3 Retrieval using composite queries

The query **intersect1** shows the `INTERSECT` operation listing the *common rows* between two resulting tables. The table that results from executing **intersect1** contains just those rows that appear in both the intermediate tables generated by the two query specifications. So **intersect1** can be used to answer the following request:

> What are the student identifier and course code of each enrolment where the student has both submitted an assignment and taken an examination?

EXERCISE 3.2

(a) Are the following two queries well-formed SQL? If not, why not? If so, what request would the query be used to answer? After you have written your answers, run both queries using the Hospital database.

```
SELECT staff_no
FROM nurse
EXCEPT
SELECT supervisor
FROM supervises
```
except2

```
SELECT prescription_no, quantity
FROM prescription
UNION
SELECT ward_name, number_of_beds
FROM ward
```
union4

(b) Write an alternative to the following filed statement which does not use the `UNION` operator.

```
SELECT *
FROM drug
WHERE type = 'Painkiller'
UNION
SELECT *
FROM drug
WHERE type = 'Antibiotic'
UNION
SELECT *
FROM drug
WHERE type = 'Sedative'
```
union5

(c) Using the University database, write and run a query which lists, for the course with code c4, the student identifier of each student who has submitted some assessed material for that course, and the mark received for that assessed material. The table generated by the query should also contain a third column named `assessment_number`, which contains the number 99 if the row represents an examination, or the assignment number if the row represents an assignment.

(d) Rewrite your answer to part (c) so that the final table shows the names of the students as well as their identification numbers. (Hint: you will need to use a join.)

EXERCISE 3.3

The `UNION` operator is said to be **commutative** because if **A** and **B** are two union compatible tables, then **A UNION B** and **B UNION A** give tables with the same rows (see also Exercise 3.21 in *Block 2*).

Are `INTERSECT` and `EXCEPT` commutative? If not, give an illustrative example.

Union and sorting

The `ORDER BY` clause may not appear in either of the query specifications involved in a `UNION` operation as it does not make sense to sort these intermediate results before completing the `UNION`. However, the combined set of query results produced by the `UNION` operation can be sorted by specifying an `ORDER BY` clause after the *last* query specification. However complex a query may be, one and only one `ORDER BY` clause can be included. This clause is the last step in the logical processing of the query, taking the table resulting from the rest of the query and sorting it according to the column(s) and order specified in the clause.

The logical processing model including the `UNION` operation and the `ORDER BY` clause is shown in Figure 3.1. This processing model also applies to queries involving the `EXCEPT` and `INTERSECT` operations.

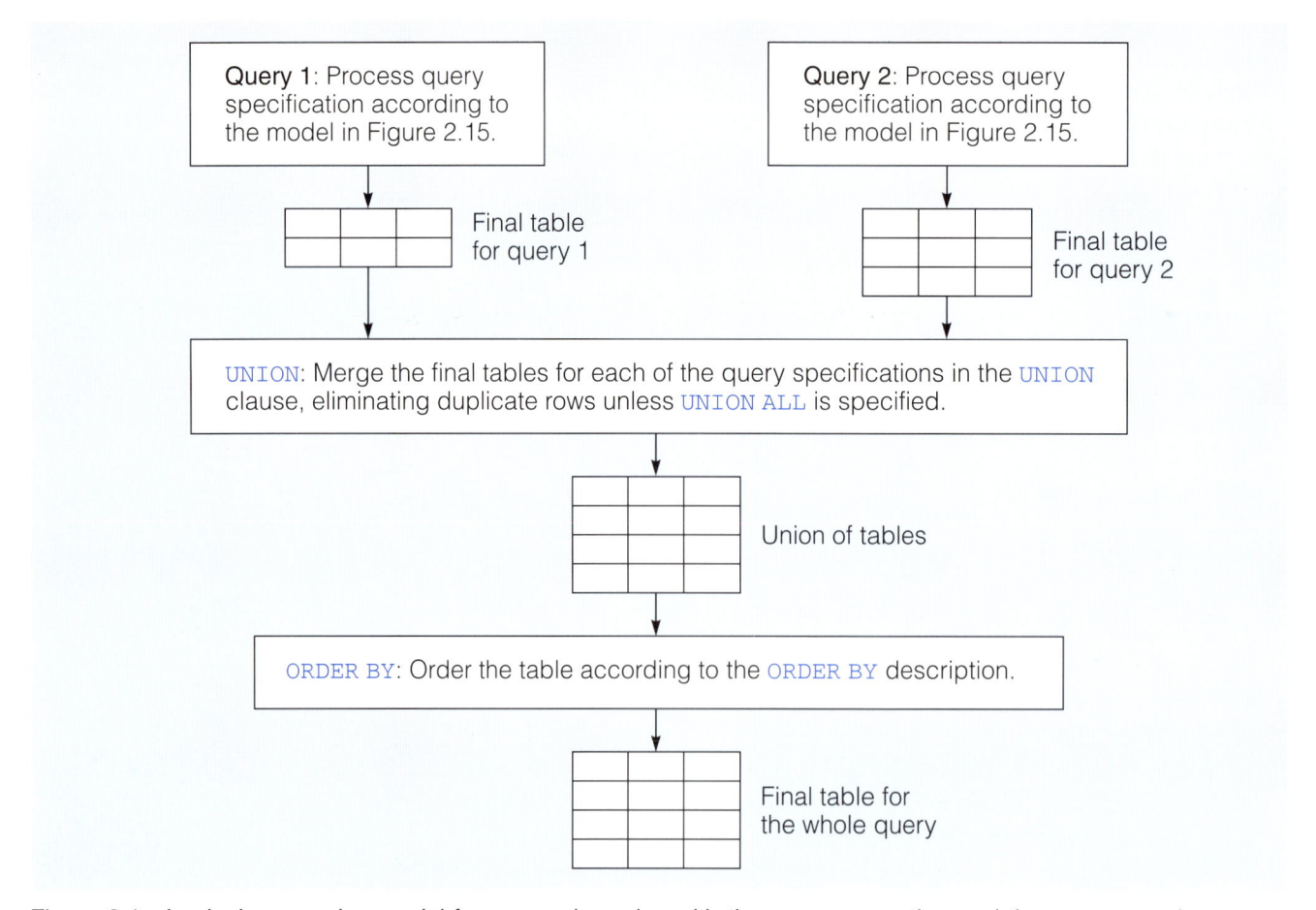

Figure 3.1   Logical processing model for grouped queries with the `UNION` operation and the `ORDER BY` clause

3.2 Subqueries

A more general form of composite query occurs when one of the clauses in a query specification itself contains a query statement (i.e. a single query specification, or several query statements joined with **UNION**, **INTERSECTION** or **EXCEPT**). In these cases, the nested query statement is evaluated, and the result is then used in the processing of the query specification containing it.

We still call the composite form a 'query specification', even if one of the clauses has a query statement embedded in it.

Consider the following request:

> List the patient identifiers and names of the male patients whose weight is below the average (for other male patients).

EXERCISE 3.4

Explain why the following query cannot be used in the Hospital database to answer the above request.

```
SELECT patient_id, patient_name
FROM patient
WHERE gender = 'M' AND weight < AVG(weight)
```
where_problem

➤ Run **where_problem** to confirm your answer.

The problem in Exercise 3.4 is very similar to that in Exercise 2.10. As in Exercise 2.10, one way to answer the query is to address the solution in two parts: one to find the average quantity and the other, using this average, to find those quantities that are less than the average quantity.

EXERCISE 3.5

Write and run two separate queries that together can be used to answer the following request:

> List the identifiers and names of the male patients whose weight is below the average (for other male patients).

ACTIVITY 3.3

Using the Hospital database, run the following filed statement.

```
SELECT patient_id, patient_name
FROM patient
WHERE gender = 'M'
  AND weight < (SELECT AVG(weight) AS avg_weight
                FROM patient
                WHERE gender = 'M')
```
subquery1

The final table produced by **subquery1** is the same as that produced by the solution to Exercise 3.5.

Notice that the subquery that appears in the **WHERE** clause of **subquery1** is just the same as **weight1** (in the solution to Exercise 3.5). However, instead of using the result of the query **weight1**, which is 75.95, in **weight2**, we have substituted the whole statement for **weight1**, within brackets, into **weight2** exactly where we previously had the result 75.95.

A query specification that is used in this subordinate way is called a **subquery** (hence the name of the filed statement). In general, subqueries can be nested, one inside another, which means that subqueries can have subqueries which themselves can have subqueries, and so on. Each subquery is part of an **outer query** specification, and in the case of **subquery1**, the outer query specification is the main query.

In general, a subquery can be used to formulate queries in which a particular row (or group of rows) of a table needs to be compared:

▶ either with values retrieved from related rows in one or more different tables,
▶ or with values derived from other rows in the same table.

The second of these comparisons is known as a *correlated subquery*, and will be discussed further in Section 3.3.

Logical processing for subqueries

The logical processing of the type of composite query shown in **subquery1** treats the subquery specification separately from the rest of the query. While both the subquery and the outer query include a `FROM` clause that specifies the `patient` table, each effectively has a separate copy of this table and, in this case, the subquery can be processed without any consideration of its outer query. Like all queries it results in a table, but this example requires that the final table is constrained to have a single column and a single row (otherwise an error is generated) so that the result can be converted to a single value, which can then be used for the comparison expression. Only when the subquery processing is complete can the rest of the main query be processed as previously described.

The logical processing of **subquery1** can be summarised as follows.

1 Process the subquery.
2 Use the result of processing the subquery to process the rest of the query.

The processing for each of these two queries is the same as that for simple queries.

A subquery can occur in a search condition for a `WHERE` or `HAVING` clause. If it is known that the subquery results in a single value, as in **subquery1**, then it can be used as the right-hand value expression with the comparison operators, `<`, `=`, and so on, which were described in Section 2.3.

More generally, a subquery results in a collection of values for the specified column, where normal comparison operators are not applicable. In this case, there are three column comparison operators that can be used: `IN`, `ALL` and `ANY`.

Column membership: `IN`

You have already seen the comparison operator `IN` in Section 2: `IN` checks whether a data value is equal to any of the values in a list. Instead of explicitly stating the values to be compared as we did in Section 2, we can now use a subquery to derive the list as a column.

ACTIVITY 3.4

Using the Hospital database, run the following filed statement.

```
SELECT drug_code
FROM drug
WHERE type = 'Painkiller'
```

painkillers

3 Retrieval using composite queries

This should produce a column of the codes of the four painkillers. We can now use **painkillers** as a subquery in place of a list of drug codes.

Now run the following two filed statements.

```
SELECT drug_name, price
FROM drug
WHERE drug_code IN ('P02', 'P27', 'P51', 'P73')
```
drug_in1

```
SELECT drug_name, price
FROM drug
WHERE drug_code IN (SELECT drug_code
                    FROM drug
                    WHERE type = 'Painkiller')
```
drug_in2

The tables returned as the result of the two queries should be identical.

3.3 Outer references and correlated subqueries

In the examples we have looked at so far, the subqueries have been evaluated independently of the query in which they appear. The queries which we have embedded in **WHERE** clauses could be evaluated independently of the main (outer) query in which they were nested. However, it is often necessary to refer to the value of a column in the current row of the outer query. This is known as an **outer reference**.

If a subquery contains an outer reference, it is known as a **correlated subquery** because the processing of the subquery depends on the (partial) processing of the main query.

As an example, consider the following request:

> What are the patient identifier, gender and weight of all the patients whose weight is more than 10% higher than the average weight of the other patients of the same gender?

This is a request that involves comparing a single value (a patient's weight) with an aggregate (10% more than the average weight of patients of the same gender).

How do we find this information just by looking at the tables on the *University Database Card*? We can start with some row of the **patient** table, for example, <p07, Tennent, M, 176.8, 70.9>, and see whether 70.9 is more than 10% higher than the average weight of the other male patients in the table, and so on, for other rows. In SQL terms, we require an expression like:

```
weight > 1.1 * <average weight for that person's gender>
```

The right-hand term can be replaced by a subquery, giving the following complete query that answers the request.

```
SELECT patient_id, gender, weight
FROM patient a
WHERE weight > 1.1 * (SELECT AVG(weight) AS avg_weight
                      FROM patient b
                      WHERE a.gender = b.gender)
```
correlated

This query can be expressed in English as follows:

> For each row in the **patient** table, list the values of **patient_id**, **gender** and **weight** if the value of **weight** is more than 10% higher than the average value of **weight** for all patients that have the same **gender**.

The query **correlated** contains a subquery in its **WHERE** clause. This subquery contains a reference to the table **a**, which is the alias of **patient** in the **FROM** clause of the outer query. To process the **WHERE** clause of the main query, we need to evaluate the subquery using the same value for **gender** as from the main query so that the processing of the subquery is based on the same gender as that of the population with which it is being compared.

This link between the two parts is the reason that it is called a correlated subquery. The comparison requires that qualified column names be used to distinguish between **gender** from the main query and **gender** from the subquery. Since the two tables have the same name (**patient**), we need to use the aliases **a** and **b** to distinguish them. Note that the columns in the main query do not need to be qualified: when a subquery appears in a **WHERE** clause, its table and column names cannot be seen outside the subquery itself.

ACTIVITY 3.5

Run the query **correlated** and check that it correctly answers the English expression of the query.

The logical processing for queries containing correlated subqueries is more complex than for the other kinds of subquery that we have examined because the subquery cannot be processed independently of the outer query. We will illustrate this by describing the logical processing of **correlated**.

```
SELECT patient_id, gender, weight                    (1)
FROM patient a                                       (2)
WHERE weight > 1.1 *                                 (3)
        (SELECT AVG(weight) AS avg_weight            (4)
         FROM patient b                              (5)
         WHERE a.gender = b.gender)                  (6)
```
correlated

For the query **correlated**, the main query and the subquery are both processed exactly according to the models given in Section 2. We have shown the query **correlated** again with the clauses numbered to illustrate the processing.

1. Processing the **FROM** clause (2) produces an intermediate table, which is a copy of the whole of the **patient** table.
2. The **WHERE** clause (3) is processed. For each row in the intermediate table:
   (i) The subquery is processed according to the model given in Figure 2.8 of Section 2. In this case, the **WHERE** clause (6) compares the value of **gender** in each row of the subquery table (i.e. **b.gender**) with the value from the current row in the main query (i.e. **a.gender**). The **SELECT** clause (4) applies an aggregate function to a single column, and so the subquery returns a single value.
   (ii) If **weight** is greater than 1.1 times the value returned by the subquery, then that row is copied into a second intermediate table.

3 Finally, processing the **SELECT** clause (1) takes the specified columns **patient_id**, **gender** and **weight** from the second intermediate table to produce the final table.

So the subquery is processed each time the **WHERE** condition is evaluated; once for each row of the **patient** table in the **FROM** clause of the outer query (or, strictly, once for each row of the intermediate table, which is identical to **patient**).

EXERCISE 3.6

(a) Explain what is meant by a correlated subquery.

(b) How does the logical processing of a correlated subquery differ from that of an ordinary subquery?

EXERCISE 3.7

(a) Write and run a query (containing a subquery) which lists the name, type and price of the drug whose price is the lowest for drugs of that type.

(b) Given the **drug** table on the *Hospital Database Card*, how many times will the subquery in your answer to part (a) be evaluated during the logical processing of the query, and how many times is the same evaluation repeated?

While part (b) in Exercise 3.7 was intended to help you understand correlated subqueries, you may also be inclined to think that the use of SQL results in an inefficient processing of such queries. However, we must again emphasise that the logical processing model does not specify *how* an implementation would execute such a query, and in practice, repeated processing may be recognised and avoided.

3.4 Quantifiers

ALL, **ANY** and **EXISTS** are known as **quantifiers**, and an expression which has a quantifier applied to it is said to be **quantified**. They are called quantifiers because they specify how many elements in a subquery must satisfy the condition. We shall now explore the use of these three keywords.

The **ALL** quantifier

ACTIVITY 3.6

Using the Hospital database, run the following filed statement.

```
SELECT ward_name
FROM ward
WHERE number_of_beds <= ALL (SELECT DISTINCT number_of_beds
                             FROM ward)
```
all1

The following exercises consider the details of this query.

EXERCISE 3.8

Using the **ward** table on the *Hospital Database Card*, describe the result of the subquery in the query **all1**.

➢ Check your answer to Exercise 3.8 by running the text of the subquery by itself.

The keyword `ALL` requires that the condition is true for every member in the collection. The answer to Exercise 3.8 causes the processing of the `WHERE` clause in **all1** to check whether the `number_of_beds` value in each row is less than or equal to every member of the set {6, 8, 8, 10, 14}.
[handwritten: collection]

EXERCISE 3.9

For what values of `number_of_beds` in the **ward** table will the condition in the `WHERE` clause be true?

EXERCISE 3.10

Using the answer to Exercise 3.9, suggest a request which the query **all1** can be used to answer.

The following points should be noted about the query **all1**.

▶ The expression is only true for those rows of the **ward** table of the main query where the value in the column `number_of_beds` is less than or equal to all the members of the collection resulting from the subquery. This collection is the same for all the rows, and so the same condition applies to all the rows.

▶ We must be able to make a comparison (using `<=`, for example) against every member of the resulting table when we use a quantifier.

The logical processing of the query **all1** is similar to that of **subquery1**. The subquery is processed first to give a result, which is a collection of values (although the values come from the `number_of_beds` column, this information cannot be used by the outer query). The rest of the main query is then processed using the result of the subquery. When processing the `WHERE` clause of the main query, a row is chosen only if the expression is true for that row's value in the `number_of_beds` column, which requires that it is less than or equal to all the values in the collection. The final table then consists of those rows that satisfy the condition.

EXERCISE 3.11

By considering the request that the query **all1** can be used to answer (see Exercise 3.10), give another query that uses an aggregate function in the subquery, rather than a quantifier, to answer the same request.

Activities 3.5 and 3.6 have illustrated the use of subqueries to answer, in one query, requests that involve a comparison of a value in each row with either an aggregate function or a collection of values, based on the whole table. A similar situation arises when answering a request that involves a grouped table and requires a comparison of some value for each group with either an aggregate function or a collection of values, based on the group.

3 Retrieval using composite queries

Consider the following, seemingly innocuous, request for information from the University database:

> What is the course code of the course on which the largest number of students are enrolled, and what is the number of students?

We shall use a method based on that employed in Section 2 to build SQL queries, taking into account that the **WHERE** and **HAVING** clauses in the query may also contain subqueries in their search conditions.

We shall build up the query in Exercise 3.12. Ideally, you should work through this whole exercise before looking at our solution, but if you are uncertain about your answers then check each part as you proceed.

EXERCISE 3.12

Using the University database, work through parts (a) to (i) to develop a query that can be used to answer the following request:

> What are the course code and the number of students for the course on which the largest number of students are enrolled?

(a) First, decide which tables will be required to develop the query.
(b) Write a **FROM** clause for the query.
(c) Write a **WHERE** clause for the query, if it needs one.
(d) Write a **GROUP BY** clause, if it is required.
(e) Explain why a **HAVING** clause may be required. Informally express the search condition that the **HAVING** clause should contain.
(f) Write and run a query that uses **COUNT** to find the number of students in each course group (as required for the above comparison).
(g) Write a **HAVING** clause for the query. Remember that you cannot use a subquery as an argument of an aggregate function, such as **MAX**. However, you can use **ALL**.
(h) Write a **SELECT** clause for the request.
(i) Write the complete query that will answer the request. This is the second stage of the method outlined earlier and it involves placing all the clauses into their correct syntactic order and resolving any ambiguities.

> Compare your final solution to Exercise 3.12 with **all2** in Solution 3.12, part (i), and check against the *University Database Card* to ensure that it answers the request.

The **ANY** quantifier

Another quantifier used in SQL is **ANY**, which is similarly used for a comparison with a set of values resulting from a subquery and requires that the associated condition is satisfied for at least one value in that set. While **ALL** requires that the comparison is true for all values in a set, **ANY** requires that it is true only for at least one value. We can think of the logical processing of **ANY** as taking each of the values in the set and applying the comparison operator in turn until one of the comparisons is true. If none of the comparisons is true the expression evaluates to FALSE.

We shall now look at some examples of **ALL** and **ANY** to illustrate their use. For these examples, we give an explicit set of values. However, note that these expressions (overleaf) are *not* well-formed SQL. In SQL, **ALL** and **ANY** must be applied to a subquery that returns a table with a single column.

- $5 = \text{ANY } (2, 4, 3, 5)$ is true because 5 is equal to at least one of the set. In this case, it is equal to exactly one element in the list, 5.
- $5 <> \text{ANY } (2, 4, 3, 5)$ is true because 5 is not equal to at least one element in the list, that is, 2, 3 or 4. SQL allows the use of the keyword **SOME** instead of **ANY**, which sometimes seems more natural: 5 is indeed not equal to *some* of 2, 3, 4, 5.
- $5 >= \text{ALL } (2, 4, 3, 5)$ is true because 5 is greater than or equal to every element in the list.
- $5 = \text{ALL } (2, 4, 3, 5)$ is false because 5 is not equal to every element in the list.
- $5 <> \text{ALL } (2, 4, 3, 5)$ is false because it is not true that 5 is not equal to every element in the list. That is, it is equal to at least one of them. This expression is equivalent to the expression `NOT (5 = ANY (2, 4, 3, 5))`, which you might find clearer.

EXERCISE 3.13

Are the following two queries well formed? If not, why not? If so, explain the result that you would expect to obtain if the queries were run in the Hospital database. After you have given your answers, run the two queries using the Hospital database.

(a) ```
SELECT doctor_name
FROM doctor
WHERE doctor_name = ANY (SELECT staff_no, doctor_name
                         FROM doctor
                         WHERE position > 'registrar')
```
any1

(b) ```
SELECT staff_no
FROM doctor
WHERE doctor_name = ANY (SELECT position
                         FROM doctor)
```
any2

EXERCISE 3.14

Write and run a query that uses a subquery with **IN** to answer the following request:

What are the patient identifier and the name of every patient who occupies a ward that is staffed by a nurse with the same name as that patient?

Notice that, applied to subqueries, the behaviour of the **IN** comparison operator is equivalent to the use of the equality operator with the **ANY** quantifier (i.e. **IN** is equivalent to **= ANY** for subqueries). However, in addition, the **IN** operator allows the use of explicit lists.

➢ Run the following filed statement, using the Hospital database.

```
SELECT drug_code, drug_name
FROM drug
WHERE drug_code = ANY (SELECT drug_code
                       FROM drug
                       WHERE type = 'Antibiotic')
```
any3

➢ Now edit the query **any3**, replacing **= ANY** with **IN**, and run the new query.

You should have found that the results are exactly the same.

3 Retrieval using composite queries

The `EXISTS` quantifier

The existence test uses the `EXISTS` quantifier to check whether or not a subquery produces any rows of query results. An expression which applies the `EXISTS` quantifier to a subquery evaluates to TRUE if the subquery returns a table containing one or more rows and FALSE otherwise. Like `ANY` and `ALL`, the `EXISTS` quantifier may be used as the search condition of a `WHERE` or `HAVING` clause.

ACTIVITY 3.7

Using the University database, run the following filed statement.

```
SELECT student_id, name
FROM student s
WHERE NOT EXISTS (SELECT *
                  FROM enrolment
                  WHERE student_id = s.student_id)
```
exists

Note that the subquery in **exists** is correlated: it refers to a column, `s.student_id`, which comes from the table of the main query. The alias, `s`, is not strictly necessary but is included to avoid having to write the full column name `student.student_id`. In a subquery, an unqualified column name relates to the table in the `FROM` clause of the subquery, so `student_id` relates to `enrolment`; of course, you can add the table name to qualify the column name if you wish.

EXERCISE 3.15

What request does the query **exists** answer?

(Hint: in trying to answer this question, study the output of the query in relation to the `student` and `enrolment` tables; also, ask yourself what are the results generated by the subquery, and then mentally 'process' the whole query.)

The following details show how we arrive at the answer to Exercise 3.15. The `WHERE` clause in the main query must process all the rows in the `student` table. Consider the row which has a `student_id` value of s42. Does it meet the search condition? The table that results from processing the subquery is empty: there is no `student_id` value of s42 in the `enrolment` table. But an expression applying `EXISTS` to a subquery is false if the subquery returns a table with no rows. Therefore, applying `EXISTS` to the result of this subquery evaluates to FALSE. This means that `NOT EXISTS` applied to the subquery evaluates to TRUE. Therefore, the row in the `student` table containing `student_id` s42 satisfies the condition of the `WHERE` clause in the main query.

Now consider the row in which the value of `student_id` is s02. The table that results from processing the subquery contains the rows corresponding to the courses on which this student is enrolled (i.e. c5 and c7). Therefore, the `EXISTS` clause is true (as there are rows in the table, the table is not empty) and the complete condition `NOT EXISTS` is false. The data for the student with student identifier s02 is therefore not included in the final table.

The query **exists** illustrates the use of the `EXISTS` quantifier with `NOT`, but can be used in a similar way without it. When `EXISTS` is applied to a subquery, the specific values in that subquery are not important: the only consideration is whether the table returned by the subquery is empty. The query **exists** uses the asterisk to specify that the subquery returns columns of the `enrolment` table, but any columns can be named in the subquery `SELECT` because the actual values contained in the result are not used.

EXERCISE 3.16

(a) If `EXISTS` instead of `NOT EXISTS` had been used in the **exists** query, what request would the query have answered?

(b) Write an alternative query for part (a) which does not use `EXISTS`.

(c) Write and run a query, which uses `EXISTS` with a subquery, that answers the following request:

For any staff member who tutors students on a course, show the staff number and the region which that staff member is contracted to.

The answer for part (b) in Exercise 3.16 shows that there are many ways of formulating a query to answer a given request. The second alternative solution uses an uncorrelated subquery with `IN` (which is equivalent to `= ANY`). Neither this form of the query nor that using `EXISTS` has an explicit join condition, as in the first alternative solution, but both still have other ways of matching the values of `student_id` in each of the two tables involved. Of course, the problem can also be solved using a join, which is a valid solution that some may find more natural.

Because there are often many queries that can answer a given request, you should always bear in mind that there may be an alternative solution. For example, there are many more complicated solutions to part (c) in Exercise 3.16. If you find that a query is complex, you may find that a different approach will give you a shorter or clearer solution: do not make things more complicated than necessary.

A query using `EXISTS` can often be expressed in other ways, but it is useful as a way of naturally representing the conditions of a request. This is particularly true when a join is not possible, and the use of `NOT EXISTS` often provides a good solution.

3.5 Subqueries versus joins

You will have noticed that many of the queries that were written using subqueries could also have been written as multiple table queries using joins. The following exercise asks you to explore this idea further.

EXERCISE 3.17

This exercise uses the University database.

(a) Using a join, write and run a query that lists the title and credit rating of each of the courses on which the student with student identifier s05 is enrolled.

(b) Using a subquery, write and run a query to answer the same request.

Either of the two queries in the solution to Exercise 3.17 will give the correct courses, and neither is better than the other. Many people find the second more natural because the English request does not ask for any information about enrolments, and it seems a little strange to join the `course` and `enrolment` tables to answer the request.

3 Retrieval using composite queries

Often either a join or a subquery may be used. However, there are cases involving data from two tables where only one formulation is suitable.

- A join is necessary when the final table includes data from both tables.
- A subquery is necessary when a comparison is to be made with an aggregate function applied to the second table or lists of values from all the rows.
- Subqueries can only be used in the `WHERE` and `HAVING` clauses of a query specification. However, when carrying out the step-by-step method for developing queries, a subquery may need to be considered at the point of formulating the `FROM` clause. If the data to be selected only references one table in the `FROM` clause, then a subquery may be used to specify data from other tables in either a `WHERE` clause or a `HAVING` clause.

When there is a genuine choice between a join and a subquery, there are two factors to consider. The first factor, as we saw in Exercise 3.17, is which formulation seems more naturally based on the English request. The second factor to consider is which formulation is likely to be most efficient in the retrieval of the required data. A subquery often makes it simpler to develop the query and, because a subquery often allows you to separate the contribution of each table to a query, the subquery can often be processed (and hence tested) independently of the main query.

3.6 Subqueries in the `FROM` clause

So far in this section, we have looked at how subqueries can occur in `WHERE` and `HAVING` clauses. The final topic which we will look at in this section is how subqueries can be embedded in a `FROM` clause. The ability to place subqueries in `FROM` clauses is a powerful technique.

ACTIVITY 3.8

Using the University database, rerun the following query.

```
SELECT region_number, COUNT(*) AS number
FROM student
GROUP BY region_number
```
group_by_region

The result of the query **group_by_region** is a table whose columns are named `region_number` and `number`, which contain the number of each region in the `student` table, and the number of rows containing that number in the `region_number` column, respectively.

Now run the query:

```
SELECT *
FROM (SELECT region_number, COUNT(*) AS number
      FROM student
      GROUP BY region_number) AS s
WHERE number > 3
```
nested_group_by

The query **nested_group_by** returns a list of those regions which have more than three students registered, along with the number of students registered in the region.

Activity 3.8 illustrates how a query can be nested in a `FROM` clause, and used in the rest of the query just as if it is a separate table. When executed, **group_by_region** returns the following table.

region_number	number
1	2
2	2
3	2
4	5

Suppose that this were a table in the database called (for example) `s`. Then to list the regions with more than three registered students, and the number of students in those regions, we would simply use the following query.

```
SELECT *
FROM s
WHERE number > 3
```

nested_group_by

SQL allows us to put a table definition in the `FROM` clause as well as the names of existing tables. So you can see that **nested_group_by** is simply this query, with the query **group_by_region** appearing in the `FROM` clause.

Notice that the table generated by the nested query has been given a name with the construction `FROM (...) AS s`. When using nested queries in this way, SQL insists that the generated table, also known as a **derived table**, is named with `AS`, even if the name is not used in the rest of the query.

Recall from Section 3.3 that when a subquery appears in a `WHERE` clause, the outer clause cannot 'see' the columns of the table generated by the subquery. This is not the case for subqueries that appear in a `FROM` clause, where the columns of the derived table can be used in the remaining clauses of the query specification. So in **nested_group_by**, the condition in the `WHERE` clause (`number > 3`) uses the `number` column that is named in the derived table. Similarly, the `SELECT` clause can refer to the columns in the derived table. If we require only the column containing the numbers of the regions where more than three students are registered, we can use the query

```
SELECT region_number
FROM (SELECT region_number, COUNT(*) AS number
      FROM student
      GROUP BY region_number) AS s
WHERE number > 3
```

derived_table_column_in_select

which selects only the `region_number` column, rather than all the columns, as in **nested_group_by**.

The `WHERE` clause in **nested_group_by** illustrates that by using nested queries in `FROM`, comparisons can be made on the results of aggregate functions. As we saw in Section 2.3, the condition in a `WHERE` clause is carried out row-by-row, so a `WHERE` clause cannot itself contain an aggregate function. However, by creating a table which contains the result of an aggregate function (here, `COUNT(*)`), we can then use the results of that table in a `WHERE` clause.

3 Retrieval using composite queries

In Exercise 2.10, you were asked to formulate a query that could be expressed in English as:

> List the student identifier, course code and mark for each assignment submission in the `assignment` table where the mark awarded is greater than the average mark for all assignment submissions.

With the SQL presented at that point in the course, two queries were needed to answer the request: one to obtain the result of the aggregate function `AVG(mark)`, and another to use the result of that function to make the comparisons in the `WHERE` clause. The first query, **average_mark**, is repeated here:

```
SELECT AVG(mark) AS average_mark
FROM assignment
```
average_mark

If you run **average_mark** in the University database, you will receive the following table.

average_mark
71.45

We can create the query that we want by joining this table to `assignment` in the `FROM` clause of a suitable query as follows.

```
SELECT student_id, course_code, mark
FROM (SELECT AVG(mark) AS average_mark
      FROM assignment) AS a1, assignment
WHERE mark > average_mark
```
nested_above_avg

The table returned by **average_mark** is used in the `FROM` clause of **nested_above_avg**. The queries **nested_above_avg** and **nested_group_by** illustrate that a subquery in a `FROM` clause can be treated and manipulated in exactly the same way as a named table.

We can now see why it is good practice to always name the columns in a table, and why such practice is necessary when we use subqueries. In **nested_group_by**, the nested query produces a column containing the result of the aggregate function, `COUNT(*)`, which is named `number`. If the column is not named in this way, the query will not execute, as you can see by running the following query.

```
SELECT *
FROM (SELECT region_number, COUNT(*)
      FROM student
      GROUP BY region_number) AS s
WHERE number > 3
```
nested_query_unnamed

We have already seen that many of the queries that use subqueries could also be written as multiple-table queries using joins. In the same way, there may be several different ways of answering a request through the different ways of using a subquery in a query. The next exercise explores this.

EXERCISE 3.18

Adapt the query **nested_above_avg** so that the subquery appears in the `WHERE` clause, rather than in the `FROM` clause. Your answer should return the same table as that generated by **nested_above_avg**.

EXERCISE 3.19

Describe the logical processing of the query **nested_above_avg**.

EXERCISE 3.20

Are the following queries well formed? If not, why not? If so, what request does the query answer?

You should attempt to answer the questions before running each query.

(a)
```sql
SELECT student_id, name, course_code
FROM (SELECT student_id AS id, course_code
      FROM assignment
      WHERE MAX(mark) > 70
      GROUP BY student_id, course_code) AS a1, student
WHERE student_id = id
```
                                                                              nested1

(b)
```sql
SELECT student_id, name, region_number
FROM (SELECT region_number AS region,
             COUNT(*) AS staff_in_region
      FROM staff
      GROUP BY region_number), student
WHERE region_number = region AND staff_in_region > 3
```
                                                                              nested2

(c)
```sql
SELECT s1.staff_number AS staff_no, name, courses_tutored
FROM (SELECT staff_number,
             COUNT(DISTINCT course_code) AS courses_tutored
      FROM tutors
      GROUP BY staff_number) AS s1, staff s2
WHERE s1.staff_number = s2.staff_number
```
                                                                              nested3

(d)
```sql
SELECT student_id, c1.course_code AS course, title
FROM (SELECT course_code AS code, title
      FROM course) AS c1, enrolment
WHERE code = course_code
```
                                                                              nested4

Writing queries with subqueries in `FROM`

We will now work through some examples that provide advice on writing queries that contain subqueries in a `FROM` clause. All the exercises in this section use the Hospital database.

EXERCISE 3.21

An SQL query is needed to answer the following request:

> Give the staff number and name of each consultant who is responsible for six or more patients, along with the number of patients that they are responsible for.

3 Retrieval using composite queries

(a) To answer this query, we need to know how many patients each consultant is responsible for. Write a query that can be expressed in English as:

List the staff number of every consultant who is responsible for a patient according to the `patient` table, along with the number of patients that the consultant is responsible for.

(b) Now write a query that answers the original request. Both the `doctor` table and your answer to part (a) should appear in the FROM clause of your query.

Exercise 3.21 illustrates how you might decompose a request into the separate tables that are required to construct the final query where an aggregate function is needed. The first part of the exercise considers what table would be generated that contains the results of the aggregate function. In this case, that involves using `COUNT(*)` on the `patient` table to find out how many patients each consultant is responsible for. The second part of the exercise considers how to use that table in the FROM clause in order to obtain a query that answers the original request.

You may also have found a query that answers the request in Exercise 3.21 that uses a HAVING clause, rather than a subquery in a FROM clause. In fact, the query **nested_group_by** could also have been written with a HAVING clause rather than a subquery, as:

```
SELECT region_number, COUNT(*) AS number
FROM student
GROUP BY region_number
HAVING COUNT(*) > 3
```

The HAVING clause was originally included in SQL because early implementations did not allow subqueries to appear in a FROM clause. Because SQL now allows subqueries to appear in a FROM clause, HAVING is no longer strictly necessary. However, it is still very widely used, and you may sometimes find it more straightforward or intuitive to use a HAVING clause rather than a subquery.

In Exercise 3.22, you are required to write a query using a subquery in the FROM clause, which you have previously written using a HAVING clause.

EXERCISE 3.22

Recall the following request that you originally saw in Exercise 2.32 of Section 2:

For each patient for whom more than one prescription has been written, list the patient identifier for that patient, the number of prescriptions that have been written for him or her, and the date of the earliest of those prescriptions.

Write a query that answers this request but does not use a HAVING clause.

Hint: start by considering a query that answers the following request.

For each patient, list the patient identifier of that patient, the number of prescriptions that have been written for him or her, and the date of the earliest of those prescriptions.

For the final example, we will see how the **correlated** subquery that you saw in Section 3.3 can be rewritten using a subquery in the FROM clause, without the need for correlating the subqueries.

EXERCISE 3.23

You require a query to answer the following request:

> What are the patient identifier, gender and weight of each of those patients whose weight is more than 10% higher than the average weight of the other patients of the same gender?

(a) To answer this query, we need to know the average weight of patients of each gender. Write a query that can be expressed in English as:

For each gender, list the average weight of patients of that gender, according to the **patient** table.

(b) Now write a query that uses the **patient** table and your answer to part (a) to answer the original request. The query that you wrote for part (a) should appear in the **FROM** clause of your query.

We have now seen that many of the queries that you have encountered in Sections 2 and 3 can be expressed using subqueries in the **FROM** clause. When to use each technique (having clauses and subqueries in **FROM**, **WHERE** or **HAVING** clauses) is largely a matter of personal preference. No method is right or wrong; you should be guided, in particular, by how readable your final query is, and choose the technique that feels most natural in that case.

3.7 Summary

In this section, you have seen that more than one query specification can be combined to form composite queries, involving either a subquery or the **UNION**, **INTERSECT** and **EXCEPT** operators.

The **UNION**, **INTERSECT** and **EXCEPT** operators merge the tables that result from different query specifications into one table, provided that the query specifications in question are union compatible, that is, they have a similar structure in terms of the number of columns and data types.

Subqueries are a powerful mechanism for retrieving data from tables. They depend on matching values in each individual row with an aggregate function or collection of values from many rows. They also provide a means of comparing data in different tables, which is often a useful alternative to a join. Correlated subqueries extend the power of this mechanism. The **IN** operator and the quantifiers **ANY** (or **SOME**), **ALL** and **EXISTS** can be used on a collection of values, by using a subquery which returns a single column.

You have also seen how many requests can be satisfied by different queries. Many queries may be written either with a join or by using a subquery. A subquery may appear in the **FROM**, **WHERE** or **HAVING** clause, and a subquery in a **FROM** clause can be used instead of a **HAVING** clause.

The consistent thread running through this section and Section 2 has been the logical processing model for queries. This model is used to provide a framework through which to understand the effect of complicated queries. It also provides a basis for a three-stage method for developing queries, as introduced in Section 2. This section has shown how further requirements need to be taken into account in the development of composite queries.

LEARNING OUTCOMES

Having completed this section, you should now be able to do the following:

▶ Use `UNION`, `EXCEPT`, `INTERSECT` and subqueries to combine the results of multiple query specifications into a single query statement.
▶ Describe the logical processing model for a query containing subqueries.
▶ Use quantifiers to write search conditions that use some, all or no values from a table returned by a subquery.
▶ Given a problem statement or an informal request, write an appropriate SQL query which satisfies the request.
▶ Provide alternative ways of formulating a query to achieve the same results.

4 Use of NULL

Throughout *Block 2* and Sections 1 to 3 of this block, we have treated database models as complete entities, where each row of a table or a relation is a complete tuple of data objects of the appropriate types. While this has allowed us to formulate a clean account of the relational theory, databases that are built for real applications may not be completely filled. Entries may be missing from a database for (at least) two reasons.

▶ There is a value but it is not known at the time. We may want to record some of the details about an entity in a row while not yet having all the information available to complete it. For example, a student's address may not be known at the time when he or she registers with a university.

▶ There is no value because an attribute may not be applicable to all the rows in a table. For example, a course may not have a quota on the number of students who may enrol on it.

In either of these cases, it is legitimate to replace the value of the attribute by a marker indicating the absence of a value. This marker is known as **NULL**. Note that NULL is a marker, not a value of the attribute, although sometimes it is loosely referred to as a '**null value**'.

In this section, we discuss the use of NULL to represent unknown or inapplicable entries in tables. SQL does not distinguish between these two different uses of NULL: using NULL to represent an unknown value, and using NULL to represent an inapplicable value. We also discuss how using NULL in SQL can lead to inconsistent or misleading results, and consider some of the issues that using NULL raises for data integrity.

> For the activities and exercises in this section (and only this section), you should use the NullUniversity database (unless directed otherwise).

4.1 Basic queries involving NULL

ACTIVITY 4.1

Using the NullUniversity database, run the following filed query.

```
SELECT *
FROM examination
```

exam_query_1

You should see that the table returned by this query is almost identical to the **examination** table on the *University Database Card*, but contains an additional row. The new row contains information about the student with student identifier s22 on the course with code c2, but it has no entry under **mark**. While a mark will presumably be awarded at some point to this student for the examination, this has not yet been entered into the database (for example, the paper may require second marking, or it may have some associated special circumstances). The default behaviour for SQL

4 Use of NULL

Anywhere in this situation is to represent an unknown value with the text '`(NULL)`'. In this case, NULL is used to show that the value for this entry is not yet known.

SQL Anywhere allows the user to set how unknown values are displayed.

It is important to note that NULL is *not* an equivalent to zero (or an empty string, or some equivalent). To see this, run the following query.

```
SELECT *
FROM examination
WHERE mark < 70
```
exam_query_2

The entry for the student s22 on c2 does not appear in this table. Because NULL indicates that the value of `mark` is not known for this row, we do not know whether or not it is lower than 70. Therefore, the expression in the `WHERE` condition cannot equate to TRUE for this row, and the row is not included in the final table for the query. In fact, as we shall see later, this expression evaluates to UNKNOWN, rather than to TRUE or FALSE.

Another effect of NULL as an unknown value can be seen by running the following query.

```
SELECT student_id, course_code, (mark + 5) AS moderated
FROM examination
```
exam_query_3

Notice that the value of `moderated` for the student s22 on c2 is NULL in this table. When an entry in a table is NULL, any numeric expression involving it will also evaluate to NULL.

To write the conditions that recognise when an entry in a table is NULL, we need to make it explicit that we are interested in the NULL entries. The keywords `IS NULL` and `IS NOT NULL` are used in this case. The filed statement **null_query** is used to find all the student identifiers, course codes and marks of all the rows in the `examination` table that have NULL in the `mark` column.

```
SELECT student_id, course_code, mark
FROM examination
WHERE mark IS NULL
```
null_query

To return a table containing only those rows for which the `mark` column does have a value, we need to use the condition `WHERE mark IS NOT NULL`, as shown in the following filed statement.

```
SELECT student_id, course_code, mark
FROM examination
WHERE mark IS NOT NULL
```
not_null_query

We will consider search conditions involving NULL in more depth later.

NULL in aggregate functions

We now need to modify the definitions of the aggregate functions described in Section 2 to accommodate the possible presence of NULL. Recall the following example that you saw in Activity 2.5.

```
SELECT AVG(height) AS average_height
FROM patient
```
avg_height

Using the Hospital database, the query **avg_height** returns a table containing a single value, which is the average height of the patients in the `patient` table.

> Run the following filed query using the NullUniversity database.

```sql
SELECT AVG(mark) AS average_mark
FROM examination
```

avg_mark

This also returns a single value, which is the average of the five values in the `mark` column in the `examination` table. Importantly, any entry in the `mark` column whose value is NULL is not included in the calculation of the average. The query **avg_mark** returns the average of the six rows that do have defined values in the `mark` column. This differs from the behaviour of numerical expressions as seen in **exam_query_3**, in which an expression evaluates to UNKNOWN if any of its arguments are NULL.

A strict expression of the query **avg_mark** in English (one that makes explicit the behaviour of the `AVG` function when NULL is present in the table) would be:

> Find the average value of `mark` for all the rows in the `examination` table for which `mark` has been defined.

We now give the full definitions of the built-in aggregate functions that we met in Section 2 to take account of the presence of NULL.

`AVG`	When applied to a collection of values defined by an expression of numeric data type, `AVG` results in the average of non-NULL values in the collection. If all the values in the collection are NULL or the collection is empty, then the function evaluates to NULL. If `DISTINCT` is included in the argument, all duplicate values are ignored.
`COUNT`	When applied to a collection of values defined by a column name of any data type, `COUNT` results in the number of non-NULL values in the collection. If all the values in the collection are NULL or the collection is empty, then the function evaluates to 0. If `DISTINCT` is included in the argument, all duplicate values are ignored.
`SUM`	When applied to a collection of values defined by an expression of numeric data type, `SUM` results in the sum of non-NULL values in the collection. If the values in the collection are all NULL or the collection is empty, then the function evaluates to NULL. If `DISTINCT` is included in the argument, all duplicate values are ignored.
`MAX`	When applied to a collection of values defined by an expression of any data type, `MAX` results in the maximum value of the non-NULL values in the collection. In the case of character string data types, the maximum value is the one that would result in the last entry in a dictionary. If all the values in the collection are NULL or the collection is empty, then the function evaluates to NULL. `DISTINCT` does not have any effect on the value that is returned, but it can be used without causing an error.
`MIN`	This function operates in exactly the same way as `MAX`, except that it selects the minimum value of the non-NULL values in the collection, rather than the maximum.

4 Use of NULL

EXERCISE 4.1

Explain why the following two queries produce different results when executed in the NullUniversity database.

```
SELECT course_code, COUNT(student_id) AS count
FROM examination
GROUP BY course_code
```
count1

```
SELECT course_code, COUNT(mark) AS count
FROM examination
GROUP BY course_code
```
count2

ACTIVITY 4.2

Run the following query to examine the contents of the **student** table in the NullUniversity database.

```
SELECT *
FROM student
```

You should see that three rows of the table contain NULL in the **address** column. This may represent, for example, students who have enrolled online and not yet provided a postal address.

➢ Now run the following query.

```
SELECT DISTINCT address
FROM student
```
distinct_null_address

The table returned by **distinct_null_address** contains only one occurrence of NULL, demonstrating that when **DISTINCT** is used in a **SELECT** clause, occurrences of NULL in the specified column are collected into a single group.

➢ Now run the following query.

```
SELECT address, COUNT(*) AS occurrences
FROM student
GROUP BY address
```
count_address

The query **count_address** returns a table with two columns: the first contains the addresses that appear in the **address** column of the **student** table, and the second contains the number of times each address appears (one occurrence per address). However, there is also a result for the number of rows where **address** is NULL (the value of 3 in the **occurrences** column). Like **DISTINCT**, a **GROUP BY** clause collects the occurrences of NULL into a single group.

Activity 4.2 demonstrates how NULL is treated by grouping functions in SQL. In general:

1. If a grouping column of a **GROUP BY** clause contains occurrences of NULL, then those occurrences are placed together in a single group.
2. Similarly, if a column in a **SELECT** clause contains occurrences of NULL and has been specified as **DISTINCT**, then the resulting table will contain only one occurrence of NULL in that column.

NULL and `ORDER BY`

The presence of NULL complicates orderings. The SQL Standard does not define how comparisons with NULL are to be treated in an `ORDER BY` clause, and therefore the behaviour in each case is implementation specific.

ACTIVITY 4.3

Before running the following query, describe what you expect it to do.

```
SELECT *
FROM student
ORDER BY address
```

order_by_null

Now run the query to check your answer. Then run it again, but this time put `ORDER BY address DESC` as the final clause. Can you draw any conclusions from your results?

When a query contains an `ORDER BY` clause, the occurrences of NULL are each considered either greater than or less than all the non-NULL values, depending on the implementation. However, those rows containing NULL in the ordering columns are grouped together in the final table.

4.2 Conditions involving NULL

We have already seen that to search for rows in which particular entries are NULL, SQL requires the expression `IS NULL` to be used. Comparisons of the form `column = NULL` cannot be used for this purpose, as NULL is not a value that can be compared with other entities in the table.

We must also consider conditional expressions involving, for example, the connectives `AND`, `OR` and `NOT` in a `WHERE` clause. If a set of tables contains no occurrences of NULL, then conditional expressions on the data in those tables evaluate to either TRUE or FALSE. However, when those tables do contain occurrences of NULL, we may not know whether those expressions evaluate to TRUE or FALSE. In these cases we require a third truth value, which we call **UNKNOWN**. It is important not to confuse UNKNOWN with NULL. UNKNOWN is used only when discussing the truth values of conditional expressions, whereas NULL is used as an entry in a table.

How do we evaluate conditional expressions if the expressions refer to columns containing occurrences of NULL? The following list gives the effects in different conditional expressions.

- If a row has NULL in a column `c`, then any expression of the form `c = <value>` evaluates to UNKNOWN.
- Expressions that involve a comparison using the operators, `<`, `=`, etc. or `LIKE`, where one or more of the values being compared is NULL, evaluate to UNKNOWN.
- Expressions that contain subexpressions that evaluate to UNKNOWN are evaluated according to the following three-valued truth tables.

AND	TRUE	UNKNOWN	FALSE
TRUE	TRUE	UNKNOWN	FALSE
UNKNOWN	UNKNOWN	UNKNOWN	FALSE
FALSE	FALSE	FALSE	FALSE

4 Use of NULL

OR	TRUE	UNKNOWN	FALSE
TRUE	TRUE	TRUE	TRUE
UNKNOWN	TRUE	UNKNOWN	UNKNOWN
FALSE	TRUE	UNKNOWN	FALSE

NOT	TRUE	UNKNOWN	FALSE
	FALSE	UNKNOWN	TRUE

These truth tables capture the behaviour of expressions whose truth value is UNKNOWN. Where the truth values of all the expressions involved are either TRUE or FALSE, the behaviour is exactly the same as for standard two-valued logic.

We will now consider some examples to illustrate the behaviour of the rows or columns of the truth table which contain UNKNOWN. Consider the expression *P* AND *Q* where *P* is an expression which evaluates to TRUE and *Q* is an expression which evaluates to UNKNOWN. Intuitively, this means that *Q* might in fact be either TRUE or FALSE, but we do not know which. If *Q* were to evaluate to TRUE, then the expression *P* AND *Q* would then evaluate to TRUE. However, if *Q* were to evaluate to FALSE, then the expression *P* AND *Q* would evaluate to FALSE. So for the expression *P* AND *Q* where *P* evaluates to TRUE and *Q* evaluates to UNKNOWN, we say *P* AND *Q* evaluates to UNKNOWN.

On the other hand, consider the expression *P* AND *Q*, where *P* evaluates to FALSE and *Q* evaluates to UNKNOWN. In this case, *P* AND *Q* would evaluate to FALSE whether *Q* were to evaluate to TRUE or to FALSE (an AND expression is TRUE only if all its conjuncts are TRUE). So in this case, we say that *P* AND *Q* is FALSE, even though *Q* is UNKNOWN.

EXERCISE 4.2

For this exercise, assume that you have the following table, `stock`, which shows the buying price and selling price (in pounds sterling) of second-hand toy cars, and the names of the original manufacturers.

`stock`

transaction	buy	sell	manufacturer
00101	1.65	2.50	dinko
00210	2.50	4.00	(NULL)
00231	1.85	(NULL)	dinko
00402	2.15	3.50	misto

(a) Why do the following two queries give different results?

```
SELECT SUM(sell - buy) AS price_difference
FROM stock
```

```
SELECT SUM(sell) - SUM(buy) AS price_difference
FROM stock
```

(b) What table would be returned by the following query?

```
SELECT *
FROM stock
WHERE NOT (buy < 2.00 AND manufacturer = 'dinko')
```

(c) Explain why the results of the following two queries are not the same.

```
SELECT *
FROM stock

SELECT *
FROM stock
WHERE manufacturer = 'misto'
   OR manufacturer <> 'misto'
```

The answers to Exercise 4.2, and in particular part (c), indicate that when NULL appears in a database, some seemingly straightforward queries may give surprising results. When expressions can evaluate to UNKNOWN as well as to TRUE or FALSE, then many well-known theorems of traditional **two-valued logic** do not hold. For example, in **classical** (two-valued) **logic**, the expression

P OR NOT(P)

This is known as the **Law of Excluded Middle**.

always evaluates to TRUE, whether P itself is TRUE or FALSE (and in classical logic, all expressions are either TRUE or FALSE). However, when the additional truth value of UNKNOWN is introduced, this expression does not always evaluate to TRUE. As shown in Exercise 4.2, the expression

```
manufacturer = 'misto' OR NOT (manufacturer = 'misto')
```

evaluates to UNKNOWN if the expression `manufacturer = 'misto'` evaluates to UNKNOWN.

So when using NULL, it is important to remember that expressions using the operators `AND`, `OR` and `NOT` may not behave in the same way as they do in classical logic. The results produced by queries containing expressions that evaluate to UNKNOWN can easily be misinterpreted.

EXERCISE 4.3

As we have seen, the presence of NULL in a table can make it easy to misinterpret the results of some queries. Write the SQL to generate a table that is the same as the `student` table, but which has the string 'Unavailable' in the `address` column where `student` has NULL. (Only consider the `address` column; your solution can have NULL values in the `email_address` column.)

(Hint: you may wish to use the `UNION` operator.)

The proposed solution to Exercise 4.3 demonstrates a commonly used technique to avoid the presence of NULL in a database by replacing NULL with a default value. In particular, this technique can make the behaviour of queries more predictable for tables that include NULL.

4 Use of NULL

4.3 Outer joins

We have already met inner joins and natural joins in Section 2.4. There is another type of join, the **outer join**, which returns tables that may contain NULL.

ACTIVITY 4.4

Suppose we wish to answer the following query:

> What are the student identifiers and names of all the registered students, and which are the courses that they are enrolled on?

The following statement does not provide a satisfactory answer to the query.

```
SELECT student.student_id, name, course_code
FROM student, enrolment
WHERE student.student_id = enrolment.student_id
```
missing_rows

> Using the NullUniversity database, run the filed statement **missing_rows**.

When you run the statement, you should see that the generated table does not list all the students who are registered: only those students who are enrolled on one or more courses are listed. So there is no row in the table returned by **missing_rows** that corresponds to the student with identifier s42.

We often want rows from one of two joined tables to appear in the final table, even if they do not contain matching entries for the join condition. To achieve this with the operators that you have seen so far requires a solution in which `UNION` is used to provide the rows that are not matched by using an inner join.

Because requests of this sort frequently occur in practice, SQL provides the outer join.

> Run the following filed statement.

```
SELECT student.student_id, name, course_code
FROM student LEFT OUTER JOIN enrolment
   ON student.student_id = enrolment.student_id
```
left_outer

The query **left_outer** can be expressed in English as:

> For each student who is registered according to the `student` table, list the student's identifier and name, along with any courses on which he or she is enrolled according to the `enrolment` table, or NULL if they are not enrolled on any courses.

In general, the **left outer join** can be described as:

> The (left) outer join returns a table in which the rows from the first joined table that do not have a matching entry in the second joined table are also included in the final table, with NULL in the missing column entries.

The logical processing of the **left_outer** query is as follows.

1. First, processing the `FROM` clause produces an intermediate table, which is the Cartesian product of the `student` table and the `enrolment` table.
2. Second, processing the `ON` part of the `FROM` clause applies the join condition to the rows of the intermediate table, choosing those rows in which `student.student_id` is equal to `enrolment.student_id`. This forms the first part of the intermediate table resulting from this clause.

3   Third, to complete the `FROM` clause a row is added for each row in the `student` table which does not satisfy the join condition, adding NULL for entries from the `enrolment` table.

4   Finally, the `SELECT` clause is processed and the specified columns give the final table.

We need to modify our logical processing model to account for outer joins, as shown in Figure 4.1.

Initial specified tables

`FROM`: Create a provisional intermediate table from the tables specified in the `FROM` clause by forming the Cartesian product of the tables (all possible combinations of each row from each table).

`ON`: Copy each row which satisfies the search condition specified in the `ON` clause to start an intermediate table.

If there are any rows which appear in the left table (the first table in the `JOIN` clause) which do not yet appear in the intermediate table, add them with NULL entries for the data in the right table. This completes the intermediate table.

Intermediate table

`SELECT`: Using the intermediate table, process each value expression specified in the `SELECT` clause to create new columns.

Copy data in these new columns and any other columns specified in the `SELECT` clause to create the final table. If the `DISTINCT` operator is used in the `SELECT` clause, each copied row is ignored if it already appears in the final table.

Final table

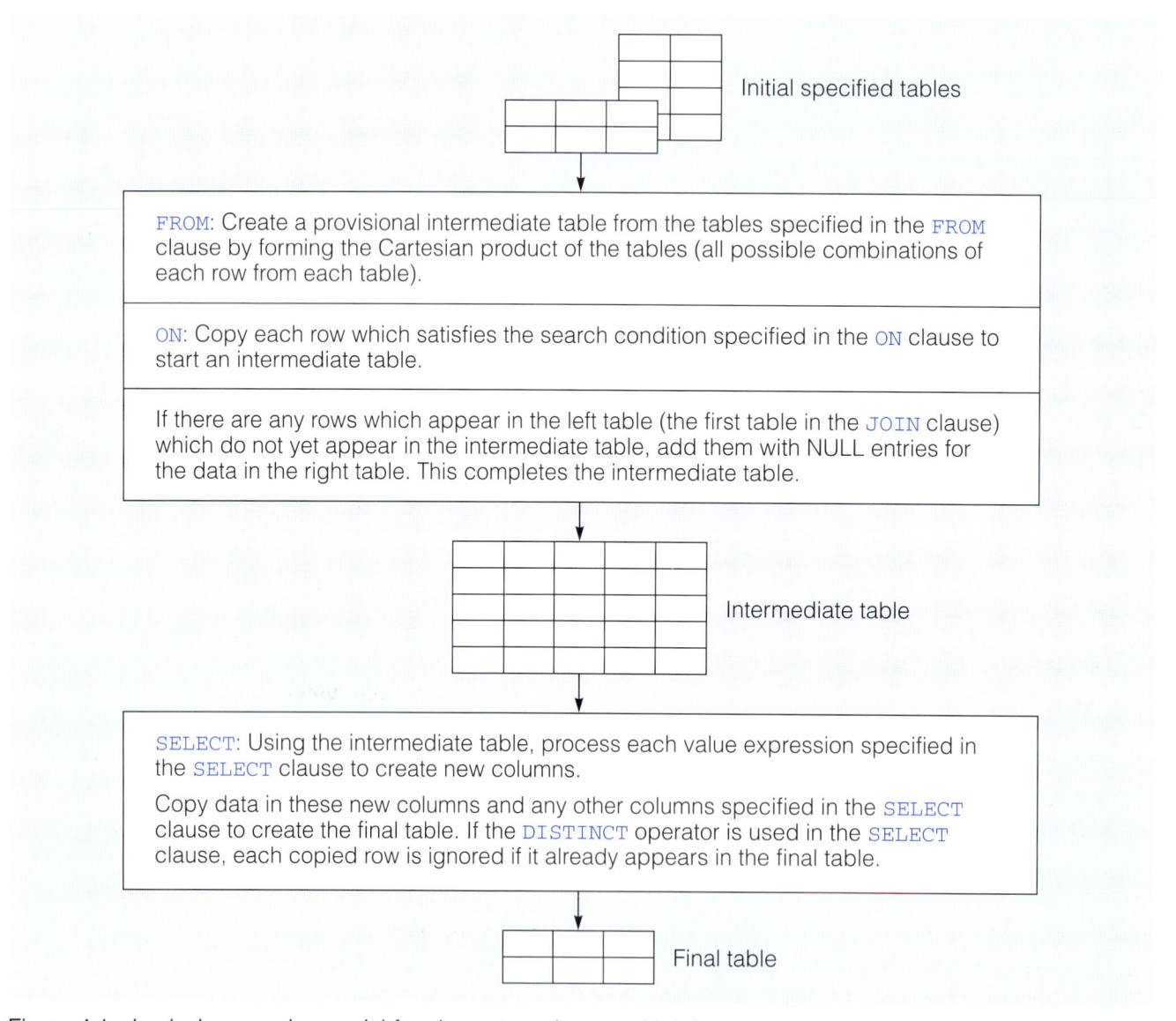

Figure 4.1   Logical processing model for elementary clauses with left outer joins

SQL also provides a **right outer join**, in which rows from the second joined table that do not match an entry in the first table are included, and missing entries from the first table are replaced with NULL. In fact, the right outer join is simply the reverse of the left outer join, so that if `p` and `q` are tables,

> `p RIGHT OUTER JOIN q`

is the same as

> `q LEFT OUTER JOIN p`

In the **full outer join**, the rows from both tables are kept, with NULL replacing missing entries from either table. In SQL, right outer joins and full outer joins are implemented with the keywords `RIGHT OUTER JOIN` and `FULL OUTER JOIN`, respectively.

4 Use of NULL

The use of a right outer join is illustrated by the result of the query **right_outer_join**.

```
SELECT student_id, c.course_code
FROM examination e RIGHT OUTER JOIN course c
   ON e.course_code = c.course_code
```
right_outer_join

NULL is used for those courses for which no students have sat an examination.

EXERCISE 4.4

Using a left outer join, write a query that can be expressed in English as:

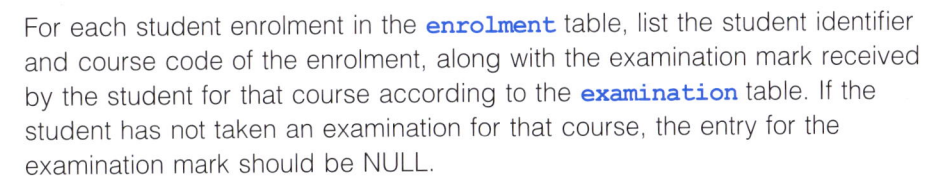

> For each student enrolment in the **enrolment** table, list the student identifier and course code of the enrolment, along with the examination mark received by the student for that course according to the **examination** table. If the student has not taken an examination for that course, the entry for the examination mark should be NULL.

Outer joins and aggregate functions

ACTIVITY 4.5

Run the following query.

```
SELECT e.student_id, e.course_code,
       COUNT(assignment_number) AS submissions
FROM enrolment e LEFT OUTER JOIN assignment a
  ON e.student_id = a.student_id
    AND e.course_code = a.course_code
GROUP BY e.student_id, e.course_code
```
count_outer

The query **count_outer** can be expressed in English as follows:

> For each enrolment in the **enrolment** table, list the student identifier and the course code, along with the number of assignments that the student has submitted for that course.

You will see that for some rows in the final table produced by **count_outer**, the number of assignments submitted is zero (for example, student s05 on course c7). We cannot obtain this information solely from the **assignment** table because the information relating to those students who are enrolled on courses but have not submitted any assignments can only be obtained from the **enrolment** table. You may wish to check the behaviour of COUNT when NULL is present (see the definition in Section 4.1) to understand the behaviour of **count_outer**.

4.4 NULL and referential integrity

From your study of Block 2, you should be aware of the part played by the various key declarations in a relational model (e.g. primary keys, alternate keys, foreign keys) in asserting the semantics of a model. While the ability to use NULL in a database model can be valuable for helping to deal with missing data, there are also implications for data integrity. We will discuss these issues in the remainder of this section. In Section 5, we will look at how keys for tables are declared.

Primary keys and entity integrity

Recall from *Block 2* that a primary key is an example of a **constraint definition**; declaring one or more columns as the primary key for a relation constrains the set of values that the primary key may take. Specifically, no two tuples of a relation may have the same value for the primary key. The declaration of a primary key is the means by which the uniqueness of tuples is guaranteed.

Primary keys are also defined on SQL tables; the primary key for a table is one or more columns, the combination of which must all have different values, just as in relational theory. For example, in the `enrolment` table, the columns `student_id` and `course_code` are defined as the primary key, meaning that no two rows in the `enrolment` table may have the same values for `student_id` and `course_code` combined. But because SQL allows the use of NULL, we must consider how that affects the primary key declarations. Because NULL indicates that the value of a table entry is not known, if the primary key of a row in a database table contains NULL, then it is not guaranteed that the primary keys of all rows are different. Therefore, to ensure that the rows of a table are unique, the whole of the primary key must be defined. This property of primary keys is reflected in the following general rule, known as the **entity integrity rule**:

> No column of a table that forms part of that table's primary key may contain a NULL value.

This entity integrity rule constrains the rows that may be added to a table, so that a row can be inserted only if it has a value defined for every column that appears in the table's primary key. The primary key's value must be different from all other existing values in the relevant columns.

Foreign keys and referential integrity

Just as primary keys are defined on tables, we can also define foreign keys on tables. The definition of a foreign key from *Block 2* is adapted to deal with columns and tables in SQL. For SQL, a foreign key is defined as follows:

> A foreign key is a column (or collection of columns) in a table, `T2`, whose values match those of a candidate key of some other table, `T1` (where `T1` and `T2` are not necessarily distinct).

As you saw in *Block 2*, a foreign key value must always have the same value as an existing value of the candidate key in a table that it references. However, SQL does allow foreign keys to be NULL, as long as no part of the foreign key is part of the table's primary key, otherwise the entity integrity rule would be violated. So if a part of a foreign key is also a part of the referencing table's primary key, for example, then that part of the foreign key must not be NULL. So we also have a form of the **referential integrity rule** for SQL tables, which is:

> If a table, `T2`, has a foreign key `F` that references a candidate key `C` in another table, `T1`, then every value in `T2.F` must either be equal to a value in `T1.C` or be NULL.

The requirement for referential integrity enforces the semantics that a foreign key value must always match some existing value of the key which it references. However, a foreign key may contain NULL, which indicates that a value is missing.

EXERCISE 4.5

What restrictions might the referential integrity rule put upon NULL values in alternate keys in an SQL table?

The referential integrity rule constrains both the referencing table (the one containing the foreign key) and the referenced table (the table to which the foreign key refers) by preventing the addition or deletion of rows that would lead to violations of referential integrity. We will deal with these issues in more depth in Section 5, where we will also consider how we can use NULL to allow us to represent optional participation with a posted key.

4.5 NULL and default values

There are advantages and disadvantages to using NULL. When managing a real database, there will almost certainly be situations where aspects of the data will be unknown, and the DBMS must be able to cope with this. However, as we have seen, using NULL can lead to misleading results when users formulate queries and interpret results, as their treatment in SQL is sometimes counter-intuitive.

As we shall see in Section 5, when defining SQL tables, **default values** can be given for columns. If that column's value is not provided for a particular row (for example, because it is not known at some time), then the default value is used. This approach can sometimes have an advantage over using NULL, because the default values are of the same type as other values in a column, and therefore they obey all the algebraic operations that you choose to apply.

However, a default value is not always appropriate, and may lead to misleading results. For example, it may be reasonable for a newly registered student to have a default value of 0 points studied rather than NULL. On the other hand, a default value of '0' for a telephone number is probably not appropriate. While zero points studied makes sense for a student's study record, an arbitrary string for a missing telephone number makes little sense. Furthermore, inappropriate default values can skew data if they are not handled carefully; we might decide to use a default value of, say, 0 kg for patient weights. However, queries returning the average weight of patients would then incorporate these defaults, returning an incorrectly low final value.

So NULL is a useful addition to SQL that helps us to deal with real world data. It should be used with care, though, and the possible effects on queries should be considered if NULL is used in a database design. In *Block 4* we discuss the use of NULL in a database's design.

4.6 Summary

In this section, you have seen how NULL is used within SQL to provide a mechanism for dealing with missing or unknown data. Using NULL is often a preferable alternative to a default value, which may not be meaningful within the database. NULL is not a value, and in conditions NULL is used in the `IS NULL` or `IS NOT NULL` constructions.

Expressions can also give surprising results when NULL appears in the database. Aggregate functions may not behave in the way that users expect. Furthermore, conditions in `WHERE` and `HAVING` may evaluate to UNKNOWN, as well as to TRUE or FALSE.

Outer joins are a further type of join which allow the rows that would be discarded in an inner join to be kept. In an outer join, NULL is used in those rows where one of the tables does not have a value to satisfy the join condition.

Using NULL raises issues for referential integrity. To maintain integrity in the database, no part of a primary key may be NULL, and foreign key values must either appear in related columns of the referenced table or be NULL.

LEARNING OUTCOMES

Having completed this section, you should now be able to do the following:

▶ Use NULL to represent unknown or inappropriate values for entries in rows in a table.

▶ Use **IS NULL** and **IS NOT NULL** in **WHERE** clauses, and understand how NULL behaves in conditional statements.

▶ Understand how the presence of NULL in a database affects the behaviour of aggregate functions.

▶ Understand why the presence of NULL requires conditional expressions to evaluate to TRUE, FALSE or UNKNOWN.

▶ Use **LEFT OUTER JOIN**, **RIGHT OUTER JOIN** and **FULL OUTER JOIN**.

▶ Understand the implications of NULL for referential integrity.

▶ Understand some of the implications of using either NULL or a default value for unknown entries in a table.

5 Database definition and population

So far, we have discussed how to construct queries to retrieve the data held in an existing database, which may be used by user processes interacting with a DBMS. We will now consider how to build our own databases. In this section and the next, we will examine the SQL facilities for managing the definition of a database using the data definition language (DDL) component of SQL as well as further data manipulation language (DML) facilities. In this section, you will see how many of the concepts that you were introduced to in *Block 2*, such as keys and constraints, are handled in SQL. In *Block 4*, we will discuss some of the issues in translating a relational model into SQL.

In Section 5.1, we describe an extension to the University model that we have been using so far. We then implement the extension throughout the rest of this section. In Section 5.2, we begin our study of the definition of tables using SQL's data definition facilities, and look specifically at the facilities used to create and remove base tables in the database you have been working with. In Section 5.3, we look at how data is inserted into and deleted from base tables and how existing data can be updated. In Section 5.4, we look at how integrity constraints are defined in SQL, and in Section 5.5, we look at how to define domains. In Section 5.6, we look at how to modify table data definitions. In Section 5.7, we look at how constraints are evaluated within SQL, and finally in Section 5.8, we discuss how indexes can be used to improve the efficiency of data retrieval.

As with previous sections, we do not aim to provide complete details of SQL capabilities, but will focus on the basic facilities that provide the foundation of how SQL may be used for managing and administering a database.

5.1 An extension to the University model

To illustrate how to use SQL to define and populate tables, we provide an extension to the University model as shown on the laminated cards, and then work through the SQL that is required to implement it.

Scenario extension:

Each course may use up to five textbooks (but might not use any). Each textbook is associated with one specific course. The title and author name, university code and number of pages are stored for each textbook. The code number of a book is a (unique) 5-digit number. Because of the way they are bound, textbooks may contain a maximum of 400 pages.

For some of its courses, the University requires an externally contracted printing company (printer) to print the textbooks (for example, where specialised diagrams are required). Each textbook is either printed by an external printing company or printed internally. Each external printing company has a unique business code that is formed from the prefix 'PX' followed by four digits. The business code, company name, address and telephone number are stored for each printer. To ensure consistent formatting, all the textbooks for any given course must be printed by the same printer.

Entity–Relationship model extension

Printer —Prints— Textbook —UsedOn— Course

Only the **Course** entity from the original diagram is shown here; assume that the rest of the diagram remains unchanged (so the **Course** entity still connects to **Quota**, **Staff** and **Enrolment**, even though these are not shown here). The **Printer** entity denotes externally contracted printers.

Entity types:
Textbook(<u>Bookcode</u>, Title, AuthorName, NoPages)
Printer(<u>BusinessCode</u>, Name, Address, TelephoneNumber)

Additional constraints:

These constraints are in addition to c.1–c.15 of the University conceptual data model.

c.16 All textbooks for the same course must be printed by the same printer.

c.17 No more than five textbooks may be used on any one course.

c.18 Textbooks contain between 1 and 400 pages.

5.2 Table definition and deletion

Base tables are the logical structure for storing data in a relational database. Before a table can be used to store data, it must first be defined so that the DBMS used to manage the database has a specification of the types of data it has to process. It is then necessary to prepare a storage structure within which the data can be kept. In this section, we show how SQL statements are used to define the structure of a table. We also show how to use SQL to remove tables and modify the structure of tables.

Creating a table

In SQL, a table is created using the **CREATE TABLE** statement. The format of this statement for a simple table is:

```
CREATE TABLE <table name> (
   <column definition list>,
   PRIMARY KEY (<column name list>) )
```

Although SQL will allow a table to be defined without the **PRIMARY KEY** clause, it is unusual to define a table without a primary key. As discussed in *Block 2*, a primary key is the standard way of ensuring that tables populated with data do not contain duplicate rows.

This is a minimal table definition statement; SQL allows many more properties of a table (such as constraints) to be declared as part of a **CREATE TABLE** statement. For example, the **CREATE TABLE** statement in Activity 5.1 contains a foreign key declaration, as well as the primary key declaration. We will introduce additional elements of **CREATE TABLE** throughout this section.

5 Database definition and population

A `CREATE TABLE` statement is executed by the DBMS in the same way as any other kind of SQL statement. During the processing of such a statement, first the table definition is checked to ensure that it is syntactically correct, then the defined properties are stored in the database schema and an empty table is constructed ready to hold new data.

ACTIVITY 5.1

In this activity, you will create the `textbook` table for the University model.

Execute the following statement.

```
CREATE TABLE textbook (
   bookcode CHAR(5),
   title VARCHAR(40) NOT NULL,
   author_name VARCHAR(20) DEFAULT 'None',
   no_pages INTEGER,
   course_code CHAR(2) NOT NULL,
   PRIMARY KEY (bookcode),
   CONSTRAINT textbook_in_used_on
      FOREIGN KEY (course_code) REFERENCES course )
```

table_creation

If there are any errors in your statement, then executing it will generate a message describing which part of the statement is wrong. If there are no errors, then there is no acknowledgement that the statement has executed successfully.

➤ Check that the `textbook` table has been created by running the query:

```
SELECT *
FROM textbook
```

You should find that a table has been created. It has the correct number of columns and the appropriate column headings, but no actual data.

The following list shows a number of features of table creation that the **table_creation** example illustrates.

- ▶ In general, the name of the table in a `CREATE TABLE` statement must be different from the name of any existing table defined by the same user. Table and column names can be a mixture of up to 128 letters, numbers and the underscore character. Table names must start with a letter, and may not be reserved words (such as `table` or `SELECT`).
- ▶ The columns of the table are defined as a list of comma-separated entries enclosed in brackets. Each column is defined by a name and a data type.
- ▶ Each column of a base table must have a distinct name, although different tables may contain a column with the same name (for example, the tables `student` and `staff` both have a column `name`).
- ▶ A primary key definition may occur anywhere in the list of column definitions, but by convention it is usually specified after the column declarations. The primary key is declared by specifying the name of the column(s) that form the primary key, which must have a unique value for each row of the table.
- ▶ We have used the declaration `NOT NULL` to state that rows in the table may not have NULL in the `title` column. In this table, entries may have NULL in the `author_name` and `no_pages` columns, but not in the `title` column.

    Additionally, because `bookcode` is the primary key, `bookcode` may not be NULL for any row either. We will discuss these **integrity constraints** further in Section 5.4.

In Section 6 we will see how to differentiate between tables with the same name that have been created by different users.

> - We have used the **DEFAULT** keyword to specify a default value for the **author_name** column. In Section 5.4, we will see how the default value is used when column values are not provided.
>
>   Note that having a default value is *not* equivalent to NULL. Rows in this table may still have NULL in the **author_name** column, meaning that the author is unknown for some reason. The default value is chosen to suggest that the textbook explicitly has no appropriate author name.
>
> - We have used a foreign key declaration to represent the relationship **UsedOn**. The foreign key declaration must state which column(s) form the foreign key (in this case, **course_code**), and the table that the foreign key references (here, **course**). The behaviour of foreign keys in SQL is similar to those of the relational models of *Block 2*, although in SQL, a column declared as (part of) a foreign key may contain NULL. We will discuss the behaviour of foreign key declarations in more depth in Section 5.4, and look at different ways of defining constraints.

Foreign keys are one of several types of constraints that we will look at in Section 5.4.

EXERCISE 5.1

If a **CREATE TABLE** statement specifies a table name that is already used for an existing table, explain why a DBMS will not allow the new definition simply to replace the existing one.

The statement **table_creation** also illustrates certain **design decisions**.

- We have chosen to allow 40 characters for the title of a book, and 20 for the author.

- We have chosen to allow **author_name** and **no_pages** to be NULL. This allows us to use NULL to show that a book might not have a single author, or that the number of pages in the expected edition is not yet known.

- Although **bookcode** and **no_pages** are both represented by a number, we have elected to use **VARCHAR** for the entries in **bookcode** and **INTEGER** for those in **no_pages**. This reflects the different properties of these columns. For example, an entry in **no_pages** represents a figure that can be manipulated by a function (for example, a pair of books of 300 and 400 pages contains a total of 300 + 400 = 700 pages). On the other hand, it does not make sense to apply mathematical functions to the entries in **bookcode**; nothing meaningful is obtained by adding together the numbers representing the codes of two different books. We will look at how to restrict a column, such as **bookcode**, to numerical values when we deal with constraints, in Section 5.4.

- We have chosen to use a foreign key declaration, rather than an additional table, to represent the **UsedOn** relationship.

Many design decisions on building a database must be made in the course of building a database. Some of these are highlighted in this block, but are discussed more fully in *Block 4*.

EXERCISE 5.2

Would you expect to represent a 12-figure telephone number using **INTEGER** or **CHAR(12)** (a 12-figure character string)? Why?

SQL data types

The possible values that may appear in columns are declared in terms of the SQL data types. You have already seen these in Section 2 but for convenience, we reproduce Figure 2.3 from Section 2 here.

Data type	Description
Character string types	
CHARACTER(len) (or **CHAR(len)**)	Fixed-length character strings of length **len**
VARCHAR(max_length)	Variable-length character strings, up to length **max_length**
Numeric data types	
INTEGER (or **INT**)	Integer numbers
SMALLINT	Small integer numbers
BIGINT	Big integer numbers
DECIMAL(p, s) (or **DEC(p, s)**)	Decimal numbers containing at least **p** digits altogether, with **s** digits after the decimal point
NUMERIC(p, s)	Decimal numbers containing exactly **p** digits altogether, with **s** digits after the decimal point
FLOAT	Single precision floating-point number
REAL	Single precision floating-point number
DOUBLE PRECISION	Double precision floating-point number
Bit string types	
BIT(len)	Fixed-length bit string of length **len**
BIT VARYING(len)	Variable-length bit string up to length **len**
Date–time types	
DATE	Calendar date
TIME(p)	Clock time of precision **p**
TIMESTAMP(p)	Date and time of precision **p**
INTERVAL	Time interval
Large object string types (but see note on page 18 for SQL Anywhere)	
CHARACTER LARGE OBJECT(size) (or **CLOB(size)**)	Character data of size up to **size**
BINARY LARGE OBJECT(size) (or **BLOB(size)**)	Binary data of size up to **size**

Figure 5.1   SQL predefined data types

Removing a table

Managing a database involves the removal of tables as well as their creation. To remove a table from a database requires the removal of the table's definition as well as any data that might have been added to it. This is accomplished by using SQL's **DROP TABLE** statement. The basic format of this statement is just:

    DROP TABLE <table name>

Executing a DROP TABLE statement removes the specified table's definition from the schema, as well as any rows of data that may have been stored in the table. So dropping a table involves the deletion of the table definition and the deletion of all data in the table.

ACTIVITY 5.2

Execute the following statement.

```
DROP TABLE textbook
```

drop1

As with CREATE TABLE, no message is given when a DROP TABLE statement has successfully executed. So check that the textbook table has been removed by running the query:

```
SELECT *
FROM textbook
```

You should receive an error message informing you that the table does not exist.

Clearly, you need to be very careful when using DROP TABLE! You are not asked to confirm that you want the table to be deleted. The dangers of losing the data in the dropped table are obvious, but other consequential changes are possible and need to be allowed for, such as the effect on foreign keys. These changes will be considered in Section 5.4.

5.3 Inserting and updating data

In this section, we introduce you to the SQL statements concerned with updating a database. SQL provides three different kinds of update statement:

1. Adding new rows to a table using the INSERT statement.
2. Modifying the values of particular columns in existing rows of a table, using the UPDATE statement.
3. Deleting one or more existing rows from a table using the DELETE statement.

Note that the UPDATE statement is only one way of updating the data.

This section is divided into four main parts. The first part explores the way in which the INSERT statement can be used to add new rows to a table. The second part deals with the DELETE statement and how it can be used to remove rows from a table. The third part explores further ways of using the INSERT statement to add new rows to a table. The final part shows how data values in a table can be modified using the UPDATE statement.

> Before starting this section, you should have the textbook table defined as in **table_creation** and containing no data. If necessary, execute **table_creation** to recreate the table.

Adding rows to a table: INSERT

The INSERT statement is used in SQL to add new rows to a specified table. There are two formats for the INSERT statement. The first format includes, as part of the statement, a collection of values that are treated as a single row to be added to the specified table. The second format includes a query specification that defines data to be retrieved from base tables that are already in a database and then added to the specified table; in this case, there may be many rows to be added. The following activity explores the first of these formats.

ACTIVITY 5.3

Run the following statement:

```
INSERT INTO textbook
    VALUES ('65281', 'Beginning Syntax', 'Kershaw, J.', 247, 'c2')
```
insert1

Display the updated table and ensure that a row containing this data has been entered into it. Now repeat the process using the following six statements. Not all of these statements will insert values into the table; you should note when an `INSERT` statement generates an error.

```
INSERT INTO textbook
    VALUES ('38572', 'Practical Pragmatics',
            'Christine Harpleton-Davies', 320, 'c7')
```
insert2

```
INSERT INTO textbook
    VALUES ('65284', 'A First Course In Logic', 'Jerry Maxwell', 115, 'c5')
```
insert3

```
INSERT INTO textbook
    VALUES (NULL, 'More Logic', 'Jerry Maxwell', 210, 'c5')
```
insert4

```
INSERT INTO textbook
    VALUES ('65290', 'Even More Logic', NULL, NULL, 'c5')
```
insert5

```
INSERT INTO textbook
    VALUES ('90326', NULL, 'Mary Jarrett', 240, 'c4')
```
insert6

```
INSERT INTO textbook
    VALUES ('81763', 'Quantifiers and Language', 'R. Young', 324, 'c8')
```
insert7

You should find that **insert4**, **insert6** and **insert7** generate errors. If you display the updated `textbook` table, you should have the following result.

bookcode	title	author_name	no_pages	course_code
65281	Beginning Syntax	Kershaw, J.	247	c2
38572	Practical Pragmatics	Christine Harpleton-	320	c7
65284	A First Course In Logic	Jerry Maxwell	115	c5
65290	Even More Logic	(NULL)	(NULL)	c5

Attempting to insert the data in these examples should illustrate the following points.

- When no column names are specified in an **INSERT** statement, the values are treated as the input to corresponding columns of the table in the order in which the columns were defined when the table was created. Because the statement **table_creation** defines five columns, we require five values in these insertions.
- If a character string that is given as the input to a column is longer than the length defined for the column's data type, the string is truncated. 'Christine Harpleton-Davies', in **insert2**, is an example of this – at 26 characters long, it will not fit into a column whose data type is defined as **VARCHAR(20)**.
- Values for primary keys may not be repeated, nor may they be NULL, as illustrated by **insert4**.
- NULL can be specified as the input to a column using the keyword **NULL** (not a character string in quotes) (**insert5**), unless the column is defined as **NOT NULL** (**insert6**) or is a primary key (**insert4**).
- Values in referring columns must refer to existing values in the referred tables: **insert7** fails because there is no course in the **course** table with course number c8.

We can also specify columns by name in an **INSERT** statement.

➢ Run the following statement.

```
INSERT INTO textbook (title, course_code, author_name, bookcode)
   VALUES ('Interpreting Semantics', 'c4', 'Hyde, E.', '63948')
```
insert_values1

If you check what has happened to **textbook**, you should see that the values in **insert_values1** have been added in the columns corresponding to the specified order. In addition, the value of the column **no_pages**, which is not specified in **insert_values1**, is NULL.

➢ Now run the following two statements, and then check the contents of **textbook**.

```
INSERT INTO textbook (bookcode, title, no_pages, course_code)
   VALUES ('12953', 'Grammatical Structures', 250)
```
insert_values2

```
INSERT INTO textbook (bookcode, title, no_pages, course_code)
   VALUES ('12953', 'Grammatical Structures', 250, 'c2')
```
insert_values3

You should find that **insert_values2** does not succeed because the number of values given does not match the number of columns specified. In general, you can specify any of the columns of a table in an **INSERT** statement, in any order, but the given values must match the corresponding columns in number and data type.

With **insert_values3**, you should see that the value of **author_name** is not NULL, but the string 'None' which was defined as the default value in **table_creation**. Compare this with the result of **insert5**: the value of the **author_name** column is NULL if we explicitly state it, but the default value is used if no value is provided in the **INSERT** statement. However, as we saw in **insert5**, if no default has been specified in the table definition, then NULL is used where no value is given in the **INSERT** statement.

EXERCISE 5.3

Which of the following statements are accepted by SQL, where the **textbook** table has been defined? In each case, state what happens when the statement is executed, and why. You may assume that there are no repeated primary keys. You should attempt to predict the behaviour of the statements before you actually execute them.

(a) `INSERT INTO textbook (bookcode, author_name, title, course_code)`
    `VALUES ('93881', 'Advances in Pragmatics', 'Farmer, S.J.', 'c7')`

columns1

(b) `INSERT INTO textbook (bookcode, title, no_pages, course_code)`
    `VALUES ('73642', 'The Semantics of Romance Languages',`
            `'Jane Hanley', 'c4')`

columns2

(c) `INSERT INTO textbook (bookcode, author_name, no_pages, course_code)`
    `VALUES ('79432', 'Richard Friedman', 194, 'c5')`

columns3

EXERCISE 5.4

From the results of Exercise 5.3, what can you infer about the columns that must be included in an **INSERT** statement?

Deleting rows from a table: DELETE

Having carried out the activities in the previous section, you should have a table **textbook** which contains several rows of data. We can now use the **DELETE** statement to clean up the data that we have added.

ACTIVITY 5.4

Check to see the contents of the **textbook** table, and then run the following statement.

`DELETE FROM textbook`

delete1

Check the contents of the **textbook** table again.

You should find that all the rows in the **textbook** table have been deleted. Clearly, using **DELETE** in this fashion is a somewhat blunt instrument for removing data from a table. However, we can delete selected rows by using a **WHERE** clause.

As with **DROPTABLE**, you are not asked to confirm that you wish to remove all the data from the table.

ACTIVITY 5.5

Check that the **textbook** table is empty (run **delete1** again if not), then run the filed statements in **fill_table** below to populate the table with data.

```
INSERT INTO textbook
  VALUES ('65281', 'Beginning Syntax', 'Kershaw, J.', 247, 'c2')

INSERT INTO textbook
  VALUES ('38572', 'Practical Pragmatics', 'Christine Davies', 320, 'c7')

INSERT INTO textbook
  VALUES ('65284', 'A First Course In Logic', 'Jerry Maxwell', 115, 'c5')
```

```
INSERT INTO textbook
  VALUES ('65285', 'More Logic', 'Jerry Maxwell', 210, 'c5')

INSERT INTO textbook
  VALUES ('65290', 'Even More Logic', NULL, NULL, 'c5')

INSERT INTO textbook
  VALUES ('63948', 'Interpreting Semantics', 'Hyde, E.', NULL, 'c4')

INSERT INTO textbook
  VALUES ('12953', 'Grammatical Structures', NULL, 258, 'c2')

INSERT INTO textbook
  VALUES ('93881', 'Advances in Pragmatics', 'Farmer, S.J.', NULL, 'c7')

INSERT INTO textbook
  VALUES ('73642', 'The Semantics of Romance Languages',
          'Jane Hanley', NULL, 'c4')
```

fill_table

Check the contents of the **textbook** table; you should have the following table.

bookcode	title	author_name	no_pages	course_code
12953	Grammatical Structures	(NULL)	258	c2
38572	Practical Pragmatics	Christine Davies	320	c7
63948	Interpreting Semantics	Hyde, E.	(NULL)	c4
65281	Beginning Syntax	Kershaw, J.	247	c2
65284	A First Course In Logic	Jerry Maxwell	115	c5
65285	More Logic	Jerry Maxwell	210	c5
65290	Even More Logic	(NULL)	(NULL)	c5
73642	The Semantics of Romance Languages	Jane Hanley	(NULL)	c4
93881	Advances in Pragmatics	Farmer, S.J.	(NULL)	c7

➤ Now run the following statement.

```
DELETE FROM textbook
WHERE author_name IS NULL
```

delete2

This time only the rows with NULL for the name of the author are deleted.

EXERCISE 5.5

How does a **DELETE** statement specify the rows to be deleted?

EXERCISE 5.6

(a) Write and run a statement to delete all the rows from the `textbook` table whose value in the column `no_pages` is less than 250.

(b) Write and run a statement to delete the remaining rows from the `textbook` table.

The basic structure of a `DELETE` statement is very simple: it uses a search condition in a `WHERE` clause to determine which rows are to be deleted from the table. Of course, the search condition can be as complex as the `WHERE` clause of any query specification, and can include subqueries.

The logical processing of a `DELETE` statement is also simple: starting with the specified table as the input, each row is examined to see if it satisfies the condition given in the `WHERE` clause, and if it does not then the row remains in the database table. However, when `DELETE` statements contain subqueries that reference the table being deleted (the **target table**), the subquery is taken to apply to the *original* target table before any deletions have been completed. So, for example, if the following statement is executed:

```
DELETE FROM textbook
  WHERE no_pages > (SELECT AVG(no_pages)
                    FROM textbook)
```

delete_above_average_pages

then the `WHERE` clause is evaluated using the same value of `AVG(no_pages)` each time. The original target table is used for the whole deletion; the subquery is not re-evaluated after each deletion of a row.

Even when all the rows of a table have been deleted, the table still exists, although it is empty. To remove the empty table from the database, we must use `DROP TABLE`.

All the `INSERT` statements in this section have inserted data into tables one row at a time. In fact, Standard SQL allows multiple rows to be inserted using a single statement. For example, the first three insertions of **fill_table** are:

```
INSERT INTO textbook
  VALUES ('65281', 'Beginning Syntax', 'Kershaw, J.', 247, 'c2')

INSERT INTO textbook
  VALUES ('38572', 'Practical Pragmatics', 'Christine Davies', 320, 'c7')

INSERT INTO textbook
  VALUES ('65284', 'A First Course In Logic', 'Jerry Maxwell', 115, 'c5')
```

In Standard SQL, these three statements can be expressed as a single statement:

```
INSERT INTO textbook
  VALUES ('65281', 'Beginning Syntax', 'Kershaw, J.', 247, 'c2'),
         ('38572', 'Practical Pragmatics', 'Christine Davies', 320, 'c7'),
         ('65284', 'A First Course In Logic', 'Jerry Maxwell', 115, 'c5')
```

SQL Anywhere has not implemented multiple-row insertion as described here. However, when using DBMSs that have implemented this feature, this example illustrates that in the general case, `VALUES` actually return a *table*, rather than a row.

Adding data from other tables

It is often the case that a table is needed to store some data from one or more existing tables in the database. The `INSERT` statement can also be used to add rows that result from executing a query specification.

ACTIVITY 5.6

We will define a temporary table and populate it with data from an existing table.

Using the Hospital database, execute the following command.

```
CREATE TABLE tmp_patient (
    patient_id CHAR(3),
    name VARCHAR(8),
    height DECIMAL(4, 1),
    PRIMARY KEY (name) )
```

create_tmp_patient

This should have created a new table called `tmp_patient`. Now execute the following statement.

```
INSERT INTO tmp_patient (patient_id, name, height)
    SELECT patient_id, patient_name, height
    FROM patient
    WHERE gender = 'F'
```

patient_insert

You should find that `tmp_patient` now contains the patient identifiers, names and heights of all the patients in the `patient` table with a `gender` value of '`F`'.

We refer to the specified table (`tmp_patient` in **patient_insert**) as the **target table** to distinguish it from the (one or more) tables referenced within the query specification. Note that a query specification may include expressions, grouping and functions to manipulate the form of the data to be stored in the target table.

Activity 5.6 illustrates the following points.

▶ As with other uses of `INSERT`, it is important to ensure that the data types are compatible. In this example, the name 'Rubinstein' that appears in `patient` is truncated to 'Rubinste' in `tmp_patient`, as we defined the `name` column to be at most 8 characters (compare **insert2**).

▶ The values are inserted in the order given by the `SELECT` clause. So although the column names do not need to be identical (here, we place the value of `patient.patient_name` into `tmp_patient.name`), the order of columns in the `INSERT` and `SELECT` clauses need to correspond. If there are an incorrect number of columns, or if columns in the `SELECT` clause contain data that cannot be converted into the appropriate data type in the target table, then the `INSERT` will fail.

▶ The condition in the `WHERE` clause uses columns that are not copied into the target table; the condition is used to obtain the rows for the `SELECT` statement, rather than applying conditions to the target table.

Some additional factors to consider are:

▶ The columns in the target table do not need to be explicitly specified in the `INSERT` statement if the `SELECT` clause contains a corresponding number of columns of the appropriate data type.

▶ A column defined as either `NOT NULL` or a primary key cannot be assigned NULL (implicitly or explicitly). This can be a problem if you do not know in advance whether the data resulting from a query specification includes NULL.

Recall the discussion of casts in Section 2.2.

We have stated that if the columns in the `SELECT` clause contain data that cannot be converted into the appropriate data type in the target table, then the `INSERT` will fail. In general, an `INSERT` statement will fail if the value being inserted cannot be cast into the data type of the column.

ACTIVITY 5.7

Still using the **tmp_patient** table as defined in Activity 5.6, run the following statement.

```
INSERT INTO tmp_patient (patient_id, name, height)
    SELECT *
    FROM nurse
```
cast_fail

The **INSERT** statement fails.

In **cast_fail**, the **SELECT** clause contains the correct number of columns for the **INSERT** statement, so we would expect the rows (**staff_no**, **nurse_name**, **ward_no**) from the **nurse** table to be mapped onto the rows (**patient_id**, **name**, **height**) in the **tmp_patient** table. However, the values in the column **ward_no** are strings that begin with a 'w'. These values cannot be cast into the **DECIMAL(4, 1)** data type of the **height** column of the **tmp_patient** table, and so the statement fails.

EXERCISE 5.7

(a) What will be the result of executing the following two statements (when the **tmp_patient** table initially contains no data in each case)?

(i)
```
INSERT INTO tmp_patient
    SELECT drug_name, price, price
    FROM drug
```

(ii)
```
INSERT INTO tmp_patient
    SELECT ward_no, nurse_name, NULL
    FROM nurse
```

(b) Write an SQL query that copies into **tmp_patient** from **patient**, the patient identifiers, names and heights of all patients who occupy a ward with ten or more beds.

This form of **INSERT** is simple, but you should remember that the query specification can be very complex and may involve joins and subqueries with a number of tables.

Modifying rows in a table: UPDATE

So far we have looked at deleting rows from, and adding rows to, a table. In this section, we consider the third way of updating a table, in which existing rows are modified by means of the **UPDATE** statement. Note that in this case, we are talking about the values of data in the table that are being modified. The term 'modify' is also used to describe changes made to the definition of a table. We will discuss these changes in Section 6 of this block.

ACTIVITY 5.8

This activity uses the University database.

Ensure that you have defined the **textbook** table, and that it is populated with the data described in **fill_table** (if not, rerun **drop1**, **table_creation**, **fill_table**).

Run the following statement.

```
UPDATE textbook
  SET author_name = 'J. K. Maxwell',
      title = title || ' (JKM)',
      no_pages = NULL
  WHERE author_name = 'Jerry Maxwell'
```

update1

You should have found that the values for the specified columns in the rows for books authored by Jerry Maxwell (i.e. containing the string 'Jerry Maxwell' in the `author_name` column), and no others, have been changed to the values given by the `SET` clause. This example illustrates how an `UPDATE` statement can modify the data in a table that satisfies a search condition given in a `WHERE` clause, according to one or more assignments given in a `SET` clause. Such an assignment specifies a new value for a named column in terms of any kind of expression, involving constants or the columns of any table (including the column being updated).

Notice that in **update1** the assignment for `title` is specified in terms of itself; for each row that is being updated, the old value for the `title` column is used to give the new value (that is, with the author's initials concatenated to the end). Also, note that `NULL` can be used as an assignment in an `UPDATE` statement; compare this with the `WHERE` conditions in which `IS NULL` must be used.

ACTIVITY 5.9

Now run the following statement.

```
UPDATE textbook
  SET author_name = 'None',
      title = title || '(' + author_name || ')'
  WHERE author_name = 'Hyde, E.'
```

update2

When you examine the `textbook` table, you should find that for the textbook with code 63948, the `author_name` column contains 'None', and the `title` column contains 'Interpreting Semantics (Hyde, E.)'.

Activity 5.9 illustrates that column values are updated together using the initial values; each expression in the `SET` clause is evaluated before they are updated. So `author_name` is not set to 'None' until after `title` has been set to 'Interpreting Semantics (Hyde, E.)'.

EXERCISE 5.8

The University has decided to add a 5-page appendix to all course books on syntax. Write an `UPDATE` statement to increase the number of pages by 5 of all the textbooks in the `textbook` table that are used on the course with code c2.

Although the examples we have given are simple, we emphasise that the search condition in the `WHERE` clause of an `UPDATE` statement can be as complex as any allowed for a query. The logical processing of an `UPDATE` statement starts with the specified table as the input. Then an intermediate table is created by copying each row from the initial table that satisfies the condition in the `WHERE` clause. The final table is created by copying each row in the intermediate table, evaluating the expressions in the `SET` clause to assign new values to the specified columns. The last stage is that the original base table is replaced by the final table of the processing, so that the table is updated.

5.4 Defining constraints

As initially described in *Block 1*, the integrity of data is vitally important to all users of a database. Data integrity is violated if there is any difference either between the data and the information about the real world which it represents, or between data in one part of the database and data in another. Here are some examples of data that would violate the integrity of the Hospital database:

- a row in the `treatment` table that refers to a patient who does not exist (**incorrect data**);
- a row in the `doctor` table with a `position` value representing a Registrar, but who is responsible for a patient according to the `staff_no` column in the `patient` table (**inconsistent data**).

You have already seen in *Block 2* how constraints are used to preserve the integrity of the database. As in the relational model, SQL allows us to define constraints for use by a DBMS in maintaining the integrity of the database. Constraints in SQL are usually included as part of a table definition within a schema; in this section, we will describe how to define them.

There are four different kinds of constraint in SQL, which may be summarised as follows.

- A **not null constraint** requires that each entry in a column is not NULL.
- A **unique constraint** requires that each value in a constrained column, or columns, is distinct. This kind of SQL constraint includes both primary key and candidate key constraints as defined in *Block 2*.
- A **referential constraint** requires that each non-NULL value in a constrained column, or columns, has a single matching value in the table to which it refers. This SQL constraint is equivalent to the foreign key constraints described in *Block 2*, Section 4.
- A **check constraint** requires that a given search condition (like a condition in a `WHERE` clause) is not false for any row of a table. This SQL constraint is comparable to a general constraint as described in *Block 2*, Section 4.3.

We have two options for expressing constraints in SQL: **column constraints** and **table constraints**. A column constraint applies to a single column and is written as part of the column definition when the table is defined, such as the not null constraints in **table_creation**. A table constraint is expressed independently of the columns as a separate entry in a table definition, such as the constraint `textbook_in_used_on` in **table_creation**. The primary key constraint in **table_creation** is a table constraint, although it could have been expressed as a column constraint with no difference in its meaning.

We will consider how constraints can be expressed as both column constraints and table constraints in this section. Generally, however, we prefer to use table constraints for compatibility with the way we define relations in *Block 2*.

Not null constraints

Not null constraints are defined on columns, rather than on tables. A column constraint is defined on a particular column at the moment a table is created, and it restricts the values that entries in that column may take. To define a column constraint at the moment the table is being defined, the following syntax is used.

```
CREATE TABLE <table name> (
    ...
    <column name> <data type> [<column constraint>],
    ... )
```

A note on syntax: Expressions contained in square brackets, such as `[<column constraint>]` here, are optional. So this description of the `CREATE TABLE` syntax states that values for `<column name>` and `<data type>` are compulsory, but the `<column constraint>` may or may not appear. This use is consistent with the SQL Anywhere online manuals.

We have already seen several examples of column constraints in **table_creation**, in which the `title` and `course_code` columns both have the declaration `NOT NULL` included as part of the column definition:

```
CREATE TABLE textbook (
    ...
    title VARCHAR(40) NOT NULL,
    ... )
```

By declaring a not null constraint on a column, it is not possible to enter a row that has a value of NULL for this column (as you saw in **insert6** in Activity 5.3).

A not null constraint applies to a single column, and is expressed by including `NOT NULL` as part of the column definition. We have seen several not null constraints in **table_creation**. As well as the explicit forms of the constraint, one not null constraint is also expressed implicitly – the primary key declaration. As we have already mentioned in Section 5.2, the primary key for a table may not contain NULL, and so the primary key declaration is itself a constraint on the values that the columns in the primary key may take.

Unique constraints

SQL does not have the additional requirement of minimality.

In *Block 2*, Section 2.4, you saw how a number of columns (or combinations of columns) may be candidate keys for a relation. The same applies in SQL tables: the values in candidate key columns uniquely identify each row. In SQL, columns are constrained to be candidate keys using the keyword `UNIQUE`.

See Block 2, Section 2.5.

For example, you have already seen that in the *Team* relation of the Hospital model, the attribute *StaffNo* can be declared as an alternate key. When we implement this in SQL, we would like to state that no two rows in the `team` table can take the same value in the `staff_no` column. This can be achieved by including in the `CREATE TABLE` statement a unique constraint on the column `staff_no`. This can be expressed as a column constraint, in the same way as a not null constraint. So, if we want to state that no two teams can be headed by the same doctor, we could write:

```
CREATE TABLE team (
    ...
    staff_no CHAR(3) UNIQUE,
    ... )
```

Using this declaration for `staff_no` to be unique will prevent any two rows having the same value in the `staff_no` column.

> In fact, SQL Anywhere does not allow a column both to have a unique constraint and to contain NULL. So if a column is constrained to be unique, an additional constraint for not null is not required; this is not the behaviour required by the Standard, which allows a column both to have a unique constraint defined upon it and to contain occurrences of NULL.

A unique constraint can also be defined as a table constraint. The standard syntax for a table constraint is:

```
CREATE TABLE <table name> (
  ...
  [CONSTRAINT <constraint name>]
    <table constraint>,
  ... )
```

A table constraint to specify that one or more rows should be unique is expressed as:

```
UNIQUE (c₁, ..., cₙ)
```

where each of the $c_1, ..., c_n$ are columns which must take distinct values. So to write a table constraint stating that every row in the **team** table should have a different value in the column **staff_no**, we would write:

```
CREATE TABLE team (
  ...
  staff_no CHAR(3),
  ...
  CONSTRAINT unique_team_head
    UNIQUE (staff_no),
  ... )
```

As you can see from the syntax, the `CONSTRAINT <constraint name>` is optional. That is, we could have simply used `UNIQUE (staff_no)` rather than the whole declaration `CONSTRAINT unique_team_head UNIQUE (staff_no)`. However, we will see in Section 5.6 that naming constraints gives us greater flexibility to redefine constraints, making the database more maintainable.

What if we require a *combination* of columns to have unique values? Suppose that, in the table **textbook**, we require that each textbook has both a title and an edition number, and that the combination of title and edition number have a unique value. We could achieve this with:

Recall from Block 2, Section 2.4 that a candidate key for a relation can be a combination of attributes.

```
CREATE TABLE textbook (
  ...
  title CHAR(40),
  edition INTEGER,
  ...
  CONSTRAINT unique_title
    UNIQUE (title, edition),
  ... )
```

If a candidate key is formed of multiple columns, the constraint is expressed as `UNIQUE (c₁, ..., cₙ)`, where no rows may contain the same values for each of the c_i. In these cases, the constraint can only be expressed as a table constraint; column constraints can be used only on single columns.

As with not null constraints, uniqueness constraints may be expressed implicitly as primary keys, rather than explicitly with the `UNIQUE` keyword. A primary key constraint is the most common form of unique constraint, in which each value of the column or columns to which it is applied is unique and not NULL. Of course, a table can have only one primary key constraint.

We have seen in **table_creation** how a primary key is defined as a table constraint; we could also have used a column constraint written as:

```
CREATE TABLE textbook (
   bookcode CHAR(5) PRIMARY KEY,
   ... )
```

When a table has a primary key involving more than one column, it cannot be expressed as a column constraint, so it must be expressed as a table constraint. For example, the table **enrolment** is defined by:

```
CREATE TABLE enrolment (
   student_id CHAR(3),
   course_code CHAR(2),
   enrolment_date CHAR(4),
   PRIMARY KEY (student_id, course_code) )
```

So although there may be repeated values in the `student_id` column, and there may be repeated values in the `course_code` column, the *combination* `(student_id, course_code)` must be different for each row. This ensures that the database only allows one enrolment for a particular student on any course.

EXERCISE 5.9

Which of the three kinds of update statement in SQL might be affected by adding a unique constraint to a table?

Referential constraints

As described in *Block 2*, Section 2.5, the foreign key mechanism is an essential part of the referential constraint for representing relationships in relational terms. Just to remind you, a foreign key is a column, or columns, in one table (the **referencing table**), which contains values that match those of a key in another table (the **referenced table**). The primary key of the referenced table is usually used, but any column or columns can be used, as long as they have a unique constraint defined upon them. The relationship is defined by these pairs of matching values.

In SQL, foreign keys are defined in the referencing table. To define a foreign key as a table constraint, we use the following syntax:

```
CREATE TABLE <table name> (
   ...
   [CONSTRAINT <constraint name>]
      FOREIGN KEY (f₁, ..., fₙ) REFERENCES <refd_table>,
   ... )
```

where `<refd_table>` is the name of the referenced table, and each of the f_i that appears in `(f₁, ..., fₙ)` is the name of a column that forms part of the foreign key.

As an example, consider the **ContractsWith** relationship in the University model. This is represented by the column `region` in the `staff` table which references the primary key of `region` (`region_number`). So `region` in the `staff` table is a foreign key, which can be expressed as:

```
CREATE TABLE staff (
    ...
    region_number SMALLINT NOT NULL,
    CONSTRAINT staff_in_contracts_with
        FOREIGN KEY (region_number) REFERENCES region )
```

In this foreign key definition, it is implicit that the foreign key `region_number` references the primary key of the `region` table, that is, `region.region_number`. However, as noted in *Block 2*, a foreign key may reference *any* key in the referenced table, not just the primary key. To reference another table using a candidate key, the column(s) should be made explicit in the foreign key declaration:

```
FOREIGN KEY (f₁, ..., fₙ) REFERENCES <refd_table> (c₁, ...,cₙ)
```

where $(f_1, ..., f_n)$ are the columns in the referencing table that reference the key $(c_1, ..., c_n)$ in the referenced table, `<refd_table>`. Where a foreign key declaration references the primary key of the referenced table, the columns in the referenced table do not need to be named explicitly, therefore we did not specify any columns for `region` in the `CREATE TABLE staff` declaration. However, we could make the choice of column explicit if we wished, by writing:

```
FOREIGN KEY (region_number) REFERENCES region (region_number)
```

To assess the impact of a foreign key declaration, we return to the referential integrity rule given in *Block 2*, which requires that a foreign key value must match a value of the key used to reference the referenced table. In other words, *a referential constraint prevents a foreign key having a value that is not a value of the key of the referenced table*.

Unlike a primary key, a foreign key may be NULL (unless this is explicitly prohibited by an additional not null constraint). So, in fact, the referential constraint only applies where the foreign key has a value (i.e. it is not NULL); where a foreign key has a value, it must match a value in the key of the referenced table.

EXERCISE 5.10

Given the definition of **textbook** in **table_creation**, which of the following statements will succeed? If not, why not?

(a) `INSERT INTO textbook`
    `VALUES ('78652', 'The Liar Paradox', 'Mitty, W.', NULL, 'c5')`
                                                                    fk_insert1

(b) `INSERT INTO textbook`
    `VALUES ('13694', 'Applied Morphology', 'Ed Hacking', 247, 'c3')`
                                                                    fk_insert2

(c) `INSERT INTO textbook`
    `VALUES ('84263', 'A Pragmatics Primer', 'Farmer, S.J.', 220, NULL)`
                                                                    fk_insert3

In Exercise 5.10, you have considered what happens if you attempt to insert rows into a table when the foreign keys do not reference keys in the referenced table (try to execute **fk_insert1**, **fk_insert2** and **fk_insert3** if you have not done so already). But what happens if we delete a referenced row in the referenced table? Maintaining referential integrity is not just a matter of preventing some changes to the referencing table – a relationship involves two tables and it is possible for changes to the referenced table to violate the constraint. For example, consider what would happen if we tried:

```
DELETE FROM course
WHERE course_code = 'c2'
```

If this command were successfully executed, the database would contain rows in `enrolment` and `textbook` that refer to `course` via the key c2, but for which no row in the referenced table exists. Clearly, this situation would violate the integrity of the database and cannot be permitted.

To prevent actions like this affecting the integrity of the database, SQL allows us to define **referential actions** as part of the referential constraint. A referential action is invoked whenever a row, being deleted from a referenced table, has any **dependent rows** (i.e. rows which themselves reference that row, such as a row in `textbook` that references a row in `course` via the key c2). The action describes what changes should be made to the dependent rows so that the changes do not violate the referential integrity of the database.

SQL provides the following four possible actions that may occur for a dependent row of a referencing table when the referenced row is deleted.

SQL:1992 uses **NO ACTION** instead of **RESTRICT**.

▶ **RESTRICT**: Prevents the referenced row from being deleted. This is the default.
▶ **SET NULL**: Sets the value of the foreign key in the dependent row to NULL.
▶ **SET DEFAULT**: Sets the value of the foreign key in the dependent row to its default value.
▶ **CASCADE**: Deletes the dependent row.

For any referential constraint it is necessary to decide whether or not to include a referential action and if so, which one. This choice has to be based on an understanding of the meaning of the relationship which is being represented by the foreign key.

EXERCISE 5.11

We have used the `course_code` column in `textbook` as a foreign key to implement the **UsedOn** relationship. From your understanding of the model, for each of the possible referential actions, explain whether it is appropriate for the referential constraint that is associated with this relationship. (You may wish to refer back to Section 5.1 to remind yourself of the description of the details of the extension to the model.)

To include the preferred referential action, **ON DELETE <action>** is added to the foreign key declaration. The complete table constraint for a referential constraint then becomes

```
FOREIGN KEY (f_1, ..., f_n) REFERENCES <refd_table> [(c_1, ..., c_n)]
  [ON DELETE <action>]
```

5 Database definition and population

and to define the **textbook** table so that the referential action is **CASCADE** rather than **RESTRICT**, we would use:

```
CREATE TABLE textbook (
  ...
  CONSTRAINT textbook_in_used_on
    FOREIGN KEY (course_code) REFERENCES course
      ON DELETE CASCADE )
```

Note that the default state is **RESTRICT**, so the original definition in **table_creation** has implicit **ON DELETE RESTRICT**.

Check constraints

> This section describes check constraints as they are defined by the SQL Standard. You should be aware that many implementations of SQL do not provide full support for check constraints. Before defining constraints on a database, you should consult the documentation for the particular SQL implementation that you are using.
>
> SQL Anywhere does support the definition of check constraints according to the description in this section. However, you should note the comments at the end of Section 5.7 which discuss how SQL Anywhere evaluates constraints.
>
> In fact, SQL usually provides several different ways of maintaining the integrity of a database. *Block 4* discusses the different options at length, and contains some guidance to selecting between the different techniques.

A check constraint is a search condition applied to values in a table. In a check constraint, the condition described must not evaluate to FALSE (so it must evaluate to either TRUE or UNKNOWN). The condition is of the same form as conditions in, for example, **WHERE** clauses. Because any search condition is possible, check constraints are a powerful and versatile tool for managing data. The general syntax to define a check constraint on a table is:

```
CREATE TABLE <table name> (
  ...
  [CONSTRAINT <constraint name>]
    CHECK (<condition>),
  ... )
```

We might use a simple check constraint to restrict the values that a column of the table might take. Consider, for example, a constraint requiring that the number of a region must be an integer between 1 and 99. This can be expressed by adding a check constraint to the **region_number** column of the **region** table:

```
CREATE TABLE region (
  ...
  region_number SMALLINT,
  ...
  CONSTRAINT region_number_limits
    CHECK (region_number BETWEEN 1 AND 99) )
```

In practice, we would probably declare this constraint in a domain definition, as we will discuss in Section 5.5.

The occurrence of **region_number** in the check constraint refers to the occurrence of **region_number** in the table that the check constraint is defined on (i.e. **region**). However, the condition in a check constraint does not have to be restricted to the table on which the constraint is defined: the condition can be as complex as required, possibly using values from other tables in the database. As an example of a more complex form of check constraint, consider the condition that students may not enrol for more than 180 points worth of courses at any one time. This might be implemented as part of the **student** table as:

```
CREATE TABLE student (
   ...
   student_id CHAR(3),
   ...
   CONSTRAINT enrolment_limit CHECK (
      180 >= (SELECT SUM(credit)
              FROM enrolment e, course c
              WHERE e.course_code = c.course_code
                AND student_id = e.student_id) )
   ... )
```

Notice that the condition behaves in the same way as a correlated subquery (see Section 3.3): the first occurrence of **student_id** in the condition **student_id = e.student_id** refers back to the value of **student_id** in the row that is being evaluated.

This constraint must not be false for any row of the table. If an update to the database would make the constraint false for any row, then the attempted update will fail. A quirk of SQL is that a constraint is always satisfied if the table on which it is defined is empty, as there is no row for which it is false.

There are often many ways of expressing the same constraint. Instead of defining the constraint on the **student** table, we could define it on the **enrolment** table by using a quantifier:

```
CREATE TABLE enrolment (
   ...
   CONSTRAINT enrolment_limit CHECK (
      180 >= ( ALL (SELECT SUM(credit)
                    FROM course c, enrolment e
                    WHERE c.course_code = e.course_code
                    GROUP BY student_id) ) )
   ... )
```

Notice that this way of expressing the constraint does not behave as a correlated subquery; no term appears in the condition that refers back to the rows being checked.

These examples show that we can often choose the table on which to define a constraint, and the constraint may need to be written differently depending upon where it is defined. You will often find that it feels more natural to define a constraint on one table rather than another. In this case, we have shown that a constraint on the number of courses that a student is enrolled on could be defined either on the **enrolment** table or the **student** table.

> Although a constraint can be defined on any table, SQL Anywhere evaluates a constraint only when the table that it is defined upon is updated. So if the constraint **enrolment_limit** were defined on the **student** table, it would be evaluated whenever **student** is updated, while if it were defined on the **enrolment** table, it would be evaluated whenever **enrolment** is updated. In this case, we would probably prefer to define the constraint on the **enrolment** table, so that it is evaluated when new enrolments are made.
>
> However, this is non-standard behaviour. Strictly, each constraint must be true whenever any change has been made to the database.

EXERCISE 5.12

The definition of **textbook** in **table_creation** defines a not null constraint on the column **title** with the following column constraint:

```
CREATE TABLE textbook (
  ...
  title VARCHAR(40) NOT NULL,
  ... )
```

Although not null constraints are applied only to columns, not to tables, the same effect as a not null constraint can be achieved by defining a check constraint on the table. How would you express this not null constraint as a check constraint on the **textbook** table?

EXERCISE 5.13

No course may use more than five textbooks. Express this as a check constraint for the **textbook** table.

You may wish to test your solution by reimplementing the **textbook** table. However, in Section 5.6, we will see how to modify a table without having to reimplement it from scratch; this includes adding and removing constraints.

Expressing referential constraints and check constraints as column constraints

So far we have looked at how referential constraints and check constraints are expressed as table constraints. As with unique constraints, when only one column is involved, it is also possible to express these constraints as column constraints.

The general form of a referential column constraint is:

```
CREATE TABLE <table name> (
  ...
  <column name> <data type> REFERENCES <refd_table>
    [ON DELETE <action>],
  ... )
```

So the referential constraint that we saw earlier

```
CREATE TABLE staff (
  ...
  region_number SMALLINT NOT NULL,
  CONSTRAINT staff_in_contracts_with
    FOREIGN KEY (region_number) REFERENCES region )
```

can also be expressed as

```
CREATE TABLE staff (
  ...
  region_number SMALLINT NOT NULL REFERENCES region )
```

Note that either **UNIQUE** or **NOT NULL** can also be included before the **REFERENCES** declaration. We can also add a referential action:

```
CREATE TABLE staff (
  ...
  region_number SMALLINT NOT NULL
    REFERENCES region ON DELETE RESTRICT )
```

Similarly, we can add a check constraint after the column definition. The constraint we defined earlier is:

```
CREATE TABLE region (
   ...
   region_number SMALLINT,
   ...
   CONSTRAINT region_number_limits
      CHECK (region_number BETWEEN 1 AND 99),
   ... )
```

We can rewrite this constraint as:

```
CREATE TABLE region (
   ...
   region_number SMALLINT CHECK (region_number BETWEEN 1 AND 99),
   ... )
```

In general, we recommend using table constraints, rather than column constraints. You will have noticed that the table constraints are named, while column constraints are not. Naming constraints allows them to be changed or replaced without affecting the rest of the table (the mechanisms for doing this are discussed in Section 5.6), and this allows greater flexibility in maintaining the database over its lifetime.

Using constraints

SQL does not force us to use the constraints that we have just described. For example, we can define tables in SQL without primary keys. But because primary keys are an essential element of the relational approach, all the tables in the databases provided for this course have primary keys defined on them. For the development of a database system, the choices about which constraints to implement are made during the process of logical schema design, as described in *Block 1*, when it is decided which of the constraints specified in a conceptual data model need to be included in an SQL schema. The issues relating to these choices, and their implications, will be considered as part of the topic of database design in *Block 4*. However, now we can look at some of the issues relating to how SQL constraints are chosen, how a given constraint may be expressed, and its impact on data manipulation.

Because check constraints are very flexible, you might be tempted to use a check constraint where another form of constraint would be more appropriate. For example, we can express the condition that each value of **course_code** in the **textbook** table must match some value of the primary key **course_code** in the **course** table with a check constraint in the **textbook** table:

```
CHECK (course_code IN (SELECT course_code
                       FROM course) )
```

Therefore, we can use a check constraint to express the same condition that we previously expressed as a referential constraint. However, where it is possible, we use a referential constraint rather than a check constraint because:

▶ a referential constraint makes the purpose of the constraint explicit – that is, that the constraint is based on a relationship;

▶ a referential constraint can take advantage of SQL's referential actions.

5.5 Use of domains in SQL

> The discussion of domains in this section describes domains as defined by the SQL Standard. SQL Anywhere correctly implements domains as defined in the current SQL Standard. However, you should be aware that many SQL implementations do not implement domains in the manner described here.

So far, when defining the range of values that a column in a table can take, you have used the SQL predefined data types (`CHAR`, `INT`, and so on). SQL provides a mechanism for constraining the possible values that may appear in a column in a table. The mechanism is based upon the relational concept of domains which you saw in *Block 2*. In *Block 2*, Section 2.2, a domain is defined as a named set of values from which one or more attributes draw their actual values.

In SQL, the purpose of a **domain** is to constrain the set of valid values that can be stored in the columns of a base table. An SQL domain is defined in terms of an SQL predefined data type (recall Section 2.2), with zero or more constraints on the values that can be taken, and possibly a default value.

For example, consider the `title` column of the `textbook` table. The column definition in **table_creation** states that entries in the `title` column have type `VARCHAR(40)` and are additionally constrained to be `NOT NULL`. We can define a domain called `book_titles` that can be used to constrain the entries in the `title` column.

The general format of a `CREATE DOMAIN` statement is:

```
CREATE DOMAIN <domain name> AS <data type>
   [[NOT] NULL]
   [DEFAULT <default value>]
   [CHECK (<condition>)]
```

For example, the domain `book_titles` is defined by the following statement:

```
CREATE DOMAIN book_titles AS VARCHAR(40)
   NOT NULL
```

A `CREATE DOMAIN` statement must include an SQL predefined data type (known as the **underlying data type**) and can optionally specify `NOT NULL`, a default value and a check constraint. Executing the statement involves checking that there is no other domain or data type with the same name, and then storing the definition as part of the schema. After execution, the domain can be used for defining a column within any table in the same way as a data type is used. So using the new domain `book_titles`, the `title` column in the `textbook` table is defined in the **table_creation** example as:

```
title book_titles
```

This definition of the column `title` now means that all entries in the column must have the properties of the domain `book_titles` – that is, `VARCHAR(40) NOT NULL`.

A check constraint can be used to further constrain the permissible values in a domain. For example, consider the column `credit` in the `course` table. Courses may only have credit values of 30 points or 60 points. Therefore, every entry in the `credit` column of the `course` table must be either 30 or 60. SQL allows a constraint to be defined as part of the domain that prevents other values appearing in the column:

```
CREATE DOMAIN credit_points AS SMALLINT
   CHECK (VALUE IN (30, 60))
```

Notice how the keyword **VALUE** is used in a check constraint in a domain definition. If a column is defined using this domain then the search condition must not be false when **VALUE** is set to any of the values in that column.

> In SQL Anywhere, you need to use **@VALUE** rather than just **VALUE**.

It would also be possible to add a constraint to the column **credit** as part of the table definition to restrict the values in the column to either 30 or 60. However, it is possible that we wish to define columns in other tables whose values are restricted to those of the **credit_points** domain. By defining this constraint at the domain level, the **credit_points** domain can be used throughout the database without requiring additional constraints at the column or table level.

We can extend the definition of the domain to include a default value. In this case, we shall assume that if no value is provided, then a default value of 60 will be used:

```
CREATE DOMAIN credit_points AS SMALLINT
    DEFAULT 60
    CHECK (VALUE IN (30, 60))
```

We could also add **NOT NULL** to prevent any occurrences of NULL in the columns defined using the **credit_points** domain. It is a design decision whether to define **NOT NULL** (or, indeed, default values and constraints) at the table level or the domain level.

As a more complex example of what is possible, consider the course codes we have adopted for the University example. They are defined so far as simply **CHAR(2)**, but they are not just any two-character string – the first character is the letter 'c' and the second character is a digit. Therefore, we could define a domain for course codes as follows:

```
CREATE DOMAIN course_codes AS CHAR(2)
    CHECK (SUBSTR(VALUE, 1, 1) = 'c'
           AND CAST(SUBSTR(VALUE, 2, 1) AS SMALLINT)
               BETWEEN 1 AND 9)
```

The check constraint here is satisfied only by a two-character string whose first character (obtained with **SUBSTR(VALUE, 1, 1)**) is a 'c', and whose second character (obtained with **SUBSTR(VALUE, 2, 1)**) can be cast into a **SMALLINT**; the second character is then checked to be between 1 and 9. The values 'cd' and 'c0' will therefore not be allowed, as 'd' cannot be cast into a **SMALLINT**, and although '0' can be cast into a **SMALLINT**, it does not satisfy the additional condition **BETWEEN 1 AND 9**.

In practice, we almost always define domains to use in the **CREATE TABLE** statements, rather than using the predefined data types.

EXERCISE 5.14

Use the description of the extension to the University scenario to give the SQL that defines domains for the columns **bookcode**, **title**, **author_name** and **no_pages** in the **textbook** table. Your definitions should include any constraints on the values that items from these domains may take. Rewrite the statement **table_creation** so that it uses your domains, rather than SQL data types. You should ensure that you give your domains meaningful names.

You may assume that the domain **course_codes** already exists, and that the primary key values of the **course** table are drawn from this domain.

To remove a domain, we use the **DROP DOMAIN** statement:

    DROP DOMAIN domain_name [RESTRICT|CASCADE]

SQL provides two possible actions that may occur if a **DROP DOMAIN** statement is executed for a domain that is in use:

- **RESTRICT**: This action prevents the domain from being dropped. This is the default.
- **CASCADE**: Any column that uses the domain is automatically changed to use the domain's underlying data type, and constraints or default clauses for the domain are replaced by the equivalent column constraints or column default clauses.

Notice that for a domain, the referential action is declared when the domain is dropped. This is different to referential constraints, for which the action is declared when the constraint is created.

There is an important difference between SQL's domains and the domains of relational theory. As you learnt in *Block 2*, Section 2.2, in relational theory, attributes can be compared only if they are defined on the same domain; attributes defined on different domains cannot be compared with each other. In SQL, values from different domains can be compared if they have the same underlying data type. In the **textbook** table, values in the **title** column are taken from the **book_titles** domain, and values in the **course_code** column are taken from the **course_codes** domain. Because the domains **book_titles** and **course_codes** are both defined in terms of the predefined data type **VARCHAR**, values from these two domains can be compared. However, values from these domains cannot be compared with values from, for example, the **credit_points** domain because **credit_points** is defined in terms of the predefined data type **SMALLINT**, and **SMALLINT** cannot in general be compared with **VARCHAR**. This also determines when tables are union compatible; in SQL, tables are union compatible if corresponding columns have the same underlying data type.

5.6 Modifying tables

In *Block 1*, the need for a database system to evolve was identified as a significant requirement. Some changes involve modifying tables, that is, changing their definition rather than just updating the data that they contain. In this section, we shall look at changing the definitions of tables.

EXERCISE 5.15

For a simple table (such as **textbook**), list the different aspects of its definition that may need to be changed. For each aspect, describe whether the change will have any effect on the data stored in the table.

Of course, most tables have more complex properties than **textbook**: for example, the table **course** requires a constraint referencing the **enrolment** table to ensure that the maximum number of enrolments is limited by the value specified by the **quota** column.

So far in this block, if we have needed to modify the definition of a table, such as by adding a new constraint or a new column, we have deleted the table using **DROP TABLE**, and reimplemented it from scratch. Clearly, we also need commands to alter the properties of existing tables. SQL provides the statement **ALTER TABLE**, which has the general format:

    ALTER TABLE <table name> <alter action>

ACTIVITY 5.10

Ensure that you have defined the **textbook** table and that it contains at least one row of data (it does not matter what the data is; if **textbook** is not defined, rerun **table_creation**, and run **fill_table** if you need to add data).

Execute the following statement:

```
ALTER TABLE textbook
   ADD publisher VARCHAR(30)
      DEFAULT 'Open University Press'
```

add_publisher

Check the contents of the **textbook** table. You should have found that an additional column, **publisher**, has been added to the table, with each row containing the default value. Delete the column with the following statement:

```
ALTER TABLE textbook
   DROP publisher
```

drop_publisher

Check that the column has been deleted from the table.

Default values have the same behaviour as column definitions in a table definition, so NULL is used if no default value is supplied.

EXERCISE 5.16

Explain why the following statement would not succeed:

```
ALTER TABLE textbook
   ADD publisher VARCHAR(30) NOT NULL
```

Standard SQL allows **ALTER TABLE** to modify a table in the following ways.
- ▶ Add a column.
- ▶ Drop a column.
- ▶ Set a column's default value.
- ▶ Drop a column's default value.
- ▶ Add an integrity constraint.
- ▶ Drop an integrity constraint.

We will look at each of these modifications in turn. Note that not all of the changes given in the solution to Exercise 5.15 are possible using an **ALTER TABLE** statement; neither a column name nor a column data type can be changed. We will consider these changes in Section 6.

Adding and dropping columns

We have already seen how to add columns and remove columns from a table; the alter actions in each case are:

```
ADD <column definition>
```

and

```
DROP <column name>
```

5 Database definition and population

Setting and dropping default values

To alter the default value for an existing column, the alter action is:

```
ALTER [COLUMN] <column name>
    SET DEFAULT <default definition>
```

and to remove a default value, the action is:

```
ALTER [COLUMN] <column name>
    DROP DEFAULT
```

> COLUMN keyword is correct standard SQL, however SQL Anywhere has not implemented the keyword

where the **COLUMN** keyword is optional in both cases, but can be included to clarify that a column, rather than a table, is being altered. So if we wished to add a default value of 0 to the **no_pages** column of our **textbook** table, we would use:

```
ALTER TABLE textbook
    ALTER no_pages SET DEFAULT 0
```
add_default

and to remove the default, we would use:

```
ALTER TABLE textbook
    ALTER no_pages DROP DEFAULT
```
drop_default

Adding and dropping constraints

We also need to consider the addition and removal of constraints in a table. We have seen already the different types of constraint and how they are expressed when a table is defined. The general form of the **ALTER TABLE** action is:

```
ALTER TABLE <table name>
    ADD [CONSTRAINT <constraint name>]
        <table constraint>
```

The syntax of the table constraint is generally similar to the table constraints that we discussed in the table definitions; we will look at the syntax for each of the constraint types identified in Section 5.4.

> Remember that not null constraints are not implemented as table constraints.

We will briefly run through the different types of table constraint that were discussed previously, and the statements that are associated with them.

Unique constraints

We have already seen that the form of a table constraint to constrain a column or a combination of columns to have unique values is:

```
UNIQUE (c_1, ..., c_n)
```

So to add a constraint to the **textbook** table to state that each book title should be unique, we would write:

```
ALTER TABLE textbook
    ADD CONSTRAINT title_in_textbook_is_unique
        UNIQUE (title)
```
add_unique

We can now see the benefit of giving a name to a constraint. Having defined the constraint on the **title** column, we can drop the constraint if necessary, by using the constraint name:

```
ALTER TABLE textbook
    DROP CONSTRAINT title_in_textbook_is_unique
```
drop_unique

Referential constraints

We have already seen that the table constraint for a referential constraint is expressed as:

```
FOREIGN KEY (f₁, ..., fₙ)
  REFERENCES <refd_table> [(c₁, ..., cₙ)]
    [ON DELETE <action>]
```

Suppose we wish to remove the existing referential constraint from **textbook**, and replace it with one that uses **CASCADE** instead of **RESTRICT**. To remove the existing referential constraint, we again take advantage of having named the constraint:

```
ALTER TABLE textbook
  DROP CONSTRAINT textbook_in_used_on
```
drop_ref_constraint

Then to define a new constraint with the required referential action, we use:

```
ALTER TABLE textbook
  ADD CONSTRAINT textbook_in_used_on
    FOREIGN KEY (course_code) REFERENCES course
      ON DELETE CASCADE
```
add_ref_constraint

> In SQL Anywhere, **add_ref_constraint** can be executed without first executing **drop_ref_constraint**, as the new referential action overrides the old one.

Check constraints

The table constraint syntax for a check constraint is simply:

```
CHECK (<check condition>)
```

So to add the constraint that was proposed as a solution to Exercise 5.13 to the existing **textbook** table, use:

```
ALTER TABLE textbook
  ADD CONSTRAINT max_5_textbooks
    CHECK (5>= (SELECT COUNT(*)
      FROM textbook
      GROUP BY course_code) <=5)
```
add_check

Referential constraints and representing relationships

We will conclude our discussion of table definitions with a discussion of how NULL can be used to represent optional participation in relationships, before going on to give the full definition of the **printer** table.

Consider the **Prints** relationship between **Printer** and **Textbook** in the extension to the University model:

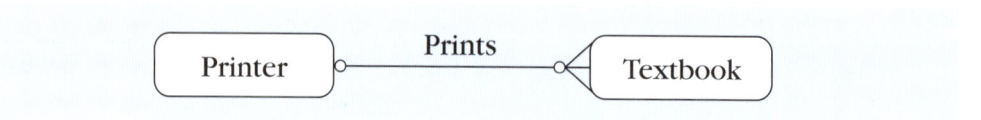

Printer —o———Prints———⊲— Textbook

In *Block 2*, you saw that relationships of this sort are generally represented with a relation for the relationship, rather than with a posted foreign key. A posted key representation is appropriate in a 1:*n* relationship, where the participation at the 1: end is mandatory because each attribute requires a value. However, in SQL, a column may take NULL as a value. This allows us to use a posted key to represent the **Prints** relationship by using NULL in the rows representing a printer that does not print any textbooks.

EXERCISE 5.17

How is NULL used to allow the optional participation of **Textbook** in the **Prints** relationship to be represented as a posted key in an SQL table?

EXERCISE 5.18

If the **Prints** relationship had been 1:1, with optional participation of both **Printer** and **Textbook**, what additional constraints would be required if the **Prints** relationship were to be implemented with a posted key?

In the remaining exercises, you will define and populate the `printer` table that represents the **Printer** entity described at the beginning of the section. You may wish to reread the description of that entity.

In this implementation, we will implement the **Prints** relationship using a posted key, and use NULL to indicate non-participation. Before starting the exercises, think about the SQL you might use to implement the relationship in this way. Also, before you start, ensure that you have defined the `textbook` table, and that it is populated with the data described in **fill_table** (if not, rerun **drop1**, **table_creation**, **fill_table**).

Our solutions are given in the filed statements for Section 5; when working through the following exercises, you can use either our proposed solutions or your own.

EXERCISE 5.19

Define domains for the business codes and names of the printing companies, choosing appropriate names. For the other fields, you should use the domains `addresses` and `telephone_numbers`, which already exist in the database. Remember that your definitions should include any appropriate constraints.

You can see the definitions of the domains in the definition script for the University database.

EXERCISE 5.20

Write a `CREATE TABLE` statement to define the `printer` table. Use the domain names that you defined in Exercise 5.19, and the domains `addresses` and `telephone_numbers` for the addresses and telephone numbers of the printers (these are already defined in the University database). Remember that your definition should include any appropriate constraints.

EXERCISE 5.21

Give the insert statements required to populate your `printer` table with the following data.

business_code	name	address	telephone_number
PX0348	Trent Press	17 Ash Street, Nottingham, NG3 2XX	0115 586423
PX8453	Vaughn and sons	Flintoff House, Manchester, M23 4QY	0186 646842
PX7129	Iliad Binding	158 Pietersen Row, Vauxhall, London, SE11	0178 352154

Now that we have defined and populated the printer table, we need to implement the **Prints** relationship. We will do this with a posted foreign key in the `textbook` table.

EXERCISE 5.22

Give an SQL statement to add a column `printed_by` to the `textbook` table, and the appropriate referential constraint so that the `printed_by` column references the `printer` table. When defining the constraint, you should consider the behaviour that you would require on deletion of a referenced row.

EXERCISE 5.23

(a) Give `UPDATE` statements so that all textbooks used on the syntax and semantics courses (course codes c2 and c4, respectively) are printed by the Trent Press printer, and all textbooks used on the pragmatics course (course code c7) are printed by Iliad Binding.

(b) What is the value in the `printed_by` column in the `textbook` table for those rows which represent textbooks used on the logic course (course code c5)? How should this be interpreted?

EXERCISE 5.24

Give a statement that adds a constraint to the `textbook` table so that all the textbooks on any course are printed by the same printer.

We leave it as an optional exercise to implement the **Prints** relationship using the relation for relationship representation, rather than the posted key. The factors affecting this kind of design decision are discussed further in *Block 4*.

5.7 Constraint evaluation

As far as SQL processing is concerned, the different kinds of constraint described in this section are optional in that they are not required in a table definition. For example, we have commented that an SQL table is not required to have a primary key, but because it is an essential element of the relational approach, we have chosen to define all tables with a primary key. So for any constraint there is an element of choice as to whether it should be included as part of the definition of a table. For the development of a database system, these choices are made during the process of logical schema design, as described in *Block 1*, when it is decided which of the constraints specified in a conceptual data model need to be included in an SQL schema. The issues relating to these choices, and their implications, are considered as part of the topic of database design in *Block 4*. At this point, we are concerned only with how a given constraint may be expressed, and its impact on data manipulation.

Constraints are a declarative description of what restrictions apply to the data in a database, and should be regarded as a part of the definition of a table. Although we have shown how constraints may be added to an existing database, where possible it is better to include them in a `CREATE TABLE` statement so that the definition of all parts of a table are kept together. This is particularly useful if a table is dropped at the development stage and then recreated, so that the developer can be confident that no `ALTER` modifications have been missed.

There is one issue that should be noted when many constraints are being defined, which is the possible dependencies between them. Like all aspects of a database, constraints may change, and so it is always a good idea to express a constraint so that it is not dependent on any other constraint. For example, a column in a table may be taken from a domain that is defined as not NULL. However, if a table requires that some of its values may not be NULL, then this constraint should also be defined on the table, in

5 Database definition and population

case the domain is modified later. So when you write constraints, you should avoid dependencies upon existing constraints that may need to be changed in the future.

Evaluation of constraints

It is important to realise how a database evaluates the constraints that are applied to it. Constraints should always be thought of as applying to the whole database, rather than to individual data items.

As an illustration, consider the **ward** table from the Hospital database.

ward_no	ward_name	number_of_beds
w2	Wessex	8
w3	Anglia	10
w4	Lakes	8
w5	Dales	6
w7	Pennines	14

Suppose that for reasons of privacy and patient comfort, a constraint were required stating that the maximum number of beds in a ward is five more than the average. We might implement this with a check constraint on the **ward** table as follows:

```
CHECK (number_of_beds <= (SELECT AVG(w.number_of_beds) + 5
                          FROM ward w) )
```

The average number of beds according to the **ward** table is 9.2. This constraint would prevent us from adding a new ward with five beds. Although 5 is smaller than the average plus five (which would be 14.2), the addition of this ward would lower the average number of beds to 8.5. Therefore the Pennines ward, with 14 beds, would violate the constraint. However, we would be able to add a new ward containing fifteen beds. Although 15 is more than five more than the *existing* average, adding the new ward would raise the average to 10.2, and so the new ward would sit within the limit of the average plus five.

To repeat: a constraint applies to the database *after* the addition of data, not to the data *before* addition to the database. In this case, the constraint applies only to one table (**ward**), although in general a constraint will apply to many tables. If the constraints on the database are violated by the addition of data, then the attempt to add the data will fail.

> SQL Anywhere behaves slightly differently from this description in its evaluation of check constraints. The SQL Standard is to behave as we have described in this section; an update to a database should fail if the state of the database after the update violates any of the constraints defined on that database. In SQL Anywhere, the constraints are evaluated before the update, rather than after. Therefore, the database can be updated with data that violates one or more check constraints in the first instance, with an error generated only on subsequent updates to the database. Note that this does not apply to unique constraints, not null constraints or foreign key constraints, all of which are evaluated immediately after the database is updated.
>
> However, the *declarative* interpretation of constraints in SQL Anywhere is as described in this block.

5.8 Defining and using indexes

> Indexes are *not* part of the SQL Standard, being concerned primarily with the implementation of the storage schema. However, they are implemented in most of the major SQL distributions, and so we will touch upon them briefly in this section. The syntax used by SQL Anywhere is similar to that in other distributions.

While any file organisation for data storage provides access to the data, there is a need for additional access methods to support efficient retrieval of data by a DBMS. Indexes are used for this purpose, and we now consider their role.

Consider the following query that gives the student identifiers of students who are tutored by the tutor with staff number 5324 on at least one course:

```
SELECT DISTINCT student_id
FROM tutors
WHERE staff_number = '5324'
```
index_req

When a DBMS executes this query, it retrieves and checks all the rows of the `tutors` table to find the ones that have the specified value for `staff_number`. This is called **sequential access**; for a query returning a small number of rows from a large table, this method can be very inefficient for returning the queried data.

An **index** is a structure that associates the values of one or more columns of a table with the stored locations of the rows which contain that value. Building an index creates a physical index object that is reused every time the table is queried.

When a DBMS executes a DML statement (retrieval or update) that references an indexed column in a condition of a `WHERE` clause, it can use the index to provide the stored locations of the particular rows that satisfy the condition. This is called **direct access**; for the example **index_req**, an index defined on the `staff_number` column would give the storage locations of the rows that have the specified value for `staff_number`. This enables the DBMS to search only those rows which satisfy the condition, rather than every row in the table. So, for an update statement such as

```
DELETE FROM tutors
WHERE staff_number = '8431'
```

execution without an index involves a search of every row in order to find the ones to be deleted, whereas using an index enables those rows that satisfy the condition to be deleted without searching through all the other rows.

The costs of using an index are:

- Indexes require space for their own storage, distinct from table data, which must be allowed for when the database is being planned.
- Indexes must be updated every time there is a change in the values in the column (or columns) on which they are based, which slows the execution of update statements.
- Indexes do not always improve execution of statements for which they can be used.

These factors need to be balanced against the possible benefits of an index in deciding whether one is appropriate for a given column (or columns). Before defining an index, you should always consult your database management system's documentation.

5 Database definition and population

Building an index

If an index is required, it must be explicitly created. There is no Standard SQL for this purpose (because indexes are not part of the SQL Standard), but there is a simple syntax that is commonly adopted, based on the SQL **CREATE** statements:

> **CREATE [UNIQUE] INDEX <index name> ON <table> (<column>)**

For example, an index may be defined for the **staff_number** column in the **tutors** table as follows:

> **CREATE INDEX tutor_index ON tutors (staff_number)**

Such a **CREATE INDEX** statement requires that a name is given for the index, in this case **tutor_index**, and specifies the table to which it relates and the column whose values are to be used for indexing. A statement to build an index for more than one column simply lists the column names separated by commas within the parentheses.

An index may be created at any time and can be removed at any time using a **DROP INDEX** statement (which has the same format as the equivalent **DROP** statements for tables and domains). In both cases, there is no effect on the data in the indexed table; the existence of an index only affects access to the table. Note that dropping a table also drops the indexes defined on that table.

Having used **CREATE INDEX** to build an index, the user does not then need to maintain it. The DBMS is responsible for maintaining the index when data is added to and removed from the table, and for using the index to improve access.

EXERCISE 5.25

Write a statement to create an index for the column **name** in the **student** table.

In fact, when an index is built, it orders the values in the columns on which the index is defined. By default this is an ascending order, although adding **ASC** to a column makes this explicit, and adding **DESC** puts the column values in descending order. The following example shows the definition for an index for two columns involving the use of **ASC** and **DESC**.

> **CREATE INDEX tutor_course_index**
> **ON enrolment (course_code ASC, enrolment_date DESC)**

create_index_order

As well as using an index to support access to data, a DBMS may also exploit an existing index when a query has an **ORDER BY** clause, if the ordering of the index corresponds to the ordering of the query result. This is a reason for specifying **ASC** or **DESC** in the index definition. If a table is frequently queried using an **ORDER BY** clause on a particular column, then the index should be defined to order the column in the way that the **ORDER BY** clause is used.

The effect of defining a primary key or unique constraint restricts values in the constrained column or columns to be unique. The same effect can be defined with a **CREATE UNIQUE INDEX** statement. The effect of such an index is to restrict values in the indexed column or columns to be unique. The use of this kind of index dates back to when DBMSs did not enable primary key and unique constraints to be explicitly defined. However, it is an alternative that should not be used, because uniqueness is a logical property that is defined in a logical schema, and not as a feature of storage. Data independence requires that the definition of data storage (which includes indexing) should not affect the result of an SQL statement. The following exercise explores the problem of unique indexes.

EXERCISE 5.26

By considering the different effects of `INSERT` and `UPDATE` statements on a table with and without a unique index, explain how a unique index may result in the violation of physical data independence.

When to use an index

As we have already stated, you should always consult your database management system's documentation before defining an index. However, there are some general principles about defining indexes, which reflect the trade-off between improvements in retrieval, and the additional time and space overheads that indexes add to updating tables. In practice, indexes are generally defined on tables after they have been in use for some time and when it is known what queries they are often used to search for.

You might consider defining an index on a column in the following situations.

- When a table is very large.
- When the queries applied to a table return a small amount of data. Indexes optimise queries that return a small amount of data, but are a heavy overhead for queries that return many rows of a table.
- When the data in the column is highly varied or contains many occurrences of NULL.
- When the column is frequently used in joins.

You would probably not use an index in the following situations.

- On small tables.
- On columns that are regularly updated. The cost of repeatedly updating the index can easily outweigh the performance benefits that the index might bring.

In this last case, it may be advisable to drop an index, carry out any necessary updates, and then rebuild the index. This can be a more efficient strategy than expecting the index to be rebuilt with each update.

In addition, an index can be used by a DBMS as a simple way of maintaining uniqueness in a column because it provides an easy way for a DBMS to check whether a given value already exists in a column. Therefore, it is normal for a DBMS to automatically create an index for any column or columns for which a primary key or a unique constraint is defined. So for such columns, a user should not create an index.

5.9 Summary

In this section, we have presented some of the facilities available in SQL for defining, modifying and deleting tables in a database and domains for the data types. We also illustrated how to define constraints on tables and domains, and briefly looked at how constraints are evaluated to maintain database integrity. Finally, we considered how indexes can be used to improve database performance.

LEARNING OUTCOMES

Having completed this section, you should be able to do the following:

- Describe the use of domains in SQL and give the necessary SQL statements to define a domain.
- Describe the main kinds of constraint in SQL, giving appropriate definitions of constraints on a table or on a domain, and understand how they will be evaluated.

5 Database definition and population

- ▶ Give an SQL statement to define a table, including a primary key and a data type or domain for each column, with possible default values and associated constraints.
- ▶ Given an update statement, describe the purpose of each clause and its effect on base tables.
- ▶ Formulate **INSERT**, **UPDATE** or **DELETE** statements to update the data in a database.
- ▶ Explain the effect of referential constraints on update commands.
- ▶ Use **ALTER TABLE** commands to modify existing tables.
- ▶ Explain the purpose of indexes, and use SQL to define indexes on columns in tables.

6 Database management and administration

In the previous sections, we have considered how to define base tables, populate them with data, and define constraints to ensure that the integrity of the data is maintained. In this section, we consider more general issues concerned with the management and administration of a database.

This section is concerned with the organisation and use of a database in the context of a shared multi-user environment. In particular, we will look at the use of views as a means of accessing and working with data without the need to work directly with the base tables and the SQL facilities for access control.

As with previous sections, we do not aim to provide complete details of SQL capabilities, but focus on the basic facilities that provide the foundation of how SQL may be used for managing and administering a database.

6.1 Views

A view is a form of **derived table** that is typically built using data in existing base tables. The view then behaves very much like a base table in the ways it can be manipulated, although in fact it contains no data itself. Since no data is stored in a database for a view, all that exists is its definition which consists of a query that produces the rows of data that are its apparent content.

A view (or rather just its *definition* since that is all that persists) can be created and dropped in a similar way to base tables. In this section we will examine how a view is defined, how it can be used like base tables in queries and what it means to update a view.

Creating views

We will look first at how views behave, and then at how to create (define) a view. A view called `occupying` has been created in the Hospital database to provide data on the identifier and name of each patient, along with the name of the ward that the patient occupies.

ACTIVITY 6.1

Using the Hospital database, run the following query to see all the data available via the view `occupying`.

```
SELECT *
FROM occupying
```

occupying1

EXERCISE 6.1

(a) Which base table(s) do you think are used to provide the data in the definition of the view `occupying`?

(b) Write a query that uses only the base tables in the Hospital model, which provides the same data as the query **occupying1**.

You can see that the queries **occupying1** and **occupying2** (given in Activity 6.1 and in Solution 6.1, respectively) both produce the same results when executed. In fact, the query **occupying2** is used in the definition of the view **occupying** as follows:

```
CREATE VIEW occupying AS
   SELECT patient_id, patient_name, ward_name
   FROM patient p, ward w
   WHERE p.ward_no = w.ward_no
```

create_occupying

The following points should be noted about this statement and about views in general.

▶ The view **occupying** is based on the pair of tables **patient** and **ward** (both base tables in this case), and is defined using a query statement containing exactly one query specification that contains multiple entries in the **FROM** clause. In general, a view can be defined by any kind of query statement (subject to certain important restrictions, which we will discuss shortly).

▶ Any of the query specifications in the definition of a view can reference other views in their **FROM** clauses, as well as base tables. So one view may be based upon one or more other views. However, the definition of a view must ultimately reference one or more base tables (possibly indirectly, via other views), which we refer to as the view's **underlying** base tables.

▶ The columns in the view **occupying** have no explicit names but, by default, inherit the names given in the **SELECT** clause of the query specification defining the view. Note that column names for a view can be explicitly specified, as you will see below. In the same way, the columns in a view inherit the data types of the columns given in the **SELECT** clause of the query specification (and so ultimately inherit the data types of the columns in the underlying base tables).

▶ A view's query statement defines the data that the table contains when it is used. The values in each column of the view are the values in the corresponding columns of the final table resulting from the logical processing of the query statement at the time the view is used.

Recall the difference between a query specification and a query statement from Section 3.

Once a view has been defined, it can be treated like any other table in the database. In particular, data can be retrieved from it in the same way as from any other table, as though it contained the data itself.

EXERCISE 6.2

Write a query using the view **occupying** to find the name of each ward in the hospital and the number of patients who currently occupy it.

EXERCISE 6.3

Give the mapping from the view **occupying** to the base tables **patient** and **ward** in terms of the column to column connection between the tables.

The view **occupying** appears very similar to the underlying **patient** and **ward** tables on which it is based. Both the sequence of columns and their names have been inherited by default, but SQL allows us to specify the names and order of columns in a view.

EXERCISE 6.4

Using the University database, write a query that, for each row in the **tutors** table, lists the student identifier, the student's name, the name of the tutor, and the course code. The columns should be presented in the given order.

While constructing your solution to Exercise 6.4, you will have noticed that you use the **name** column from the **student** table, and the **name** column from the **staff** table. This is fine in a table that is returned by a query, but when creating a view, SQL requires that the columns have distinct names. We can give columns distinct names by using **AS** in the query, as shown in the Activity 6.2.

ACTIVITY 6.2

Using the University database, define a view by executing the following statement, and check that it provides the same data as the query in the solution to Exercise 6.4.

```
CREATE VIEW tutoring AS
   SELECT s.student_id, s.name AS student_name,
          c.name AS staff_name, course_code
   FROM student s, staff c, tutors t
   WHERE t.student_id = s.student_id
     AND t.staff_number = c.staff_number
```

tutoring_view

Processing the statement **tutoring_view** results in the view definition being checked as syntactically correct and consistent with the underlying tables – that is, it confirms that the query statement can be executed. The details of the definition are then stored in the schema tables. No data is ever kept in a view: when a query is written to retrieve data from a view (such as **occupying1**), then the DBMS uses the view *definition* to obtain data from the base tables.

The general format of the **CREATE VIEW** statement is:

```
CREATE VIEW <view name> [(<column list>)] AS <query statement>
```

This general form contains an optional list of column names. This allows the columns of the view to be named in the view declaration, rather than in the query. In the list of column names, the number of names must be the same as the number of columns in the **SELECT** clause of the query specification.

For the view definition **tutoring_view**, we could have defined the column names in the view declaration rather than in the query by writing:

```
CREATE VIEW tutoring2 (student_id, student_name,
                      staff_name, course_code) AS
   SELECT s.student_id, s.name, c.name, course_code
   FROM student s, staff c, tutors t
   WHERE t.student_id = s.student_id
     AND t.staff_number = c.staff_number
```

tutoring_view_2

For **tutoring_view_2**, the view declaration specifies the names of the columns as required, independently of the names used in the underlying table(s), or names assigned within the query. Each specified column name refers to the column of the final table in the order determined by the **SELECT** clause of the query specification. So `student_name`, the second column name, refers to the second column in the `SELECT` clause, which contains the data resulting from the column `name` in the `student` table.

Column names *must* be specified for a view:

▶ either when the inherited column names would be duplicated and hence cause conflict;

▶ or when a column in a view is formed from an expression and has not been assigned a column alias with `AS`, and so there is no name to inherit.

In either of these cases, the column names of the view can be stated either in the view declaration or by naming the columns in the query with `AS`.

EXERCISE 6.5

Explain how the columns of the following view are named.

```
CREATE VIEW long_course AS
   SELECT *
   FROM course
   WHERE credit = 60
```

Note that when the `CREATE VIEW` statement is processed, the column names from `course` are included in the definition of the view. However, if the `course` table is later altered by adding another column, the definition of the view does not change and so will not include the new column. The view then appears inconsistent with its definition as given by the query.

EXERCISE 6.6

(a) Write and run a query which uses the view `tutoring` to return a table containing the code of each course, and the number of students enrolled on those courses. The table generated should have column names `course` and `students_per_course` respectively.

(b) Define a view called `course_numbers` using the query you wrote in part (a).

We can now consider a processing model of how views access a database. We have shown how a view is defined using a query statement and, in turn, how that view itself can then be used in any other query statement. So when a query contains a view, the logical processing model has two distinct processing steps:

▶ evaluating the view to access the underlying base tables;

▶ processing the query using those base tables.

This is illustrated in Figure 6.1 (overleaf) for a query using a view.

The first step in the processing model illustrated in Figure 6.1 suggests that evaluating the query statement in the view definition results immediately in a final table for the view query. It may be, of course, that the view is defined in terms of other views, rather than base tables. In this case, those views must be evaluated in turn, and so on.

It is important that this logical processing does not lead you to imagine that a view ever contains any data. As always, a logical processing model is intended only to help you understand what the result of a query will be.

```
1. Process the view definition:
   Obtain the query statement from the view
   definition and process it according to the logical
   processing models of Sections 2 and 3 providing
   a 'final table' for the view query.
```

↓ View table – that is, a table populated with rows

```
2. In the FROM clause of the query of the view:
   Use the final table from the view definition as
   the input to the FROM clause.
   Rest of query:
   Process according to the logical processing
   models of Sections 2 and 3.
```

Figure 6.1   Logical processing of a query involving a view

Some of the common uses of views are as follows.

▶ A database expert, such as a database administrator, can define views which include a complex query statement to allow other users to retrieve data they want with just simple queries – they do not have to know about grouping or joins. For example, users of the view `tutoring` do not have to know that it involves a join, nor users of `course_numbers` that it involves grouping, as long as they understand the data as it appears in the view.

▶ A user may have a repeated need for different queries relating to the same collection of data, such as data from a number of base tables. For example, people concerned with student counselling might want the data given by the view `tutoring`. Defining such a collection of data as a view makes repeated use of it simpler.

▶ Some requests, even some apparently simple ones, can be very difficult to answer using a single query. By using two queries, the first of which is the definition of a view, a request can often be answered more clearly.

ACTIVITY 6.3

In this activity, we will look at an example where defining a view can considerably simplify the processing of a query. Suppose we want a table with the following properties:

> For each student registered at the university, list the student's identifier and name, the codes of the courses on which they are enrolled and the average mark for the assignments that they have submitted for that course. If the student is not enrolled on any courses, then the table should contain NULL in the columns for course code and average mark. If the student has not submitted any assignments for a course on which they are enrolled, then the table should contain NULL in the column for the average mark.

We require a table with four columns to list the student's identifier, name, enrolled course and average mark for the assignments. The definition of the table is made more complicated by the requirement for NULL values where the student is not enrolled on any courses, or has not submitted any assignments. We first define a view that contains the average marks for the courses that each student is enrolled on, using a left outer join to give NULL if the student is not enrolled on any courses.

```
CREATE VIEW average_mark AS
  SELECT e.student_id, e.course_code, AVG(mark) AS avg_mark
  FROM enrolment e LEFT OUTER JOIN assignment a
    ON e.student_id = a.student_id
      AND e.course_code = a.course_code
  GROUP BY e.student_id, e.course_code
```
avg_mark_view

If you execute **avg_mark_view** and display the contents of the resulting view, you should find that it contains the average assignment mark for each course that a student is enrolled on, and NULL for those courses where a student has submitted no assignment. We can now write a query that uses this view to form the final query.

```
SELECT s.student_id, name, course_code, avg_mark
FROM student s LEFT OUTER JOIN average_mark a
  ON s.student_id = a.student_id
```
final_avg_marks

By using **avg_mark_view**, the request **final_avg_marks** is clearer and can be written more naturally. When writing SQL, if you find that using a single query is becoming unnecessarily complex, consider defining a separate view to deal with some of the first processing steps.

EXERCISE 6.7

Explain why the table generated by the query **final_avg_marks** could not have been defined as a base table.

All the view definitions so far have referenced base tables from the University and Hospital databases. A view can be defined on any query statement: the following view definition is based on the query **dummy_no_table_expression** from Section 2.2:

```
CREATE VIEW view_no_table AS
  SELECT 5+8 AS thirteen
  FROM SYS.DUMMY
```
view_dummy_no_table_statement

This statement defines a view called **view_no_table** with one column, **thirteen**, and one row which contains the value 13. **view_dummy_no_table_statement** demonstrates that any query that returns a table can be used to define a view.

Remember that **SYS.DUMMY** is a feature of SQL Anywhere, rather than of Standard SQL.

The reasons that we have given so far for using views may all be considered to relate to ease of use. We will consider more reasons for using views later.

Removing views

Removing a view from a database can be done using a statement similar to that used to remove base tables. The basic format of this statement is:

```
DROP VIEW <view name>
```

The result of processing such a statement is that the view definition is removed from the database.

In most cases this **DROP** statement is all you need. However, since a view is defined by a query involving other base tables or views, it is dependent on those other tables or views (and, of course, other views may be dependent on it). A view definition becomes meaningless if the underlying tables or views are deleted. This is comparable to the situation we described for referential integrity, whereby referential actions determine what happens to dependent rows. SQL enables a similar behaviour to be defined when dropping a view. This behaviour may be **RESTRICT**, which prevents a drop where there are dependent views, or **CASCADE**, which causes all dependent views to be dropped as well.

> Unfortunately, SQL Anywhere supports neither of these behaviours, so when using SQL Anywhere, you can drop a table or a view and then have a dependent view which becomes unusable. We will not demonstrate this anomalous behaviour here, but it is an issue to be aware of while administering databases.

Updating views

Throughout this section, we have emphasised that a view does not itself contain data. Rather, the data apparently in a view is in fact data in the view's underlying base tables. Updating a view therefore actually means updating the view's underlying base tables. To understand what this involves, we need another perspective of a view and return to the ideas originally introduced in *Block 1*. There, we described a general schema architecture, one component of which is an external schema that defines data as required by user processes. Associated with an external schema is a mapping, which defines how data defined in the external schema is derived from data defined in a logical schema – that is, the data in a database. So the mapping provides a connection between data as represented in a database and data as it is represented within a user process.

A view should be considered as part of an *external* schema, and the query statement defining a view is a mapping that determines how data gets from a database to a viewed table, when required. If we want to update a view, we can think of it in terms of simply reversing the connection between a database and a viewed table.

ACTIVITY 6.4

In this activity and many of the remaining activities in this section, you will use the `textbook` table as defined in Section 5. In particular, you will use the original definition as defined by the **table_creation** statement, rather than the altered table with the posted key (recall Exercise 5.22). When you start this activity, the `textbook` table should contain no data.

Rerun **drop1** to delete any existing version of the `textbook` table, followed by **table_creation** to redefine it.

First, put some data into the `textbook` table using the following statement.

```
INSERT INTO textbook
    VALUES ('65281', 'Beginning Syntax', 'Kershaw, J.', 247, 'c2')
```
insert1

Next, define a view by running the query:

```
CREATE VIEW course_text AS
    SELECT bookcode, title, course_code
    FROM textbook
```
course_text_view

Write and execute two queries to show the contents of the `textbook` table and the `course_text` view. You should find that they contain the same data, although the view `course_text` does not contain all the columns of the `textbook` table.

Now run the following query:

```
INSERT INTO course_text
    VALUES ('47521', 'Computational Semantics', 'c4')
```

view_insert

Write and execute two queries to show the contents of the `textbook` table and the `course_text` view. How do you explain the results of these two queries?

After running **view_insert**, you should have found that the `course_text` table presents one more row, containing the data described in **view_insert**. However, because a view does not contain any data itself, the data is inserted into the underlying base table, `textbook`, on which the view is based.

Displaying the table `textbook` shows that a new row has been inserted, containing the data from the `INSERT` statement in the `bookcode`, `title` and `course_code` columns of the new row. The other values are of interest: the new row has NULL in the `no_pages` column, and 'None' in the `author_name` column. When a row is inserted into a table via a view, columns with missing values are set to NULL, unless a default has been defined, in which case the default value defined on the column is used.

So when the `INSERT` statement is executed, the new data is inserted into the `textbook` table. It is only when the query to display the view `course_text` is executed that data is retrieved from the table `textbook`. This makes it appear as if the new row was inserted into the view.

If you try other updating statements for this view, including an explicit list of the names of columns being assigned values, you should find that the apparent effect of updating, as far as this view is concerned, is the same as that described for base tables in Section 5.

EXERCISE 6.8

What behaviour would you expect on executing the following pair of queries?

```
CREATE VIEW course_text2 AS
    SELECT bookcode, title, author_name
    FROM textbook

INSERT INTO course_text2
    VALUES ('97584', 'Parsing Algorithms', 'R. Jones')
```

The restriction on updating views described in the solution to Exercise 6.8 is based upon the principles established in Section 5 on integrity constraints. However, there are other situations in which a view cannot be updated. The general reason for this is that the connection defined by the mapping for a view, that is, its query statement, cannot always be reversed. This is not surprising if you consider the final table that results from the logical processing of a query statement. In many cases, the logical processing of the original tables results in a final table with a different number of rows and columns from the original base table(s). In other words, a DBMS cannot always infer from the query statement how a row inserted into the view would result in changes to the base tables.

ACTIVITY 6.5

First, create the view `enrolment_count` by running the following statement.

```
CREATE VIEW enrolment_count AS
    SELECT course_code, COUNT(student_id) AS enrolments
    FROM enrolment
    GROUP BY course_code
```
enrolment_count_view

The first column of the view `enrolment_count` shows the code of each course, and the second shows the number of students enrolled on that course according to the `enrolment` table.

Now execute the following UPDATE statement to update the view `enrolment_count`.

```
UPDATE enrolment_count
    SET enrolments = 3
    WHERE course_code = 'c2'
```
invalid_update

Attempting to execute the statement **invalid_update** will generate an error. To understand why this is the case, you should go back and identify the base table upon which the view `enrolment_count` is based. It should not be surprising that this update is not allowed; there is no single, unambiguous way that the base table `enrolment` can be changed so that the view retains the required data. There are currently five students enrolled on course c2, and this statement states that it should be changed to three. How can that relate to a change in the underlying base table `enrolment`? If we were to change the table so that only three students were enrolled on this course, which students are no longer enrolled? This example shows that there are often very good reasons why some views should not be updatable.

What are the restrictions on modifying a view – by updating, deleting or inserting into it? In terms of the idea of reversing the connection to the database, we can say that a view may be modified if each value in an entry of the view corresponds to exactly one entry of an identifiable underlying base table.

For many views, this requirement is not satisfied, and you should not expect to be able to modify them. This is the case for views based on query statements involving value expressions, GROUP BY and most kinds of join. However, even when a query statement could, in principle, satisfy these requirements for update, in practice it may be difficult to establish the correspondences necessary to identify exactly which base table values are to be updated. The problem is that it is not always possible for a DBMS to reverse the query mapping to go from a view to base tables, even when, in principle, that mapping exists.

For SQL, this problem is resolved pragmatically by specifying a number of rules that a view has to satisfy for it to be classified as **updatable**, in which case it is certain that a mapping to a base table can be established. These rules require that the query statement defining the view satisfies the following restrictions.

1. The FROM clause can include only tables and views that are themselves updatable.
2. The SELECT clause can include only column names (i.e. there must be no value expressions) and cannot include DISTINCT.
3. None of the underlying tables of the tables in a query specification's FROM clause can also be an underlying table of any table appearing in that query specification's WHERE clause.
4. There should be no joins (although see the note below).

6 Database management and administration

5   There can be no **GROUP BY** clause and no **HAVING** clause.
6   The results of two or more queries can be combined only by using **UNION ALL** (i.e. **EXCEPT** and **INTERSECT** are not allowed, and **UNION** is not allowed unless **UNION ALL** is used).

Point 3 is conceptually tricky. Broadly, it states that a query specification in the definition of an updatable view cannot contain the same table both in the **FROM** clause and as part of a condition in the **WHERE** clause. However, because a table might be referenced indirectly via a view, the definition must refer to the underlying tables, rather than to the tables themselves.

The condition in point 4 that there should be no joins is more restrictive than the current SQL Standard requires. SQL does allow updates on joins under certain circumstances. However, the complete definition of updatable joins is complex, and is beyond the scope of this course.

EXERCISE 6.9

Explain why the query specification for an updatable view must not use **DISTINCT**.

In general, an updatable view is a part of a single base table, having a subset of either the rows or the columns or both. We have already considered an updatable view, `course_texts`, which has a subset of the columns of its underlying base table. Now we consider an example of an updatable table with a subset of the *rows* of the underlying base table.

ACTIVITY 6.6

Run the following statements.

```
CREATE VIEW long_textbook AS
    SELECT *
    FROM textbook
    WHERE no_pages > 200
```
long_view

```
INSERT INTO long_textbook
    VALUES ('38572', 'Practical Pragmatics', 'Christine Davies', 320, 'c7')

INSERT INTO long_textbook
    VALUES ('65284', 'A First Course In Logic', 'Jerry Maxwell', 115, 'c5')
```
insert_long_view

If you use a simple query to display the contents of the base table **textbook**, you should see that the two rows in **insert_long_view** have been inserted as you would expect. However, if you use a query to display the rows in the view **long_textbook**, you will find that only the first of the two rows can be seen. While surprising, this effect can be explained by the way that a view is modified separately from the query that displays it. The **INSERT** statement inserts the rows into the base table. Then a **SELECT** statement applied to the view returns those rows which satisfy the condition in the view's definition, that is, textbooks that have more than 200 pages.

A similar situation could arise if you used this view with an **UPDATE** statement. Such a statement affects only the rows that belong to the view, but without restricting how they may change. The following activity gives an example of changing a row so that it is no longer part of the view because it no longer satisfies the condition in the view definition.

ACTIVITY 6.7

Execute the following statement (we assume that you still have the results from executing **insert_long_view** in `long_textbook`).

```
UPDATE long_textbook
   SET no_pages = 180
   WHERE bookcode = '38572'
```
view_update

If you now display both the view `long_textbook` and the base table `textbook` to examine the effect of **view_update**, you should see that the row in which the value of `bookcode` is 38572 no longer appears. However, the row does appear in `textbook`, with the new value of 180 in `no_pages`.

Note that while operations carried out on views are interpreted as changes to the underlying base tables, only the rows that appear in a view are affected by an operation on that view.

➢ Execute the following statement.

```
DELETE FROM long_textbook
```
view_delete

You should find that all the rows which appeared in the view (i.e. those with a value greater than 200 in the `no_pages` column) have been deleted from the underlying base table `textbook`.

SQL `WITH CHECK OPTION`

When using an `INSERT` statement to insert a row into a view, the statement may result in a row being added to the base table which is not visible in the view itself (as you saw in Activity 6.6). Similarly, by using an `UPDATE` statement on the rows in a view, the data in the base tables may be affected in such a way that they no longer appear in the view (as you saw in Activity 6.7).

SQL provides a mechanism to prevent rows from being inserted into a view which do not then appear in the view itself, and rows in a view being updated so that they no longer appear in the view. This is achieved with the SQL `WITH CHECK OPTION`, explored in Activity 6.8.

ACTIVITY 6.8

Execute the following statements; check the contents of the view `short_textbook` and the base table `textbook` before and after each of the update statements to see the effects.

```
CREATE VIEW short_textbook AS
   SELECT *
   FROM textbook
   WHERE no_pages < 200
   WITH CHECK OPTION
```
with_check_option1

```
INSERT INTO short_textbook
  VALUES ('83569', 'A Logic Primer', 'Jerry Maxwell', 130, 'c5')
```
with_check_option2

```
UPDATE short_textbook
  SET no_pages = 210
  WHERE bookcode = '83569'
```
with_check_option3

You should find that the **UPDATE** statement in **with_check_option3** fails. This is because a successful update would change the value of **no_pages** in the base table to 210, and the row would no longer be shown in the view. This is the behaviour that **WITH CHECK OPTION** prevents.

We will be considering further reasons for using views in Section 6.5. In many ways, particularly for queries, views can be used in essentially the same way as base tables. However, when updating views, you need to be aware that updating a view is often more complicated than updating a base table.

6.2 Sharing data

We have already emphasised that an essential feature of a database system is the ability for many users to share data. It is now time to examine this aspect for SQL databases. We first consider how users are identified in a DBMS. We then consider how we use SQL to define and use tables in a multi-user environment. In *Block 1*, we also discussed the need to control users' access to data in such an environment, and this section describes SQL's access control capabilities to provide a complete perspective on sharing data. We generally refer to database administration as though it were the responsibility of a single person, the *database administrator* (DBA), but in practice it is likely to be the responsibility of a team of people.

Identifying users

Up to this point, you have had full access to the data in the University and Hospital databases. However, in most real database systems, it is not usually the case that all users of a database should have unlimited access to read or modify the data in that database. So SQL statements can only be executed in the context of a database connection, and the DBMS can restrict the operations that a user can carry out, depending on the user who has made the connection to the database.

Before a user can do anything with a database, a connection must be established which requires that the DBMS has an **authorisation identifier** (also referred to as a **user ID**) for that user. An authorisation identifier is a string like `smith` or `user1`.

You have already seen one way in which a user may provide his or her authorisation identifier to the DBMS; when you connect to the database, SQL Anywhere asks for a user ID and a password. In this case, the authorisation identifier is provided explicitly by the user; so far, you have been using the identifier `m359` to query the database.

An authorisation identifier can also be provided implicitly. For example, a user might access the database via an application process. In these cases, the authorisation identifier is typically provided through the application, rather than directly by the user.

The DBMS uses the authorisation identifier to determine what data in the database a user may query or modify. For example, the authorisation identifier given to a student could allow that student to look at their own examination grades, but not those of other

> Note that the password is the DBMS's method of ensuring that the person who logs on is a legitimate user of that identifier (the **authentication** mechanism); it is not part of SQL.

students. Similarly, the authorisation identifier given to a member of staff could allow that staff member to look at the results of the students that they tutor, but not the results of other students. It is the responsibility of a database administrator to create an authorisation identifier for each user of a database, and (because there is no connection between databases) for each database that a user wants to access.

There is no statement in Standard SQL for defining authorisation identifiers, so the way a DBMS enables authorisation identifiers to be defined depends on the implementation.

> In SQL Anywhere, a new user can be created by the user with identifier dba by using the command:
>
> `GRANT CONNECT TO <new authorisation identifier>`
>
> The user with identifier dba has special privileges, which we discuss in Section 6.4.

Authorisation identifiers do not need to be unique either to users, or to databases. A single user who requires access to several databases may require a different authorisation identifier for each database, or they may need only a single identifier. Nor is it necessary for the authorisation identifiers to be unique to users; several users may share the same identifier, if their needs of the database are similar. The choice and allocation of authorisation identifiers to users are organisational issues for a database administrator to resolve in deciding how a database may be used.

During the course we use the term 'user' to correspond to a unique authorisation identifier, and such a user is considered to be named by their authorisation identifier.

Logging on as different users

So far, you have been logging onto the database using the user ID **m359**. In addition to **m359**, we have created several more user IDs for this database. For the rest of this section, we will use these different user IDs to explore some of the issues that are raised by using a database in a multi-user environment.

ACTIVITY 6.9

First, disconnect from the database and reconnect to the University database using the ID **admin**. The instructions for connecting as a different user are contained in the *Software Guide*. The user **admin** uses the same password as m359. In a professional database environment, giving all users the same password would normally be very poor practice!

Having logged on as **admin**, execute the following SQL statement.

`SELECT *`
`FROM student`

show_student

You are presented with the error message stating `table 'student' not found`. Although you know that **student** is a table in the database, you cannot currently access it because you are not the table's owner. Tables in SQL are *owned* by the user who created them, in this case, the user **m359**. In general, a table is accessed by prefixing it with the owner's authorisation identifier.

6 Database management and administration

ACTIVITY 6.10

Execute the following statement.

```
SELECT *
FROM m359.student
```

show_m359.student

You now receive the error message `Permission denied: you do not have permission to select from "student"`, showing that the table has been found using the prefix, but you are still not permitted to select or display any data from it. In this case, it is not possible for user `admin` to share the data that user `m359` has created. While we have emphasised that databases are for sharing data, we have also said that there is a need for control, and in Activity 6.9 and this activity, these controls have prevented you from accessing `m359`'s data.

In fact, a widely held principle of computer security is that a user who is denied access to data should not even be told that it exists.

User identity is essential to understanding how data can be shared and controlled in an SQL database. We will start by examining the definition of tables.

EXERCISE 6.10

What are the two essential steps that have to be performed before an SQL DBMS allows a user to access data in a database?

You can see which authorisation identifier you have used to log on at any time by using a system variable called **USER**, and it can be included in any statement to give the authorisation identifier of the current user. The simplest query to demonstrate its use is:

```
SELECT USER
FROM SYS.DUMMY
```

If you execute this query, you will see a table with one row and one column, containing the value for the variable **USER**.

6.3 Table definition

Having an authorisation identifier enables a user to access a database, but that is all! As you have just seen, such a user cannot access other users' data, nor can they necessarily create their own tables. It is reasonable to expect that not all users should be allowed to create base tables, in order to limit the amount of data in a database. This means that there should be some way of specifying whether a user is allowed to create tables, but there is no SQL statement to enable a user to be given this capability.

> In SQL Anywhere, a user must have resource authority to be able to create tables (and other database objects, such as functions and triggers, which we will meet in the next section). Resource authority is granted by dba with the statement:
>
> ```
> GRANT RESOURCE TO <authorisation identifier>
> ```
>
> The user with identifier dba has special privileges, which we discuss in Section 6.4.

When a user with the appropriate capability defines a base table, that user is considered to be the **owner** of the table. There is no restriction on what the owner of a table may do with it: for example, inserting and deleting data, altering the table's definition, updating or deleting it.

For an SQL database, which may have many users who are allowed to define base tables, the tables owned by each user are not automatically shared and so there is a partitioning of the data according to user. The definitions of the tables are also partitioned according to user and are said to be in an SQL schema belonging to that user. The many SQL schemas of all users together constitute the complete database schema.

Let us now see what happens when you, as user `admin`, try to create a new table called `student`. The user `admin` has been granted the appropriate privileges to create tables.

ACTIVITY 6.11

As user `admin`, execute the following statement.

```
CREATE TABLE student (
  student_id CHAR(3),
  name VARCHAR(20),
  region SMALLINT,
  PRIMARY KEY (student_id) )
```

create_student

The statement **create_student** should execute without giving a confirmation message (showing that it has executed successfully).

EXERCISE 6.11

What would you expect as the result of executing the statement **create_student** as user m359?

You can confirm that executing **create_student** has created the new table by adding data, such as

```
INSERT INTO student
  VALUES ('s24', 'Bates', 1)
```

student_data

and then executing a simple query to check that the table contains only this one row. So as user `admin`, you create and use tables in the same way as you did in Section 5, when you were logged on as m359. However, you have now been working with the table `admin.student`, rather than `m359.student`. This demonstrates that it is essential to know the authorisation identifier of the user (more precisely, the connection) in order to determine the effect of any SQL statement.

To resolve the problem that we now appear to have two tables named `student`, SQL uses the name of the SQL schema to specify where the definition of each table is to be found. In the simple case where a user has just one schema with a name given by their authorisation identifier, this identifier is used as a prefix. Hence we distinguish the tables as `m359.student` and `admin.student`, and while we continue to say that the name of each table is **student**, we use the qualified table name whenever it is necessary to include the schema name – that is, the authorisation identifier of the owner.

So in general, a table is referred to with the expression:

`<authorisation identifier>.<table name>`

where `<authorisation identifier>` defaults to the identifier of the connected user.

Combining the schema name and the table name uses the dot notation in the same way as that used to qualify column names. In SQL statements which include both qualified table names and qualified column names, there is a double qualification. For example, in the **student** table owned by user **m359**, a fully qualified reference to the column **student_id** is **m359.student.student_id**.

EXERCISE 6.12

(a) The column **name** occurs in both the **student** and **staff** tables. If the owner of both these tables is user **m359**, how would another user refer to these columns?

(b) How would user **m359** refer to these columns?

Using shared tables

By using qualified names to refer to other users' tables, all the SQL statements that we have seen in the previous sections can now be applied to a multi-user database. The only inconvenience is that the writing of the statements becomes longer.

When aliases are used in SQL statements, the alias covers the whole of the qualified name. For example, suppose a user wished to find the student identifiers and the courses of all students in the **enrolment** table, along with the quota for each of the courses on which they are enrolled. If the user had permission to query the tables owned by user **m359**, the query might be:

```
SELECT student_id, e.course_code, limit
FROM m359.enrolment e LEFT OUTER JOIN m359.quota q
  ON e.course_code = q.course_code
```

qualified_name_aliases

The alias **e**, for example, aliases the whole of the expression **m359.enrolment**; we do not use **m359.e** to refer to the table. If aliases had not been used in this example, all references to **course_code** would have had to be expressed in full, in the way described in the solution to Exercise 6.12.

View definitions can include references to other users' tables, and provide an alternative way of simplifying the way queries are expressed. The definition of such a view is contained in the schema of the user who creates it and, in this sense, the user owns the view (but not the data it relates to, if based on another user's table). For example, if the user **admin** needs to access the **staff** table of user **m359** (and has appropriate access rights), **admin** may usefully define a view as follows.

```
CREATE VIEW staff AS
  SELECT *
  FROM m359.staff
```

admin_create_view

Having defined this view, `admin` can now use the unqualified name `staff` in SQL queries to access the base table `m359.staff`. Its definition ensures that it has the same columns and content as the base table, and returns the same content when used in a query. This view allows only the user `admin` to write more concise queries; any other users wishing to use the same technique will need to create their own version of the view.

EXERCISE 6.13

The dot notation is used both for qualifying a table name with the appropriate schema name, and for qualifying a column name with the appropriate table name. For any SQL statement, describe when each qualification must be used and when it is optional.

EXERCISE 6.14

Given two tables, both named `student`, one of which is a base table owned by `m359` and the other a view owned by `admin`, how would another user, say with authorisation identifier `faculty`, refer to each of these tables?

6.4 Access control

By including references to other users' data, a user can write statements to access any of the tables within a database. However, we have seen that a user must have authorisation to access tables. Users have the authorisation to access the tables that they own, but we have not yet considered how users obtain the authorisation to access another user's tables.

The task of ensuring that users are only able to access the tables for which they have the necessary authorisation is known as **access control**. As we described in *Block 1*, Section 3, this is an essential DBMS function that is required to maintain both the quality and the confidentiality of data in a database. The rest of this section describes the SQL facilities that enable access to the tables in a database to be controlled.

Privileges

When a base table is first defined, the only user who is able to do anything with it is its owner. The owner may then grant *privileges*, which allow specified users to perform certain actions on that table. The privileges are what the DBMS refers to when controlling access to tables.

Privileges are granted with an SQL GRANT statement, having the following syntax:

```
GRANT <privileges> ON <table> TO <users>
```

A GRANT statement specifies that the users identified in the TO clause (consisting of one or more authorisation identifiers, separated by commas) are granted the stated privileges for the named table (a user is granted privileges for only one table per GRANT specification). One or more of the following privileges can be specified.

- ▶ A SELECT privilege allows a user to retrieve data from the named table.
- ▶ An INSERT privilege allows a user to insert rows into the named table.
- ▶ A DELETE privilege allows a user to delete rows from the named table.
- ▶ An UPDATE privilege allows a user to change existing values in the named table.
- ▶ A REFERENCES privilege allows a user to create constraints that reference the named table.

A user who is granted a privilege is then able to execute a corresponding SQL statement involving the named table, so a **SELECT** privilege enables a user to execute a statement that reads data from the named table. A statement involving another user's table will fail to execute unless the user executing the statement has all the privileges required to execute that statement. The owner of a table automatically has all privileges on that table.

A user who is granted a **REFERENCES** privilege on a named table can declare a foreign key for one of their own tables, referencing that named table. To understand why such a privilege is necessary, imagine what happens when another user declares a foreign key on a table that you own. If the foreign key is defined without any referential action (or with **RESTRICT**), you are prevented from making any deletions or updates in your table when there are any dependent rows in the referencing table. You may no longer be able to do what you want with your own table if another user has added rows to their table which reference rows of your table.

Similarly, a user who has been granted a **REFERENCES** privilege on a named table can write check constraints that reference that table in the constraint's condition. And as with a foreign key constraint, such check constraints may prevent the table's owner making certain updates to the table.

EXERCISE 6.15

A user of a database with authorisation identifier `fred` owns a table named `t_fred`, and a user with authorisation identifier `bill` owns a table named `t_bill`. `bill` grants **REFERENCES** privilege to `fred` on the table `t_bill`.

When connected to the database, `fred` then adds a constraint to his table by executing the following statement.

```
ALTER TABLE t_fred
   ADD CONSTRAINT fred_constraint
      CHECK ((SELECT COUNT(*)
              FROM t_fred) >= (SELECT COUNT(*)
                               FROM bill.t_bill))
```

How does this affect how `bill` may update his table, `t_bill`?

Exercise 6.15 illustrates how granting a **REFERENCES** privilege can result in users losing some control over their own tables; by default, `bill` would not be able to remove `fred`'s constraint. Requiring the **REFERENCES** privilege to declare foreign keys or check constraints does not prevent this situation occurring, but ensures it happens only in a controlled manner, that is, if the owner of the table finds it acceptable.

In addition to the basic privileges given above, a **GRANT** statement can also specify **ALL PRIVILEGES**, which gives the specified users all the privileges for the named table, and can also include a list of column names to limit the privilege that is given to those columns.

Use `SELECT USER FROM SYS.DUMMY` to check that you are logged on as `admin`.

> You are logged on as user `admin`, and have already seen that you cannot retrieve or update any of the tables owned by user `m359`, even if you use a fully qualified table name.
>
> ➤ Disconnect from the database, and reconnect to the University database using the user ID dba. The password for dba is `lqs`. This is different from the password for the other users defined for the databases, to emphasise that dba has special privileges.
>
> As user dba you do not own any of the tables in the database, including the table `admin.student` that you created as user `admin`. You should not be able to access it since you have not been granted the necessary privileges.
>
> Check user dba's access rights for the table `admin.student` by executing the following query.
>
> ```
> SELECT *
> FROM admin.student
> ```
> *show_admin.student*
>
> By executing **show_admin.student** you should see that the lack of privileges did not prevent user dba accessing another user's table.
>
> SQL Anywhere gives this particular user (dba) access rights to do anything to any user's tables. Although this extension is not part of the Standard, it is widely implemented in DBMSs because it is envisaged that a database administrator needs complete control over the whole database. Whether this is a good idea from the point of view of the privacy of each user's data is another matter.
>
> For SQL Anywhere, the description of how privileges are needed to access other users' tables applies to all users except dba. However, user dba still needs to *grant* privileges to other users to enable them to access dba's tables. In addition, we have already seen that in SQL Anywhere, the user dba has the right to grant `CONNECT` and `RESOURCE` privileges. We will not discuss dba further in this block.

➤ If you are not connected using the user ID m359, disconnect from the database and reconnect using the user ID m359. If the table `textbook` is not defined, define it using **table_creation**. Now execute the following `GRANT` statements.

```
GRANT SELECT ON student TO admin, faculty
GRANT ALL PRIVILEGES ON textbook TO admin
GRANT UPDATE (author_name) ON textbook TO faculty
```
grant_statements

As user m359, executing these `GRANT` statements has no effect on what you can or cannot do (yet). To test their effect, you need to see how they affect the behaviour of queries that are executed by different users of the database.

➤ Disconnect from the database and reconnect using the user ID `admin`. Then execute the following query that was given previously as **show_m359.student**, which failed when you first tried it.

```
SELECT *
FROM m359.student
```
show_m359.student

The successful execution of this statement shows that you now have the necessary privileges to use `SELECT` on this table owned by m359.

➢ Now execute the following `INSERT` statement.

```
INSERT INTO m359.student
    VALUES ('s24', 'Bates', 'The Motel, Mumford', NULL, NULL, '1')
```
m359.student_data

You should receive an error message stating `Permission denied: you do not have permission to insert into "student"`. Of course, this message refers to the `student` table owned by m359, as specified in the `INSERT` statement. You do not have permission because m359 has not granted the necessary privilege.

However, you do have `ALL PRIVILEGES` granted for the table `textbook`.

➢ Execute the following `INSERT` statement, and a simple query to ensure that it has been successful.

```
INSERT INTO m359.textbook (bookcode, title, no_pages,
                          course_code)
    VALUES ('80862', 'Dependency Grammar', 220, 'c2')
```
m359.textbook_insert

You may like to test the other privileges which allow you to execute all the data manipulation statements for m359's table `textbook`.

Now we will look in particular at the `REFERENCES` privilege. Suppose that the user `admin` needs to define a table `availability` which contains the quantity of each textbook currently available for dispatch to students. The table will contain a foreign key referencing the primary key of `textbook`.

➢ If you have not already executed the statement **m359.textbook_insert** to insert into the table `m359.textbook`, do it now. Then disconnect from the database, and reconnect using the user ID `admin`. Now execute the following sequence of statements to create a table with a foreign key.

```
CREATE TABLE availability (
    bookcode CHAR(5) PRIMARY KEY,
    quantity INTEGER,
    FOREIGN KEY (bookcode) REFERENCES m359.textbook)
```
reference_m359.textbook

```
INSERT INTO availability
    VALUES ('66778', 500)
```
bad_availability_data

```
INSERT INTO availability
    VALUES ('80862', 450)
```
good_availability_data

You should find that **bad_availability_data** fails, because there is no primary key to be referenced in `m359.textbook`, while **good_availability_data** succeeds.

For the final step in testing the foreign key you have just defined, you need to connect as user m359, and then check the restriction on deleting a row in the table `m359.textbook`, which has a dependent row in the table `admin.availability`.

➢ Reconnect as user m359 and execute the following statement.

```
DELETE FROM textbook
    WHERE bookcode = '80862'
```
restrict_delete

The prevention of this deletion demonstrates that the foreign key you defined works in the way we described in Section 5.4; as before, the default behaviour is to prevent the deletion of dependent rows, even though it references a table owned by another user.

You should appreciate the need for the **REFERENCES** privilege as well as the **SELECT** privilege. When another user is granted a **SELECT** privilege on a table, the owner of that table retains full control over that table. However, because granting a **REFERENCES** privilege allows another user to define foreign keys that reference a table, the owner of the referenced table can then lose some control over the content of their table. In SQL Anywhere, this still applies to the user **dba**; despite having all privileges on all tables, **dba** cannot create data that violates the database's integrity.

Note that the **GRANT** statements you executed included a user `faculty`, mainly to show how multiple users can be granted privileges. This user has been defined in the University and Hospital databases (with the same password as `m359` and `admin`) and you may wish to use this user ID to practise what you have learnt in this section.

EXERCISE 6.16

Earlier you were shown **qualified_name_aliases**, which is an example query to demonstrate the use of qualified names. For this query, user `admin` requires access to user `m359`'s tables in order to list the total number of students allowed on each course that a student is enrolled on. Give the **GRANT** statements that must be executed before the query **qualified_name_aliases** can be executed by user `admin`, and state which user must execute those statements.

The privileges for a table are regarded as part of its definition. When a **GRANT** statement is executed, the granted privileges for the named table are included in the owner's schema. When any user inputs an SQL statement that references one or more tables, a DBMS checks the defined privileges for those tables to ensure that the user has been granted the required privileges.

Granting privileges to all users

A **GRANT** statement for a table can include many authorisation identifiers, but if all users of a database are to be allowed access to a table this can be specified simply by granting privileges to **PUBLIC**. For example, user `m359`, as owner of the **textbook** table, can give all users the **SELECT** privilege and the **UPDATE** privilege for the **author_name** column by executing the following statement.

```
GRANT SELECT, UPDATE (author_name) ON textbook TO PUBLIC
```

Privileges need to change according to varying user requirements, since data requirements and users themselves may be expected to change. Additional privileges can be granted at any time, and it is also possible for the owner to remove privileges using a **REVOKE** statement. For example, the **UPDATE** privilege just given for the table **textbook** can be revoked by the owner executing the statement:

```
REVOKE UPDATE (author_name) ON textbook FROM PUBLIC
```

Note that this is a different use of the **FROM** keyword from that in a query.

Note that **PUBLIC** means all users at all times. If, for example, the **SELECT** privilege has been granted to **PUBLIC** on some table, then any user who is allowed to connect to the database has the **SELECT** privilege on that table.

EXERCISE 6.17

Give a sequence of two statements that grant all privileges for the table `textbook` to users `admin`, `clerk` and `faculty`, with the exception that user `clerk` does not have the privilege to `DELETE`.

EXERCISE 6.18

What are the three means by which a database user may obtain access privileges to a particular table?

A user who has been granted privileges on a table explicitly, retains those privileges if they are revoked from `PUBLIC`. Suppose, for example, that `admin` owns a table `t`, and executes the following statements.

    GRANT SELECT ON t TO faculty
    REVOKE SELECT ON t FROM PUBLIC

The user `faculty` was explicitly given the `SELECT` privilege on `admin.t`, and therefore retains it even if `admin` revokes that privilege from `PUBLIC`. Having explicitly granted `faculty`'s privilege on this table, `admin` also needs to revoke it explicitly, with:

    REVOKE SELECT ON t FROM faculty

The WITH GRANT OPTION clause

So far, the discussion has been in terms of users being granted privileges directly by the owner of a table. SQL provides a more complex facility that allows a user to be given not only privileges for a table but also the capability to grant those privileges to other users. So users may be granted privileges for a table by someone who is not the owner of the table.

For example, suppose that user `admin` is responsible for certain uses of the data in the `student` table, although it is owned by user `m359`. User `faculty` now asks user `admin` to be allowed access to the `student` table. The previous form of the `GRANT` statement implies that only the owner of the table, user `m359`, can grant the appropriate privilege(s). However, user `m359` can enable user `admin` to grant some privileges by using `WITH GRANT OPTION` in the `GRANT` statement. For example, user `m359` can give user `admin` the ability to pass on the `SELECT` privilege for the `student` table as follows.

    GRANT SELECT ON student TO admin WITH GRANT OPTION

The additional clause `WITH GRANT OPTION` means that user `admin` has been authorised to grant the same privilege (and only that one) to another user. User `admin` may satisfy the request from user `faculty` with the following statement.

    GRANT SELECT ON m359.student TO faculty

Note that this is a statement executed for user `admin`, but the table is not owned by that user and so the table name needs to be qualified with the ID of the table's owner.

In this complex situation, there are three user roles involved: the owner of a table is the user who created it; a grantee is a user who is granted a privilege to use a table; and a grantor is a user who executes a `GRANT` statement to grant a privilege to a grantee.

EXERCISE 6.19

Describe the roles of the users `m359`, `admin` and `faculty` with respect to the two **GRANT** statements above.

Note that when privileges on a table are being granted by a grantor who is not the owner, it is possible to use **ALL PRIVILEGES** in the **GRANT** statement, but in this case only those privileges that have been granted to the grantor with a grant option are then granted to the grantee.

6.5 Using views to limit access

All the activities and exercises in this section use the Hospital database.

The possession of privileges is the only SQL facility that determines what each user may do with data in a database, but used with base tables they do not provide a sufficiently flexible access control mechanism. The main problem is that most privileges apply to complete tables, or columns within the table; they do not allow access to be limited to just some rows in a table – users must be granted access to all the data in the specified columns, or none at all.

However, there are many cases where users of a database should be allowed access only to particular columns or rows in a table (or tables). As an example, consider the table `patient`. This table has columns that contain data about the patients' height and weight. There are many users who may require access to various parts of the `patient` table, but not necessarily all of it. For example, a secretary may need to know where each patient is located and who their doctor is, but should not have access to personal data such as the patient's height and weight. However, any user who is granted the **SELECT** privilege for the base table `patient` has complete access to every row and every column of the table. It is not possible to grant access to the `staff_no` and `ward_no` columns but exclude access to the columns `height` and `weight`. Similarly, a nurse might require access to all of a patient's medical information, but should only have access to information about those patients in their own ward. Again, this means having access to only part of the table, but this time by limiting the rows.

In SQL, the general solution to this problem is for the owner of a base table to grant privileges for *views* of the base table rather than for the base table itself. For the example we described above, in which someone should have access to all the columns in the `patient` table except `height` and `weight`, the owner of the table should define a view as follows.

```
CREATE VIEW patient_public AS
   SELECT patient_id, patient_name, gender, staff_no, ward_no
   FROM patient
```

public_patient_view

Then, if all users are to be allowed to retrieve this data, the owner can grant them the necessary privilege with a simple **GRANT** statement:

```
GRANT SELECT ON patient_public TO PUBLIC
```

So limiting access to a base table is carried out in two stages. First, create a view of the base table containing the data that the user needs, which can be a subset of the rows and columns in the base table. Second, grant the user privileges that are required to access the data in that view.

Views are not the only solution to the problem of limiting access because, as we have already noted, there is an option of specifying columns for some privileges, which does limit the privilege to only those columns. However, basic SQL allows this column limit for only **UPDATE** and **REFERENCES** privileges, and it does not help when there is a need to limit access to certain rows of a table. So specifying columns does not provide a general solution to the problem, though it should be considered in some situations.

EXERCISE 6.20

A nurse has authorisation identifier **n113**. This nurse needs to retrieve data from all columns of the **patient** table, and to be able to add and remove patient data from the table. However, **n113** should only have these privileges for patients in ward w2 (the ward staffed by that nurse). Give the SQL that the owner of the **patient** table should give to:

1. Create a view called **patient2** that contains the appropriate data from **patient**.
2. Grant the necessary privileges to the user **n113**.

The use of views allows the owner of a table to limit that part of the table being made available to another user to match exactly what that user requires (or is allowed). However, since many users want to share the data in a table, defining a view for each one is an onerous task. For example, it is likely that several of the nurses have similar requirements to nurse **n113** in Exercise 6.20, each requiring a view to be defined containing the data for the patients in their own ward. It is not possible to 'parametrise' a view such as **nurse(ward)**, where **ward** is some variable that represents the ward for which the view is produced.

However, we can make use of the SQL system variable **USER** to 'personalise' a view. Remember **USER** has the value of the authorisation identifier for the user executing a statement, so **USER** can be used in the definition of a view to provide different data content according to who is using it.

ACTIVITY 6.12

Nurses of the Hospital database are defined as users with authorisation identifiers that consists of an 'n' followed by their 3-digit staff number.

As user m359, create a view of the **patient** table by executing the following statement.

```
CREATE VIEW my_patient AS
  SELECT *
  FROM patient
  WHERE ward_no = (SELECT ward_no
                   FROM nurse
                   WHERE staff_no = SUBSTR(USER, 2, 3) )
```
create_my_patient

Still as user m359, grant public access to this view with the statement:

```
GRANT SELECT ON my_patient TO PUBLIC
```
grant_my_patient

Now disconnect from the database and reconnect using the authorisation identifier n192. Execute the following query.

```
SELECT *
FROM m359.my_patient
```
select_my_patient

You should find that only the rows from the `patient` table containing data about the patients in ward w4 (the ward staffed by the nurse with staff number 192) are displayed.

Executing **select_my_patient** involves the view `m359.my_patient`. According to the logical processing model described in Section 3, the subquery is processed first. Processing the subquery requires the value of `SUBSTR(USER, 2, 3)` for the `WHERE` clause which, in this case, is '192', and so the subquery returns a table containing just the ward number w4. In the main query, this means that the view contains only the data from those rows in the `patient` table where the value of `ward_no` is w4, i.e. the same as that of the nurse making the query.

If this view were to be used by a nurse with a different staff number and authorisation identifier, it might contain different data because the `WHERE` clause in the subquery depends upon the identifier of the user making the query.

EXERCISE 6.21

What behaviour would you expect if user `admin` executed the query **select_my_patient**?

EXERCISE 6.22

Suppose patients have access to the Hospital database using authorisation identifiers that are the same as their patient identification numbers. Define a view of the `treatment` table that enables each patient to retrieve the rows of data that correspond to the treatment that they have received.

As a general perspective on sharing data, you should appreciate by now that there are few new principles concerned with SQL data definition or data manipulation, when compared with your work in previous sections, but access control introduces a new level of complexity from the point of view of database administration. A database administrator has to decide which users may define tables, which users require access to the data in those tables, and what views should be defined in order to provide access to just those parts of the tables that are required by those users. For those users who are granted privileges, it must also be decided whether they can have a grant option, which is not recommended if the owner of a table wants to control who has access to data. This complexity cannot be avoided because SQL's access control is an intrinsic part of enabling data to be shared.

While this perspective is based on a centrally controlled database, as described in *Block 1*, you should realise that this is not required by SQL. It is possible to administer an SQL database in many ways, even the uncontrolled situation of every user being quite independent and defining their own tables, which they may or may not choose to share with other users.

Finally, note that a further aspect of sharing data is concurrent processing which involves transactions. Transactions involve more than just sharing data, and so this topic will be considered separately in Section 7.

Roles

We conclude this section with a discussion of SQL **roles**. Roles are extremely useful for allowing many users' access privileges to be managed together.

Recall the earlier example in which the view `my_patient` was created so that nurses were able to see the information about patients (only) occupying their own ward. The view was made accessible to PUBLIC. In fact, most users connecting to the system without a nurse's identifier would find the view empty, as you saw in Exercise 6.21. However, the database administrator might prefer it if only nurses were able to query the view at all; even the column names of an empty view inform others what information is recorded.

It would be extremely tedious to write a GRANT SELECT statement for each nurse on an individual basis, particularly if there were several views to which only nurses were expected to have access. A role associates a set of authorisation identifiers with a set of access privileges on database objects. In this case, a role might be created with the name nurse; then any user assigned that role would be granted all the privileges associated with that role.

To create the role, use the following CREATE ROLE statement.

    CREATE ROLE nurse

Then privileges can be assigned to roles in the same way as to individuals:

    GRANT SELECT ON my_patient TO nurse

The privileges associated with the role nurse are then granted to any user who has been assigned that role. So to assign the role nurse to users n126 and n424, the following GRANT ROLE statements are used:

    GRANT ROLE nurse TO n126
    GRANT ROLE nurse TO n424

The users with authorisation identifiers n126 and n424 will then have access to the view my_patient. Note that a role can be granted to other roles, as well as to users, creating a hierarchy of roles. The DROP ROLE statement is used to remove a role.

Having assigned individual users to the role of nurse, the administrator can then grant or revoke further permissions to all nurses in the database without the need to go through all the nurses' authorisation identifiers one at a time.

> A user requires the CREATE ROLE privilege to create roles; **dba** has this privilege, as does any other user to whom **dba** has granted that privilege.

SQL Anywhere does not implement roles as described here. However, similar behaviour can be achieved with SQL Anywhere's groups.

You can see the syntax used for groups in SQL Anywhere in the Hospital script in \M359\SupportMaterials\Hospital, which also describes the Standard SQL equivalents.

All the SQL used in Activity 6.13 is Standard SQL.

ACTIVITY 6.13

In this activity, we will look at how roles can be used to simplify the granting and revoking of privileges.

For each nurse in the nurse table of the Hospital database, an authorisation identifier has been set up of the form nXXX, where the XXX is a nurse's staff number. It is assumed that each nurse has their own authorisation identifier, so that the nurse with staff number XYZ has the authorisation identifier nXYZ. In addition, a role (or group in SQL Anywhere) has been created called nurse_role, to which all the identifiers of the form nXXX are assigned.

Apart from the name, there is no difference between a 'group' in SQL Anywhere and a 'role' in Standard SQL.

Connect to the database as m359 and execute the following statement.

```
CREATE VIEW responsible_doctor AS
  SELECT patient_id, patient_name, d.staff_no, doctor_name
  FROM patient p, doctor d
  WHERE p.staff_no = d.staff_no
    AND ward_no = (SELECT ward_no
                   FROM nurse
                   WHERE staff_no = SUBSTR(USER, 2, 3))
```

create_responsible_doctor

Grant the SELECT privilege to the members of nurse_role with the statement:

```
GRANT SELECT ON responsible_doctor TO nurse_role
```

grant_to_role

Disconnect from the Hospital database, and reconnect using the identifier n838. Execute the following query.

```
SELECT *
FROM m359.responsible_doctor
```

select_responsible_doctor

Disconnect from the Hospital database, and reconnect, this time using the identifier admin. Execute **select_responsible_doctor** again. An error message should be generated, indicating that the user admin does not have the SELECT privilege on the view.

Activity 6.13 demonstrates that by associating users with roles, the task of granting privileges to many users at a time can be made quicker and simpler.

EXERCISE 6.23

This exercise considers nested roles.

You are asked to set up a role medical_staff_role to contain the authorisation identifiers of the hospital's nurses and doctors. Why might you prefer to associate nurse_role with medical_staff_role, using

```
GRANT ROLE medical_staff_role TO nurse_role
```

to associate the nurses with medical_staff_role, rather than granting the roles one identifier at a time?

6.6 Summary

In this section we have presented a number of aspects of SQL related to the more general needs of database management and administration – that is, distinct from the use of SQL for retrieval and update by user processes.

In Section 6.1 we looked at views, in particular the statements used to create and remove a view, and how views can be used in the same way as base tables except for certain updating restrictions. In Sections 6.2 and 6.3, we examined sharing data in a multi-user environment, in particular the need for distinguishing users by authorisation identifiers and how the ownership of tables affects their use in SQL statements. Then in Sections 6.4 and 6.5, we looked at the mechanisms in SQL to provide access controls based on granting privileges, and how views may be used to provide more flexible control of data.

6 Database management and administration

LEARNING OUTCOMES

Having completed this section, you should now be able to do the following:

▶ Describe the use of views in SQL, with an explanation of the effect of updates, and give a statement that defines a simple view.

▶ Describe the sharing of data in a multi-user environment and explain how to reference a table that is owned by another user.

▶ Give an SQL statement to grant privileges, including a possible **WITH GRANT OPTION** clause, and explain its effect.

▶ Explain how views are used in access control.

▶ Describe how roles are used to manage the privileges of groups of users.

7 SQL control statements

In this section, we look at some of the constructions provided in SQL that allow statements to be combined so that complex processing can be simplified. We also look at new ways of processing information in a database and, in particular, cursors for row-by-row processing of the results of queries. This discussion provides the basis for embedding SQL within external applications, which we discuss in *Block 5*.

We compare user-defined queries, which are executed by a user request, and triggers which execute automatically in response to updates of tables in the database. The section concludes with a discussion of how transactions are managed using SQL.

7.1 SQL routines

We now examine ways in which SQL enables a number of statements to be defined as a **routine**. A routine is a (potentially complex) series of statements which is stored by the DBMS and executed as a single action. By defining routines for frequently used series of statements, accessing and manipulating the data in the database can be simplified, and coding time reduced. We will discuss additional uses of routines in more depth after looking at the facilities provided by SQL to define them.

We look at two kinds of routine in this section: **functions** and **procedures**. There are considerable differences in the way these facilities are supported by different DBMSs, even though there is now a standard specification given by what is known as SQL/PSM – that is, SQL Persistent Stored Modules, which was published as an International Standard in 1996. SQL Anywhere is very similar to the standard specification, and is used for the examples in this section.

Compound statements

Before looking at how SQL allows us to define functions and procedures, we look at **compound statements**, in which a number of statements can be defined as a single statement using the keywords `BEGIN` and `END`.

ACTIVITY 7.1

Connect to the University database as user `m359` and execute the following compound statement.

```sql
BEGIN
  CREATE VIEW tmp_view (student_id, course_title) AS (
    SELECT e.student_id, title
    FROM enrolment e, course c
    WHERE e.course_code = c.course_code);
  SELECT *
  FROM tmp_view;
END
```

compound_statement

You should find that the view `tmp_view` is created, and the contents of the view displayed via the `SELECT` statement.

7 SQL control statements

A compound statement has the same effect as executing two or more SQL statements separately, but the DBMS treats the compound statement as a single action without further interaction with any user processes. The **BEGIN ... END** construction allows us to put several SQL statements into functions and procedures to be executed consecutively.

A compound statement can also be defined as **ATOMIC**. An atomic compound statement must either succeed completely or fail completely.

ACTIVITY 7.2

Still connected to the University database as user m359, execute the following statement to create a table with a single column.

```
CREATE TABLE t (
  c INTEGER,
  PRIMARY KEY (c) )
```

test_table

Now execute the following compound statement.

```
BEGIN ATOMIC
  INSERT INTO t VALUES (1);
  INSERT INTO t VALUES (NULL);
  INSERT INTO t VALUES (3);
END
```

atomic_compound

Because primary keys cannot contain NULL, the second **INSERT** of the compound statement fails (select `Continue` when SQL Anywhere prompts you to state whether you wish to stop or continue execution). When execution has completed, you should find that `t` is empty. The compound statement must either completely succeed or completely fail, and so none of the **INSERT**s has taken place.

➤ Now execute the following compound statement.

```
BEGIN NOT ATOMIC
  INSERT INTO t VALUES (1);
  INSERT INTO t VALUES (NULL);
  INSERT INTO t VALUES (3);
END
```

not_atomic_compound

You will find that SQL executes until the second **INSERT** raises an exception, and then the compound statement ends. When execution has completed, you should find that `t` contains a single row, containing the value 1.

As you work through the examples for defining functions and procedures, we will introduce you to further control flow statements in compound statements.

Functions

You have already used built-in SQL functions in Section 2.1, where we described a number of functions that are a predefined part of an SQL implementation and may be used with any database. One example is the function **LENGTH**, which has a single argument of a character string data type that is formed from an expression involving one or more columns. For example, in Section 2, you used the function **LENGTH** in the following query.

This description does not apply to aggregate functions, which give a single result for groups of rows in a table.

```sql
SELECT patient_name, LENGTH(patient_name) AS name_length
FROM patient
```
length

For each row of the `patient` table, the function takes the value in the `patient_name` column as an argument and returns the number of characters in that argument as an integer. In general, a built-in function takes one or more arguments of a given data type, and when evaluated provides a result based on the value of each argument.

The SQL functions we are now considering are used in the same way as built-in functions, but are defined by a user, and therefore are often referred to as **user-defined functions**. These functions are often intended to apply only to the specific database in which they are defined.

To define these functions, SQL includes facilities that allow a user to define conditions on any data, rather than that which currently exists in a table. For example, a function to return the greater of two integer numbers can be defined as follows.

```sql
CREATE FUNCTION greater (par1 INTEGER, par2 INTEGER)
            RETURNS INTEGER
  BEGIN
    IF par1 > par2
    THEN RETURN par1;
    ELSE RETURN par2;
    END IF;
  END
```
create_greater

ACTIVITY 7.3

In the University database, create the function `greater` by executing the filed statement **create_greater**. Then test the new function with the following simple query.

```sql
SELECT greater(582,947)
FROM SYS.DUMMY
```
test_greater

Repeat the test by changing the values of the arguments to show that the greater of the two arguments is returned. (We are using `SYS.DUMMY` in the same way as in **dummy_no_table_expression** in Section 2.2.)

The general structure of the `CREATE FUNCTION` statement is:

```sql
CREATE FUNCTION <function name> ([parameter, ...])
            RETURNS <data type>
  <compound statement>
```

The function is defined with a name `<function name>` and a list of parameters separated by commas. A parameter for a function is a pair of a variable name and the variable's data type (such as `par1 INTEGER` in **create_greater**). The data type that follows `RETURNS` is the data type of the expression returned in the `RETURNS` clause of the function.

The **body** of the function is a compound statement which is defined by a block of statements between the keywords `BEGIN [ATOMIC]` and `END`, and is treated as a complete unit. When used in a function, the compound statement should also

7 SQL control statements

contain one or more **RETURN** clauses. When the **RETURN** is executed, the function is immediately exited, and the value of the expression in the **RETURN** clause is returned as the value of the function. Once a compound statement has been exited, the statements following the **RETURN** statement are not executed. The expression that follows **RETURN** should be of the same data type as the function's **RETURNS** data type.

> Although SQL Anywhere requires that the body of a routine (either a function or, as we shall see, a procedure) be a compound statement defined by a **BEGIN ... END** block, Standard SQL does not have this requirement. For the function definition **create_greater**, the body is composed of only a single statement (the **IF ... END IF** block is considered a single statement, displayed over several lines) and so, in Standard SQL, is not required to be bounded by **BEGIN ... END**. Although Standard SQL does not require the body of a routine to be a compound statement, declaring it a compound statement is not incorrect either.

Having defined the function **greater**, we can now use it in any kind of SQL clause where an expression is allowed. Just as with built-in functions, an expression using **greater** can be evaluated for each row of a table being processed. For example, suppose we want to list the fees owed by each student, which are £100 per enrolled course and £50 for those who are registered but not enrolled on a course. The following query can be used to obtain this data.

➢ Execute the following query.

```
SELECT s.student_id,
       greater (50, 100 * COUNT(course_code)) AS fee
FROM student s LEFT OUTER JOIN enrolment e
  ON s.student_id = e.student_id
GROUP BY s.student_id
```

student_fees

When this query is executed, the function is evaluated for each row. The function's second argument (`100 * COUNT(course_code)`) is evaluated for that row, then the function itself is evaluated.

In our example, the name of the function is **greater**, and there are two parameters named **par1** and **par2**, both of which are **INTEGER**s. The result returned is also an **INTEGER**. When the function is called, **par1** and **par2** are set to the values that the function is called with, and then in the body of the function, the two **RETURN** clauses return the value of either **par1** or **par2**, depending on which is the greater.

Notice that an **IF** statement is used to determine which value of **par1** and **par2** to return. This is one of the SQL **control statements**; we will introduce the control statements throughout this section, and give a summary when we discuss cursors.

Having defined the function, it can be used within queries and other SQL statements at any point where an expression is allowed in the form:

```
<function name> (<argument list>)
```

The next function definition illustrates the use of a query embedded in the compound statement, and an example of a local variable definition. When defined in the Hospital database, the function **get_price** takes the name of a drug as its argument and returns the price of the drug with that name.

```
CREATE FUNCTION get_price (d_name VARCHAR(24))
            RETURNS DECIMAL(5, 2)
  BEGIN
    DECLARE my_price DECIMAL(5, 2);
    SELECT price
      INTO my_price
    FROM drug
    WHERE drug_name = d_name;
    RETURN my_price;
  END
```

create_get_price

In this example, a `DECLARE` statement is used to define a variable, `my_price`, with an associated data type, `DECIMAL(5, 2)`. This variable is local to the compound statement that it appears in, and so is not visible outside the compound statement in which it is declared. Each local variable used within a compound statement must be defined with a `DECLARE` statement at the beginning of the compound statement. The definition of the variable specifies a data type for that variable, and this must be compatible with the values it may receive when the statement is executed. For example, a variable that is expected to receive data from a column of integer numbers should itself have type `INTEGER`.

When the function is called with a particular value, that value is put into the parameter `d_name`, and can be used within the body of the function (such as in the condition of the `WHERE` clause in the definition of `get_price`). The definition of `get_price` also uses a `SELECT` statement to retrieve a value for `price` from the `drug` table, and the value is assigned to the variable `my_price` in the `INTO` clause. The `RETURN` statement then uses the variable `my_price` as the result of the function. The `INTO` clause can be used to input many values into variables using the general form:

```
SELECT col₁, col₂, ..., colₙ
  INTO var₁, var₂, ..., varₙ
```

ACTIVITY 7.4

In the Hospital database, create the function `get_price` using the statement **create_get_price**. Now use `get_price` to find the price of the drug 'Agonese' by executing the following statement.

```
SELECT get_price ('Agonese')
FROM SYS.DUMMY
```

test_get_price

EXERCISE 7.1

Define a function, `hw_fun`, which takes a patient identification code, and returns the height-to-weight ratio (in cm/kg) of that patient, correct to one decimal place.

Procedures

The second kind of SQL routine is **procedures**, which are often referred to as **stored procedures** or **database procedures**. Procedures are similar to functions in that they are routines with a body containing a compound statement. Unlike a function, a procedure does not return a value and so does not have a **RETURNS** clause or a **RETURN** statement in the body. However, a procedure can be used to put values into one or more variables; Activity 7.5 illustrates this.

ACTIVITY 7.5

In this activity, you will use a very simple procedure to put values into variables. This activity illustrates how procedures are called, using a procedure `prescription_length_cost` that is defined as part of the Hospital database. (You can find the code defining `prescription_length_cost` in the SQL Hospital script.)

Using the Hospital database, execute the following compound statement.

```
BEGIN
   DECLARE duration INTEGER;
   DECLARE cost prices;
   CALL prescription_length_cost ('P0101', duration, cost);
   SELECT duration, cost AS total_cost
   FROM SYS.DUMMY;
END
```
call_proc

The procedure `prescription_length_cost` has three arguments: the first is a prescription number, and the second and third are variables. In this example, we have defined the first variable, `duration`, to be of type **INTEGER**, and the second, `cost`, to be of type `prices`, which is a user-defined data type, defined in the Hospital database.

When the procedure is executed with the **CALL** statement, the value of the first variable is set to the number of days that the treatment is due to last, and is calculated as the quantity divided by the daily dosage, according to the `prescription` table (for the prescription P0101 in this case). The value of the second variable is set to the cost of the drug used in the treatment, and is defined as the `quantity` in the `prescription` table multiplied by the drug price in the `drug` table for the prescribed drug (P0101).

The final statement of the compound statement is a **SELECT** query to display the values of the variables. Note that by default, the column is given the name of the variable (as with `duration`), but can be renamed (as with `cost` renamed to `total_cost`).

As you can see from **call_proc**, procedures must be invoked directly with a **CALL** statement. This contrasts with functions, which are generally called as part of an expression within a query. The general syntax for calling a procedure is:

`CALL <procedure name> (<argument list>)`

where the arguments in `<argument list>` are separated by commas, and can contain expressions (such as the string expression `'P0101'` in **call_proc**), or output variables (`duration` and `cost` in **call_proc**).

To show how to specify whether an argument for a procedure is used for input or output, we will look at the definition for `prescription_length_cost` (overleaf).

```sql
CREATE PROCEDURE prescription_length_cost
                (IN pn prescription_nos,
                 OUT duration INTEGER,
                 OUT cost prices)
  BEGIN
    SELECT (quantity/daily_dosage)
      INTO duration
    FROM prescription
    WHERE prescription_no = pn;
    SELECT (quantity * price)
      INTO cost
    FROM prescription p, drug d
    WHERE prescription_no = pn
      AND p.drug_code = d.drug_code;
  END
```

The general structure of the **CREATE PROCEDURE** statement is:

```
CREATE PROCEDURE <procedure name> ([parameter, ...])
  <compound statement>
```

> As with functions, if the body of the procedure is a single statement, Standard SQL does not require it to be written as a compound statement.

The syntax is similar to that for creating a function, but a procedure has no **RETURNS** clause. Furthermore, for a procedure, each parameter is a triple of an input/output type, variable name and data type. The first of these is **IN**, **OUT** or **INOUT** depending upon whether the parameter is expected to provide a value into the procedure, have its value set by the procedure, or both. For example, in the definition of **prescription_length_cost**, the first parameter definition is:

*For a function definition, all the parameters are implicitly preceded by **IN**.*

    IN pn prescription_nos

The variable is named **pn** and has type **prescription_nos** (a domain defined in the Hospital database). Because **pn** is preceded by **IN**, when the procedure is called, it is expected to have a value in its second argument (in **call_proc**, this argument has the value '**P0101**'). The second parameter definition is:

    OUT duration INTEGER

The variable name is **duration**, and takes values of type **INTEGER**. Because the first part of the parameter is **OUT**, when the procedure is called, the second argument is expected to be a variable which will be assigned a value as the procedure executes.

The declaration **INOUT** can be used if an argument is to be used to provide both input and output; that is, when the procedure is called with a variable which has an initial value and whose value is also set to an output value as the procedure executes.

When a procedure has exactly one **OUT** parameter, and all the rest of the parameters are **IN**, we can often choose whether we use a procedure or a function. For example, the following procedure has the same purpose as the function **hw_fun**.

```sql
CREATE PROCEDURE hw_proc (IN p_id CHAR(3),
                          OUT hw_ratio DECIMAL(4, 1))
  BEGIN
    SELECT height/weight
      INTO hw_ratio
    FROM patient
    WHERE patient_id = p_id;
  END
```

create_hw_proc

You may recognise the compound statement in the body of the definition of **hw_proc**: it is almost the same as the compound statement in the body of the function **hw_fun**, given in **create_hw_fun**, proposed as the solution to Exercise 7.1. There are two differences:

1. In the procedure, the variable **hw_ratio** is defined in the parameter list rather than in the compound statement.
2. In the function, the value of the variable **hw_ratio** is explicitly returned with a **RETURN** clause, while in the procedure, the value is put into the **hw_ratio** variable, which has been defined as **OUT**.

We can use this procedure to obtain the same data as that in the example of the function **hw_fun** by invoking the procedure as follows:

```
CALL hw_proc ('p15', harris_hw)
```

So what is **harris_hw** (or whatever name might be used in its place) in the context of this **CALL** statement? You have seen that the second parameter, **hw_ratio**, is specified as **OUT**, and when the procedure is executed it assigns a value to **hw_ratio** in the **INTO** clause. So when the **CALL** statement is executed it needs some variable for the second argument, which can receive the value assigned to the variable **hw_ratio** in the procedure. In this case, the height-to-weight ratio of the patient with patient identifier p15 will be placed into the variable **harris_hw**.

We now consider in what context such a procedure may be invoked, and what variable is appropriate to that context. One possible context is within another routine – a function or procedure may include a call to another function or procedure. The function **hw_fun2** shows how we can define a function to return the height-to-weight ratio for a particular patient in inches per pound (in/lb) using the procedure **hw_proc**, which finds the height-to-weight ratio in cm/kg (recall from Section 2.2 that the conversion factor is 0.179).

```
CREATE FUNCTION hw_fun2 (p_id CHAR(3))
             RETURNS DECIMAL(4, 1)
  BEGIN
    DECLARE hw_var DECIMAL(4, 1);
    CALL hw_proc (p_id, hw_var);
    RETURN hw_var * 0.179;
  END
```

create_hw_fun_2

The variable **hw_var** is declared at the start of the compound statement. Then when **hw_proc** is called, it is set to the value of the height-to-weight ratio of the patient with identifier **p_id** (obtained from the parameters of the embedding function) when the procedure is called. The **RETURN** statement then returns the value multiplied by the appropriate conversion factor.

EXERCISE 7.2

You have just seen how a procedure may be embedded in a function; this exercise looks at how to embed the same procedure within another procedure.

Define a procedure **hw_proc2** with two parameters, the first of which is the identifier of a patient (specified as **IN**), and the second contains the height-to-weight ratio of that patient in inches per pound (specified as **OUT**). You should use the existing procedure **hw_proc** in your solution.

Deleting routines

Functions and procedures can be deleted with a **DROP** statement:

```
DROP FUNCTION <function name> ([<data_type>, ...])
DROP PROCEDURE <procedure name> ([<data_type>, ...])
```

> In Standard SQL, it is possible to define functions and procedures which have the same name, but which take different numbers or types of parameters (known as different **signatures**). Therefore, a list of the types of parameter must be provided to ensure that the correct routine is deleted by a **DROP** statement.
>
> SQL Anywhere does not allow you to define different functions or procedures with the same name, and so to delete routines in SQL Anywhere, only the function name is required in a **DROP** statement:
>
> ```
> DROP FUNCTION <function name>
> DROP PROCEDURE <procedure name>
> ```

Using SQL routines

Which of the two types of routine, a function or a procedure, is appropriate in a given situation? A function provides more flexibility than a procedure, where it can be used, since it may be included in an expression for any SQL statement, whereas a procedure has to be invoked by a **CALL** statement. However, a procedure offers more options than a function in the results it provides, since it can be defined with multiple parameters to return as many values as required, whereas a function can return only a single result. Apart from these differences, the processing that functions and procedures are capable of performing is the same, since the same SQL statements can be included in the body of each. So the choice of whether to use a function or a procedure is based on the results of the processing. If only one result is to be returned, a function is the better choice, but to return many values requires a procedure.

We will also consider here the benefits of using SQL routines. There are three major reasons for using routines: to standardise the location of functionality, to improve security, and to improve efficiency. We will discuss some of these further in *Block 4*, but introduce the issues here.

Location of functionality

As you saw in *Block 1*, a particular database may be used by many application programs. It will often be the case that several applications will require similar functionality in the database. For example, the membership of different hospital teams may be required both by applications used by the HR department, and (different) applications used by the finance department. By defining a routine to return a table containing data about the membership of hospital teams, a single routine can be kept by the database rather than requiring each of the different application programs to define their own routines.

Routines can also be used to hide unnecessary complexity from database users. In the previous example, developers of application programs which need to use information about team membership do not need to know the underlying database structure if routines have been developed to provide that information. Rather than having to query individual tables, a single call to a routine should be all that is necessary. Furthermore, if the database is restructured, all applications using the

7 SQL control statements

procedure do not need to be updated if the procedure itself is redefined, whereas direct querying of the database would require that all applications would need to be modified.

As another example of how we might use a procedure to hide the complexity of a query, consider how we might want to update a table. If we wish to *change* the values in a row of a table, we need to use an **UPDATE** statement. However, if we wish to *add* a row to the table, then we need to use an **INSERT** statement. By using an appropriate procedure, the user can make alterations with a single **CALL**, having the processing decisions hidden.

ACTIVITY 7.6

This activity uses the University database. Assume that for each course run by the University, a member of staff is nominated as that course's leader. Each course has exactly one leader, and a member of staff can lead more than one course.

In the University database, execute the following statement.

```
CREATE TABLE course_leader (
   course_code course_codes,
   staff_number staff_numbers,
   PRIMARY KEY (course_code) )
```
create_course_leader

The domains `course_codes` and `staff_numbers` are defined as part of the University database (you can find the definitions in the University definition script). We would generally define appropriate foreign keys and other constraints on this table; but as we are using this table only to illustrate the use of procedures, we will omit such constraints for simplicity.

Now execute the following statement to create a procedure.

```
CREATE PROCEDURE new_course_leader (IN c_code CHAR(2),
                                    IN s_no CHAR(4))
   BEGIN
     IF EXISTS (SELECT *
                FROM course_leader
                WHERE course_code = c_code)
     THEN UPDATE course_leader
       SET staff_number = s_no
       WHERE course_code = c_code;
     ELSE INSERT INTO course_leader
       VALUES (c_code, s_no);
     END IF;
   END
```
create_new_course_leader

Next, execute the following two **CALL** statements to first insert data into the table, and then update the data. After executing each statement, check the contents of `course_leader` to ensure that a row is first inserted, and then updated.

```
CALL new_course_leader ('c4', '6451')
```
insert_course_leader

```
CALL new_course_leader ('c4', '7774')
```
update_course_leader

You should have found that there is no difference between the two calls; whether **UPDATE** or **INSERT** is required is determined within the procedure and is hidden from the user.

Security

Routines may also be used to provide restricted access to the underlying data in a database to users who do not have the right to modify or access that data directly. When a routine is created it is considered as being owned by the user who executed the **CREATE** statement in the same way as for tables and views. The owner of a routine must have appropriate privileges for all the tables referenced within the routine. In other words, a routine can include only statements that its owner is allowed to execute independently of the routine.

To enable a routine to be used by a user other than its owner requires that the user has been granted a privilege to do so. The particular privilege is **EXECUTE**, which can be granted in a **GRANT** statement. For example, suppose a function `new_student` existed to add rows to the `student` table. The owner of `new_student` would use the following statement to allow a user `admin` to use the function `new_student`.

    GRANT EXECUTE ON `new_student` **TO** `admin`

The important point about an **EXECUTE** privilege for a routine is that a user with such a privilege can use the routine to access the tables referenced by the routine without requiring other privileges for those tables. So routines enable many users to access a database for a specific purpose, and nothing more. This is particularly important for updating, both for controlling how a table may be updated and for hiding from users any complexities that may occur during updating.

So by granting an **EXECUTE** privilege on a procedure such as `new_student`, the user `admin` could make limited updates to the table `student`, without having to be granted **SELECT**, **INSERT** and **UPDATE** privileges on the table `student`. Only the **EXECUTE** privilege on the procedure needs to be granted.

Efficiency

When a routine defined in an application program requires data from the database, that program must access the data from the database server via a network. This reduces the speed of execution. Routines that are defined within the DBMS can access the data that they require without needing to communicate, as they execute on the DBMS server. In addition, when a single routine is required by many application programs, the concurrency in the execution can be handled by the DBMS, rather than relying upon access by several (probably independently developed) application programs.

7.2 Temporary tables

We have seen how variables can be declared in a compound statement. It is also possible to declare tables at the beginning of a compound statement. To declare a temporary table within a compound statement, use the following expression:

    DECLARE LOCAL TEMPORARY TABLE

Activity 7.7 illustrates how the declaration is used.

7 SQL control statements

ACTIVITY 7.7

Using the University database, execute the following statement.

```
BEGIN
  DECLARE LOCAL TEMPORARY TABLE tmp_result (
    student_id student_ids,
    name names,
    exams_taken INTEGER,
    PRIMARY KEY (student_id));
  INSERT INTO tmp_result
    SELECT e.student_id, name, COUNT(*)
    FROM examination e, student s
    WHERE e.student_id = s.student_id
    GROUP BY e.student_id, name;
  SELECT *
  FROM tmp_result;
END
```
temporary_table

This compound statement returns a table containing the student identifier and name of each student who has taken one or more examinations, along with the number of examinations. The table is returned by the final `SELECT` query specification in the compound statement. If you now execute the query

```
SELECT *
FROM tmp_result
```
temporary_table_query

you will find that the table `tmp_result` does not exist. Like a variable, the table exists only within the compound statement in which it is declared.

There are several situations in which temporary tables are useful. If several statements within a compound statement use a common query specification, the efficiency and clarity can be improved by using a temporary table to hold the result of that query specification. This result can then be used by subsequent statements, without the need to repeatedly re-evaluate the query statement. Although Activity 7.7 only shows the temporary table `tmp_result` being used for a single further statement, any number of subsequent statements could make use of `tmp_result`, without the need for the contents of `tmp_result` to be repeatedly re-evaluated.

Temporary tables are also valuable for restructuring tables. When tables are restructured, it is often necessary to store the data in those tables somewhere else while the table is being altered. By using a temporary table, data can be safely stored while the restructuring is carried out.

7.3 Cursors for row-by-row processing

The functions and procedures that you have seen so far have been used to simplify commonly used queries. We now want to consider the problem of how a function or procedure in SQL can process a table one row at a time. This capability is essential for application programs to communicate with a DBMS. We will discuss the development of such application programs in *Block 5*, but we will provide the necessary SQL here for use within an SQL routine.

The technique used in SQL is to use the concept of a cursor (which is a kind of pointer) to refer to each row of the table to be accessed in turn. To make use of this technique, it is necessary to declare that a named cursor is to be used to refer to the data retrieved by a query statement. We will present a procedure that uses a cursor in Activity 7.8, and then describe the processing.

ACTIVITY 7.8

In this activity, we will use cursors to define a procedure to copy the rows of the `examination` table one at a time into a second table, `exam_mod`.

Using the University database, execute the following statement to create the table `exam_mod`.

```sql
CREATE TABLE exam_mod (
    s_id CHAR(3),
    course CHAR(3),
    percentage INTEGER,
    PRIMARY KEY (s_id, course) )
```

create_exam_mod

Execute the following statement to create the procedure `high_mark`.

```sql
CREATE PROCEDURE high_mark (IN lim INTEGER)
  BEGIN
    DECLARE s CHAR(3);
    DECLARE c CHAR(3);
    DECLARE m INTEGER;
    DECLARE loop_control CHAR(5);
    DECLARE exam_marks CURSOR FOR
        SELECT student_id, course_code, mark
        FROM examination;
    OPEN exam_marks;
    SET loop_control = '00000';
    WHILE loop_control <> '02000' LOOP
      FETCH exam_marks INTO s, c, m;
      SET loop_control = SQLSTATE;
      IF m > lim AND loop_control <> '02000'
      THEN INSERT INTO exam_mod (s_id, course, percentage)
        VALUES (s, c, m);
      END IF;
    END LOOP;
    CLOSE exam_marks;
  END
```

create_high_mark

Finally, ensure that the procedure works by calling it with:

```sql
CALL high_mark(50)
```

call_high_mark

You should find that the table `exam_mod` now contains the student identifier, course code and final mark of every student in the `examination` table with an examination mark of 50 or higher.

7 SQL control statements

There is nothing in Activity 7.8 that cannot be carried out using the SQL that you have already seen, but the procedure **high_mark** implements the behaviour in a very different way; row-by-row processing, rather than using a single query.

In Activity 7.8, you should recognise the definition of the procedure, the use of **BEGIN** and **END** to delimit a compound statement, and the declaration of local variables. The new points that are covered by this example are:

- the declaration and use of the cursor,
- the use of **SQLSTATE**,
- the use of a **WHILE** loop.

We will discuss each of these in turn.

Cursor declaration and use

The general form of a cursor declaration is:

> **DECLARE <cursor name> CURSOR FOR <query statement>**

Such declarations can include any form of query statement, not just simple queries, so subqueries and unions are allowed.

For example, in **create_high_mark**, the cursor declaration is:

> **DECLARE exam_marks CURSOR FOR**
>   **SELECT student_id, course_code, mark**
>   **FROM examination**

This defines a cursor that will access rows from the **examination** table, allowing a process to access the values of the **student_id**, **course_code** and **mark** columns.

Having declared a cursor, an **OPEN** statement is used to initiate retrieval of data from the table. To make the cursor **exam_marks** available for use, the following statement is used:

> **OPEN exam_marks**

Once an application program has opened a cursor, the table that results from the query statement can be processed, one row at a time, using a **FETCH** statement, for example:

> **FETCH exam_marks INTO s, c, m**

which places each of the three values from the **student_id**, **course_code** and **mark** columns into the local variables **s**, **c** and **m**. The **INTO** clause should have a list of variables that match in number and data type the columns that are given in the cursor's query statement. Execution of a **FETCH** statement assigns a value for each of the columns in one row to each of the host variables. Repeated execution of a **FETCH** statement assigns values from succeeding rows of the retrieved table into the variables. The global variable **SQLSTATE** is used here to determine when there are no more rows to **FETCH**.

When the cursor is no longer needed, it should be closed with the statement:

> **CLOSE exam_marks**

To specify the order in which the rows are to be retrieved from a table, the cursor declaration can include an **ORDER BY** clause. If no **ORDER BY** clause is used, then the rows will be retrieved in an arbitrary order determined by the DBMS. So, for example, if **create_high_mark** had contained the declaration

```
DECLARE exam_marks CURSOR FOR
    SELECT student_id, course_code, mark
    FROM examination
    ORDER BY mark
```

then the rows would be returned from **examination** in increasing order of **mark**. This would not affect the overall behaviour of the procedure **high_mark**. However, cursors are the main means by which external applications interface with SQL, as we will discuss in *Block 5*, and it is often important for an external application to know the order in which it fetches data from the database.

The SQLSTATE variable

There is one special global variable, **SQLSTATE**, whose value is set by a DBMS following the execution of every SQL statement to indicate the status of the processing of that statement.

The **SQLSTATE** variable consists of two parts concatenated together:

1. a two-character class value, which identifies a general classification of a status, and
2. a three-character subclass value, which identifies a specific status within a class.

A limited set of class and subclass values are defined for SQL but, in general, they are defined by the implementation. Examples of some typical **SQLSTATE** values are shown in Figure 7.1. Note that some of the rows in Figure 7.1 give general classifications (such as '22xxx', which is the general format of data exceptions), while others give specific exceptions (such as '22012', which is the specific value for a division by zero exception).

Value	Meaning
00000	Successful completion
01xxx	Warnings
01003	NULL value eliminated in aggregate function
02000	Row not found
22xxx	Data exceptions
22012	Division by zero
23xxx	Integrity constraint violations
23502	Column 'c' in table 't' cannot be NULL
99999	User-defined exception

Figure 7.1 Some values for **SQLSTATE**

The particular use of **SQLSTATE** that we saw in the **WHILE** loop of the procedure **high_mark** was to recognise when the cursor had finished collecting data; the value of **SQLSTATE** immediately after executing a **FETCH** statement when there are no rows left for the cursor to read is 02000.

Figure 7.1 gives only a few of the most common values of **SQLSTATE** that you might find useful. For SQL Anywhere, a complete list of possible values for **SQLSTATE** is available in the online documentation.

Control flow statements

SQL provides two control flow statements for loops; the `WHILE` statement and the `FOR` statement. The general form of a `WHILE` loop is:

```
WHILE <condition> LOOP
   <compound statement>
END LOOP
```

The statements in `<compound statement>` are repeatedly executed while `<condition>` evaluates to TRUE. `<condition>` is evaluated before each iteration of the `<compound statement>`, and if it does not evaluate to TRUE (i.e. if it is FALSE or UNKNOWN), control jumps straight to `END LOOP`, and then continues to the next statement after `END LOOP`. It is important to recognise that `<condition>` is evaluated *before* each iteration, and so `<compound statement>` might not execute at all if `<condition>` does not evaluate to TRUE the first time that the loop is executed.

In Standard SQL, a single statement can be used instead of a compound statement.

In the procedure **high_mark**, we want to repeatedly execute the loop until the cursor is unable to fetch any more values from the `examination` table, shown when `SQLSTATE` has the value 02000. However, even if `examination` is empty, we need to execute `FETCH` at least once so that the value of `SQLSTATE` indicates whether there are remaining rows. Therefore, we give `loop_control` an initial value that ensures that the loop is executed at least once, and thereafter, `loop_control` is given the value of `SQLSTATE` as each row is fetched. Then `loop_control` can be used to determine when the cursor has fetched all the rows from its own query. We will discuss the processing of cursors in more depth after looking at `FOR` loops.

EXERCISE 7.3

Why must the value of `SQLSTATE` be placed in the local variable `loop_control`, rather than writing the `WHILE` clause as `WHILE SQLSTATE <> '02000'`?

When a loop is defined using a `WHILE` statement, the cursor must be explicitly opened, the `FETCH` statement must be made explicit, and the loop must be terminated using `SQLSTATE`. An alternative to the `WHILE` loop is the `FOR` loop, in which these stages do not need to be made explicit. The general form of the `FOR` loop for use with cursors is:

```
FOR <for loop name> AS <cursor name> CURSOR FOR <statement>
DO
   <statement list>
END FOR
```

For a `FOR` statement, most of the cursor controls that need to be stated explicitly with a `WHILE` statement are implicit in the initial declaration of the `FOR` statement. In particular:

▶ The cursor does not require an explicit `OPEN` statement.

▶ The `<statement list>` does not require an explicit `FETCH` – the column names act as variables in the statement list.

▶ The loop does not need to be explicitly terminated – `<statement list>` is executed once for each row retrieved by the cursor.

We can rewrite the body of the definition of the procedure **high_mark** using a **FOR** loop as:

```
BEGIN
  FOR my_loop AS exam_marks CURSOR FOR
    SELECT student_id, course_code, mark
    FROM examination
  DO
    IF mark > lim
    THEN INSERT INTO exam_mod (s_id, course, percentage)
      VALUES (student_id, course_code, mark);
    END IF;
  END FOR;
END
```

Each time the control passes through the **DO** ... **END FOR** loop, the variables **student_id**, **course_code** and **mark** are updated with the values from a different row of the **examination** table. An important point to note is that we need to rename the column **percentage** in the **SELECT** statement to ensure that there is not a conflict of variable names in the **INSERT INTO** expression.

If you want to try using the procedure **high_mark** with this **FOR** loop, remember that the table **exam_mod** must be empty when you call **high_mark**. Otherwise, the procedure will attempt to insert duplicate rows into **exam_mod**, and an error message will be given as entity integrity is violated.

Processing model for cursors

A processing model can be used to explain the combined effect of the **OPEN** and **FETCH** statements. When an **OPEN** statement is executed, the query given in the cursor declaration is processed, using the value at the time of execution of any variables specified in the query. A DBMS retrieves the data as defined in the query and constructs the resulting table, which we shall refer to as a **cursor table**, with the specified columns and required rows, sorted according to any **ORDER BY** clause that may be specified (the DBMS determines the order if there is no **ORDER BY** clause). An **OPEN** statement positions the cursor *before* the first row of the cursor table.

Execution of a **FETCH** statement combines two actions: first, the cursor named in the statement is moved to the next row of the cursor table; then, the data values from that row are assigned to the variables. So the first time a **FETCH** statement is executed (after its cursor has been opened), the cursor is moved to the first row and the data from this row is transferred to the variables in the **INTO** clause. Repeated execution of the **FETCH** statement moves the cursor, one row at a time, to the next row of the cursor table and assigns its data to the variables. This process continues to the last row, when the next execution of **FETCH** results in the cursor being positioned after the last row and the global variable **SQLSTATE** being assigned a value of '02000'.

So a simple routine to process a cursor table has a general framework that includes an initial cursor declaration (specifying the data required for the cursor table), followed somewhere later by an **OPEN** statement (executed just once), and then by a **FETCH** statement (which may be executed repeatedly for each of many rows of the cursor table). The data for each row that is 'fetched' is assigned to variables, which can then be processed according to the requirements of the application.

When the program has finished with the cursor table (the cursor does not have to be positioned after the last row), the cursor can be closed with a **CLOSE** statement. If no

CLOSE statement is given, the cursor cannot be used outside the compound statement in which it was declared.

Once it has been defined, a cursor may be opened and closed many times during the execution of a routine. A base table may be referenced in the query definition of many cursors, and any number of those cursors may be opened at the same time. For example, we could define two cursors called `c_student` and `c_course`, both referencing the `tutors` table, to allow the retrieval of details that relate to the students and courses a particular member of staff tutors. Both of those cursors can be opened at the same time, retrieving data from the same base table.

More generally, it is possible to define cursors that are 'scrollable', which allows the application program to move a cursor a number of rows forwards and backwards through a table.

EXERCISE 7.4

Give a declaration for a cursor called `tutor` which provides a cursor table containing the name and staff number of each of the staff members who tutor the student whose identification number is stored in the variable `StudentId`.

EXERCISE 7.5

Describe when a cursor may be considered as having a position during the execution of a routine. Explain how that position may be used by the routine.

Updating using cursors

In conjunction with the use of a cursor for retrieving data, there is also a form of the UPDATE and DELETE statements that may be used to modify or delete the row in the current cursor position. Such statements are known as **positioned updates**.

Apart from the WHERE clause, the form of both the UPDATE and DELETE statements for a positioned update are the same as described in Section 5, except that the cursor is specified rather than the table being updated. The WHERE clause for a positioned update statement is of the following form (with no other conditions allowed):

    WHERE CURRENT OF <cursor name>

In Section 5, an UPDATE (or DELETE) statement resulted in the modification (or deletion) of all the rows which satisfied the condition in the WHERE clause. For a positioned UPDATE (or DELETE) statement, only the one row in the position given by the named cursor is modified (or deleted). A positioned UPDATE does not affect the position of the cursor, but after a positioned DELETE the cursor is placed so that a subsequent FETCH statement retrieves the next row.

Positioned UPDATE statements are used within the program framework already described for retrieval, and depend on prior use of FETCH, because the FETCH statement causes the cursor to move from row to row.

EXERCISE 7.6

If a cursor named `failed` is declared with a query involving the table `assignment`, give an appropriate DELETE statement that could be used to delete a row of assignment after fetching the row to be deleted.

Because cursors can be declared for any columns in a table, care is sometimes needed to ensure that the correct rows are updated. For example, consider the following sequence of statements:

```
DECLARE c CURSOR FOR SELECT name FROM staff;
OPEN c;
FETCH c INTO n;
DELETE WHERE CURRENT OF c;
```

Suppose these statements were executed using the University database, and the variable `n` subsequently contained the value 'Sanderson'. Then we would know that the `DELETE` statement had removed a row from the `staff` table in which the value of `name` was Sanderson. However, we would not know whether it was the row with `staff_number` equal to '3678' or '4219'. This example illustrates a possible danger when cursors are defined on columns that may contain duplicate values.

EXERCISE 7.7

Distinguish each of the different kinds of variable that may occur within a procedure, and describe where they are declared.

7.4 Triggers

We have already seen that procedures and functions must be explicitly invoked by a user, that they make use of a compound statement to process data from the database, and often return a result. SQL also provides the **trigger**, a type of stored procedure that uses a compound statement but does not normally return a result. A trigger is associated with a single named table, known as its **subject table**. A trigger is implicitly invoked as a consequence of some modification of its subject table, quite likely without the user who caused the modification being aware of the triggered action. When a table is dropped, so are its triggers.

When the subject table is modified by an `INSERT`, `DELETE` or `UPDATE` event, the triggers (a subject table can have zero, one or more triggers associated with each possible modification) associated with the particular operation on that table are fired, and the compound statement defined within the trigger is executed. The compound statement may involve data from the modified subject table and/or data from other table(s) in the database.

This 'hidden' effect of a trigger is directly comparable to the referential actions associated with foreign keys, and triggers can be used to provide the same effect as referential actions when the latter are not supported by an implementation.

As an example of how triggers can be used, we will build a table that contains the number of books used on each course. This table must be updated whenever a row is added or removed from the `textbook` table. We will use a trigger to automate the update of the new table. We will discuss how the trigger works after the activity.

ACTIVITY 7.9

This activity uses the University database. Before starting this activity, ensure that the `textbook` table is defined and contains no data. If it is not defined, execute **table_creation**. If the `textbook` table is defined but is not empty, then use

```
DELETE FROM textbook
```

to remove the data from it.

7 SQL control statements

Execute the following statement to create a table containing the number of books used on each course.

```
CREATE TABLE books_per_course (
    course_code CHAR(2),
    book_count INTEGER,
    PRIMARY KEY (course_code) )
```
create_books_per_course

(As in Activity 7.6, for simplicity we have omitted the foreign keys and other constraints that we would normally expect to be part of the table definition.)

Execute the following statement to populate `books_per_course` with the course codes and initial counts of 0 (zero) books per course.

```
INSERT INTO books_per_course (course_code, book_count)
    SELECT course_code, 0
    FROM course
```
initial_books_data

We can now define a trigger so that whenever a row is added to the `textbook` table, the `book_count` value is increased in the row for that textbook's course.

Execute the following statement.

```
CREATE TRIGGER add_textbook
    AFTER INSERT ON textbook
    REFERENCING NEW AS new_textbook
    FOR EACH ROW
      BEGIN ATOMIC
        UPDATE books_per_course
          SET book_count = book_count + 1
          WHERE books_per_course.course_code =
                new_textbook.course_code;
      END
```
create_textbook_trigger

To test the trigger, execute the following statement.

```
INSERT INTO textbook
    VALUES ('65281', 'Beginning Syntax', 'Kershaw, J.', 247, 'c2')
```
check_textbook_trigger

You should find that the row with `course_code` c2 in the `books_per_course` table now has a value 1 in the `book_count` column.

To explain the behaviour of the trigger, we will examine the definition in **create_textbook_trigger**, and give some of the variants that may be used to define different behaviours. The definition is in two parts – an initial declaration and the trigger action.

1. The first line defines the trigger name, `add_textbook`.
2. `AFTER INSERT ON textbook` states that the trigger is fired when an `INSERT` event is carried out on the `textbook` table. Other possible trigger events are `DELETE` and `UPDATE` (`UPDATE` can optionally include named columns). The trigger timing is specified as `AFTER` – that is, the trigger is fired *after* the insertion into the table is complete. Triggers can also be specified as `BEFORE`, so that the trigger is fired before the insertion into the table.

3   **REFERENCING NEW AS new_textbook** states that the new row of data (i.e. the data that has been inserted) can be referred to as **new_textbook** within the body of the trigger action. Similarly, for a trigger defined for a **DELETE** event, it is possible to specify a name to refer to **OLD** data. A trigger for an **UPDATE** event may specify names to refer to both **OLD** and **NEW** data (for those rows which have changed).

4   **FOR EACH ROW** states that the trigger action is fired as each row is updated; so if many rows are being inserted, the qualifier **new_textbook** is a reference to the current row. An alternative is **FOR EACH STATEMENT**, which means that all processing of the triggering statement is completed before the trigger is fired. In this case, **new_textbook** refers to a *table* consisting of all the inserted rows.

> Do not confuse this use of **FOR EACH ROW** with a **FOR** statement.

5   Finally, the compound statement specifies the action that will occur when the trigger is fired. In this example, the trigger uses the value of the column **course_code** in **new_textbook** (from the row inserted into **textbook**) to determine the row in the **books_per_course** table that is to be updated by adding one to the number of textbooks used on the course.

The general form of a trigger definition is:

```
CREATE TRIGGER <trigger name>
  {BEFORE|AFTER} {INSERT|DELETE|UPDATE|
                                UPDATE OF <column name> [, <column name>, ...]}
    ON <table name>
  REFERENCING [OLD AS <old name>] [NEW AS <new name>]
  FOR EACH {ROW|STATEMENT}
  [WHEN <condition>]
    <atomic compound statement>
```

The additional **WHEN** condition allows a condition to be specified in the same way as a **WHERE** clause to restrict the firing of the trigger to those rows that satisfy the condition. We give an example of this in the next section.

SQL requires that the statement in the body of a trigger be declared as **ATOMIC**. The body of the trigger definition must therefore be declared as **BEGIN ATOMIC ... END**.

> As with functions and procedures, if the body of the trigger is a single statement, then Standard SQL does not require that it be declared as a compound statement using the **BEGIN ATOMIC ... END** format.

An important subtlety to note about triggers that fire when an **UPDATE** occurs on a row in the subject table is that if the trigger is defined as **BEFORE UPDATE**, then it will fire whenever an update occurs on that row, whether or not the values of that row change. If the trigger is defined to fire **AFTER UPDATE**, then it will fire only if the new values are different from the old values.

EXERCISE 7.8

The trigger **add_textbook** only fires when a new row is added to the **textbook** table. Write triggers that maintain the correct count of textbooks per course when rows in **textbook** are removed with a **DELETE** statement, or modified with an **UPDATE** statement.

Execution of triggers

Triggers can be used whenever a change to one table requires a change to be made to another table, and so can be used for a variety of tasks. There are no privileges associated with a trigger because it has to execute whenever a triggering event occurs for its subject table – though the user causing that event needs appropriate privileges on the subject table. If the triggered action includes any reference to another table, then the owner of the trigger must have privileges for that table.

When defining triggers, it is also necessary to think about the interaction of the triggers with constraints that may also have been defined. If the actions of a trigger violate a constraint that has already been defined, an exception will be raised and the execution of statements in the body of the trigger will be halted.

You should note that a single SQL statement is atomic. This is relevant to triggers, because a failure in a triggered action causes the triggering update statement to fail as well. An SQL statement can cause many rows to be inserted, deleted or updated. A DBMS must automatically ensure that either the modification operation (`INSERT`, `DELETE` or `UPDATE`) on a table and the actions triggered by the event are both successfully completed, or that there is no change.

For example, consider an `INSERT` statement that is being used to copy many rows from one table to another. If a row being inserted into a table violates any of the constraints on that table (for example, the row has NULL in a column constrained to be `NOT NULL`), then the `INSERT` statement must fail and no rows will be inserted.

Note that it is the use of the statement `REFERENCING [OLD AS <old name>][NEW AS <new name>]` that makes this **rollback** of the trigger possible (we will discuss rollback at more length in the next section, on transactions).

Removing triggers

Triggers are explicitly removed with a `DROP` statement:

`DROP TRIGGER <trigger name>`

Triggers are also automatically dropped when their subject table is dropped.

Use of triggers

One particular use of triggers is for a kind of constraint that cannot be handled by the constraint definition facilities that we described in Section 5. Such constraints are often called **dynamic constraints** because they restrict how a database may change from one state to another. The constraints described in Section 5 must be true for all the data at any instant and are referred to as **static constraints**. Static constraints cannot constrain how the database may change.

Let us consider an example of a dynamic constraint. The definition of the `textbook` table allows the number of pages for a book to be NULL; this means that a book can be recorded even if the number of pages is not known at first. Suppose that, for the benefit of the printer, once a value for this column has been set, then a later update must not change it back to NULL. This behaviour cannot be achieved with a not null constraint, because it is about how the table is allowed to *change*, rather than about the values that the table may contain.

We can use the following trigger to prevent a user from modifying a row in the `textbook` table so that a value in the `no_pages` column is set to NULL. (The new features are discussed below.)

```
CREATE TRIGGER update_page_nums
  BEFORE UPDATE OF no_pages ON textbook
  REFERENCING OLD AS old_textbook
              NEW AS new_textbook
FOR EACH ROW
WHEN (new_textbook.no_pages IS NULL
  AND old_textbook.no_pages IS NOT NULL)
  BEGIN ATOMIC
    DECLARE pages_not_null
      EXCEPTION FOR SQLSTATE '99999';
    SIGNAL pages_not_null;
  END
```

create_update_page_nums

The `BEFORE UPDATE` statement means that any row from the original table that would be changed is held in `new_textbook`. The condition `WHEN` checks to see whether an attempt has been made to change the value of `no_pages` in any row to NULL. Only if this is the case will the body of the trigger be executed. Note that the trigger can compare the updated row both before and after the update because of the use of both `OLD` and `NEW` in the `REFERENCING` clause.

The body of the trigger declares a variable `pages_not_null`, and defines it as an exception with an `SQLSTATE` of '99999'. An exception is an event that causes normal SQL processing to be terminated; we have already seen that different kinds of exception have different values for `SQLSTATE`. The value '99999' is the value for a user-defined exception. When the `SIGNAL` statement in the trigger is executed, it sets `SQLSTATE` to the given value and terminates execution of the trigger and the statement that fired the trigger. This combination is a general rule: a trigger should be seen as part of the processing of the triggering statement, and all processing must complete successfully or not at all, like a transaction.

ACTIVITY 7.10

This activity uses the University database. Before starting this activity, ensure that the `textbook` table is defined. If it is not defined, execute **table_creation**. It does not matter whether or not the table contains data.

Execute the statement **create_update_page_nums** to create the trigger `update_page_nums`. Next, execute the following statement.

```
INSERT INTO textbook
  VALUES ('39631', 'Branching Quantification', 'Melia, R.', NULL, 'c5')
```

trigger_test_1

Check the contents of `textbook` to ensure that this row has been added, and that it contains NULL in the `no_pages` column. Having added the row to the table, now update the `no_pages` column by executing the statement

```
UPDATE textbook
  SET no_pages = 180
  WHERE bookcode = '39631'
```

trigger_test_2

and note that the row has been updated. If you now execute the following statement to return `no_pages` to NULL, the update will fail with a user-defined exception.

```
UPDATE textbook
   SET no_pages = NULL
   WHERE bookcode = '39631'
```

trigger_test_3

As Activity 7.10 shows, triggers can be used to prevent certain *changes* to the data. A row can be added to the table with NULL as the value in the `no_pages` row; what is prevented is an attempt to change an existing value back to NULL.

EXERCISE 7.9

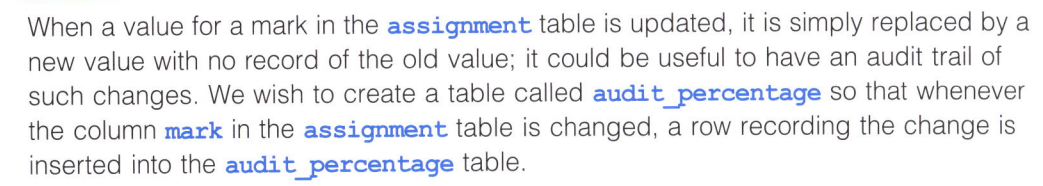

When a value for a mark in the `assignment` table is updated, it is simply replaced by a new value with no record of the old value; it could be useful to have an audit trail of such changes. We wish to create a table called `audit_percentage` so that whenever the column `mark` in the `assignment` table is changed, a row recording the change is inserted into the `audit_percentage` table.

The database development team propose two possible solutions to this task.

1 A procedure can be written that both updates the `mark` column in the `assignment` table and inserts the change into `audit_percentage`. Users will then be given an `EXECUTE` privilege for the procedure but no `UPDATE` privilege for `assignment`.

2 A trigger can be created on `assignment` for the event `UPDATE OF mark`, whose triggered action inserts the change into the `audit_percentage` table.

Which method might you prefer to ensure that all changes to mark are properly recorded in the `audit_percentage` table? (You are not expected to implement the proposed solutions.)

7.5 Transaction management

This final section considers another aspect of SQL concerning the processing of a number of statements together. It relates to managing **transactions**, which were introduced in *Block 1*, Section 3, as units of work that either succeed completely or fail without causing any change to the database. Transactions are necessary to maintain consistency when a database is being updated.

The need for transactions

A simple example of the need for transactions arises in the context of banking, where a sum of money is to be transferred from account A to account B – a business transaction, which in this case is also a database transaction (they are not always the same). This involves first checking that there is enough money in account A, followed by two update statements, to subtract the money from account A and add it to account B. The order in which the update statements are executed should not matter. The end result should be the same – both updates must be completed for the result to be consistent, otherwise the totals of money into, and out of, accounts do not balance.

However, there are various situations to be considered in which such updates are not completely satisfactory.

- ▶ A failure in the hardware, system software or application program that happens after the first update but before the second can prevent the second update from being executed. When restarted, the database includes only the first update. There is then an inconsistency in the database as the accounts will not balance.
- ▶ After executing part of the transaction, the system may determine that there is a problem with the transfer, for example, finding that the number for account B is invalid after subtracting money from account A.
- ▶ Other programs that are allowed to update the same data at the same time may lead to an unsatisfactory final state. For example, the program could read details of account A and, while it is assessing whether there is enough money for the transfer, another program could withdraw money from the account. This results in the first program basing its assessment on data that is no longer valid.

Each of these three situations is an example of a different kind of problem that a DBMS can be expected to prevent. In the first situation, updating was only partially completed and a DBMS must ensure that the database is returned to a consistent state after a failure of the machinery, at either the hardware or software level. This requires that all the updates that have been executed for an incomplete transaction are undone, or rolled back, so that the database appears to its users as if nothing has happened. The same requirement applies to any other program with incomplete transactions that was using the database when the failure occurred. Just as importantly, a DBMS also needs to ensure that successfully completed transactions are preserved in the database. These capabilities of a DBMS are aspects of **recovery**, and our description treats a transaction as a unit of work – that is, when a system is recovering from a failure, a DBMS recovers all or nothing of a transaction. We are assuming that a DBMS provides recovery, but we will not cover the details of the mechanisms involved. It is enough to say that recovery depends on a DBMS receiving a request for the appropriate action when each transaction is complete, so that it can ensure that changes made during all successful transactions are persistent, and incomplete transactions have no effect.

In the second situation, the program itself determines when it cannot proceed with a successful transaction, in which case there is a similar requirement that any changes already executed must be undone – the transaction cannot be allowed to remain partially complete, so it must fail. So a program determines what happens, according to the user requirements, and requests a DBMS to take action when a transaction fails, so that any prior updating is undone. Similarly, a request is required when a transaction succeeds, to **commit** those changes to the database, so that all updates are confirmed, and cannot be lost in possible future failures. Note that it is the final status of a transaction which matters, rather than the success or failure of any of the statements within the transaction.

The final situation in which a transaction may be unsatisfactory is a consequence of concurrent use of data when a database is shared. To prevent such a situation, a DBMS has to ensure that a transaction completes its processing without the data involved being affected by other programs. When a program requests a DBMS to complete a transaction, the DBMS can then allow the data to be accessed by other users. We shall explore more of these issues related to concurrent transactions below.

So to enable a DBMS to support recovery and provide concurrency, and to enable a program to control its database updates, a program needs to be able to request a DBMS to take action on completion of a transaction, allowing for either of the following two (and only these two) situations.

1. A transaction succeeds, so the program requests the DBMS to **commit** all the changes made during the course of the transaction to the database, that is, to make all the changes permanent.
2. A transaction fails, so the program requests the DBMS to **rollback** all the changes made during the course of the transaction so that the database returns to its state at the start of the transaction.

EXERCISE 7.10

Excluding concurrency, describe the roles of an application program and a DBMS in managing transactions.

SQL transaction management

We have already seen that single statements, or compound statements that are declared `ATOMIC`, must either completely succeed or completely fail. So the transactions that we need to consider are formed from multiple statements, any of which may fail without necessarily causing the whole transaction to fail. A transaction can make a test at any time during its execution (for example, testing the value of `SQLSTATE`) and can choose to continue with a transaction even though a statement failure was indicated.

An SQL transaction should be defined whenever a unit of work involving one or more SQL statements updates a database. We have already described the two situations a program needs to cater for, success or failure of a transaction, and SQL provides this capability by means of the following statements (where, in each case, `WORK` is optional):

```
COMMIT WORK
ROLLBACK WORK
```

Each of these two statements corresponds to the completion of a transaction. A `COMMIT` statement causes all statements in a transaction to be recorded in a database. Conversely, a `ROLLBACK` statement ensures that a transaction being completed has no effect on a database.

While the `COMMIT` and `ROLLBACK` statements specify the end of a transaction, there is no statement to specify the beginning. A new transaction is considered to have started automatically either at the beginning of a program or where the previous transaction ended. During the running of a program, a transaction consists of those SQL statements executed from one `COMMIT` or `ROLLBACK` statement to the next.

As a simple example of using the `COMMIT` and `ROLLBACK` statements, we will consider a case where an `UPDATE` statement for the `textbook` table increases the page counts for all books by 30. In the absence of any constraint on the maximum value for page numbers, this would be successful. However, as part of the transaction, the maximum value of `no_pages` for each row will be checked, and the transaction will fail if this value exceeds 360 for any row. If the transaction fails, the changes of the update will be rolled back; otherwise, the update can remain and the transaction is committed.

We can express this transaction by the following sequence of statements which we have written for the `textbook` table.

```
BEGIN
  DECLARE max_length INTEGER;
  UPDATE textbook
    SET no_pages = no_pages + 30;
  SELECT MAX(no_pages)
    INTO max_length
  FROM textbook;
  IF max_length > 360
  THEN ROLLBACK WORK;
  ELSE COMMIT WORK;
  END IF;
END
```

textbook_transaction

ACTIVITY 7.11

Before starting this activity, ensure that the `textbook` table is defined and is populated only with the data defined with the SQL in **fill_table**.

Execute a query to examine the contents of the `textbook` table. Then execute the compound statement **textbook_transaction**, and repeat your query to show that the transaction is successful and that the table has been updated. Execute **textbook_transaction** for a second time, and repeat your query to show that the transaction is unsuccessful and that the table has not been updated, because the textbook numbered 38572 would then have 380 pages.

EXERCISE 7.11

From your examination of the updated contents of the `textbook` table, explain how the compound statement in **textbook_transaction** prevents the update from happening if any of the rows has a value greater than 360 in the `no_pages` column.

EXERCISE 7.12

Exercise 7.9 described the use of a table called `audit_percentage` to record changes to the `mark` column of the `assignment` table. Describe how you would organise a transaction to update a value in the `mark` column in the `assignment` table and record the change in the `audit_percentage` table. (You are not expected to write SQL here, but rather to give the outline for the stages of the transaction.)

Savepoints in transactions

A **savepoint** is a marker that can be put in the transaction so that when a `ROLLBACK` statement is used, all the work up to that savepoint is kept, and only the work that comes after the savepoint is rolled back. Using several named savepoints in a transaction gives you more control over the execution of the transaction than `COMMIT`. With `COMMIT`, you must confirm all the work that was carried out during the transaction, while savepoints allow parts of the work to be undone.

ACTIVITY 7.12

Before starting this activity, ensure that the `textbook` table is defined and contains no data. Execute **table_creation** if `textbook` is not already defined, otherwise execute `DELETE FROM textbook`.

Execute the following compound statement.

```
BEGIN
  DECLARE max_length INTEGER;
  INSERT INTO textbook
    VALUES ('38572', 'Practical Pragmatics', 'Christine Davies', 320, 'c7');
  SAVEPOINT save1;
  INSERT INTO textbook
    VALUES ('65284', 'A First Course In Logic', 'Jerry Maxwell', 115, 'c5');
  SELECT MAX(no_pages)
    INTO max_length
  FROM textbook;
  IF max_length > 300
  THEN ROLLBACK TO SAVEPOINT save1;
  END IF;
  COMMIT WORK;
END
```

rollback_transaction

If you now examine the contents of the **textbook** table, you will find that only the content of the first **INSERT** statement has been added to the table.

When **rollback_transaction** is initially executed, both **INSERT** statements succeed, and so the **SELECT** statement places the value 320 into the variable **max_length**. Then as the value of **max_length** is greater than 300, the **ROLLBACK TO SAVEPOINT save1** is executed. This rolls back everything after the savepoint and so only the data from the first **INSERT** statement remains in the **textbook** table. Finally, the **COMMIT** clause confirms the addition of this data. Note that the maximum value in the **no_pages** column is still greater than 300.

The savepoint is declared with the declaration:

SAVEPOINT <savepoint_name>

A savepoint can be removed at any time after its declaration with the statement:

RELEASE SAVEPOINT <savepoint_name>

A savepoint can no longer be used after **COMMIT** has been used to confirm changes.

We shall not consider any further details of the way programs have to be written for managing transactions, but there are many details that have to be taken into account, particularly when using embedded SQL. You should note, however, that the use of triggers and referential actions, which are executed as part of an atomic SQL statement, can simplify the organisation of transactions.

Concurrent transaction problems

So far, we have concentrated on transactions designed to maintain the consistency of data for a sequence of updates for an individual user. However, real database systems are generally used by many users, and as we showed in the introductory banking example, other problems can arise when many users wish to access the database at the same time. In these cases, we must consider **concurrent transactions**. There are four fundamental problems that can occur with concurrent transactions, each in a situation in which a user is affected in some way by other users. Each of these situations is a problem in a context where the behaviour does not match the user's requirements or expectations.

We shall illustrate each of the problems by considering concurrent transactions involving a tutor administrator A and a student administrator B, both accessing the **tutors** table.

Lost update

Suppose that the member of staff with staff number 8431 stops tutoring on courses and their students must be assigned new tutors. User A queries the **tutors** table for students tutored by this member of staff and finds that student s09 on course c2 must be reallocated. Meanwhile, user B also queries the **tutors** table with the same query and obtains the same result. User A updates the **tutors** table to allocate tutor number 5324 to student s09 for course c2. For the same reason, user B updates the same table to allocate tutor number 5212 to student s09 for course c2. As a consequence the update made by user A is 'lost', so that user A thinks they have allocated one tutor when another tutor is recorded in the database. This is known as the **lost update** problem. This problem is illustrated in Figure 7.2, where the sequence of events (1 to 4) is shown at the top left-hand corner of each box.

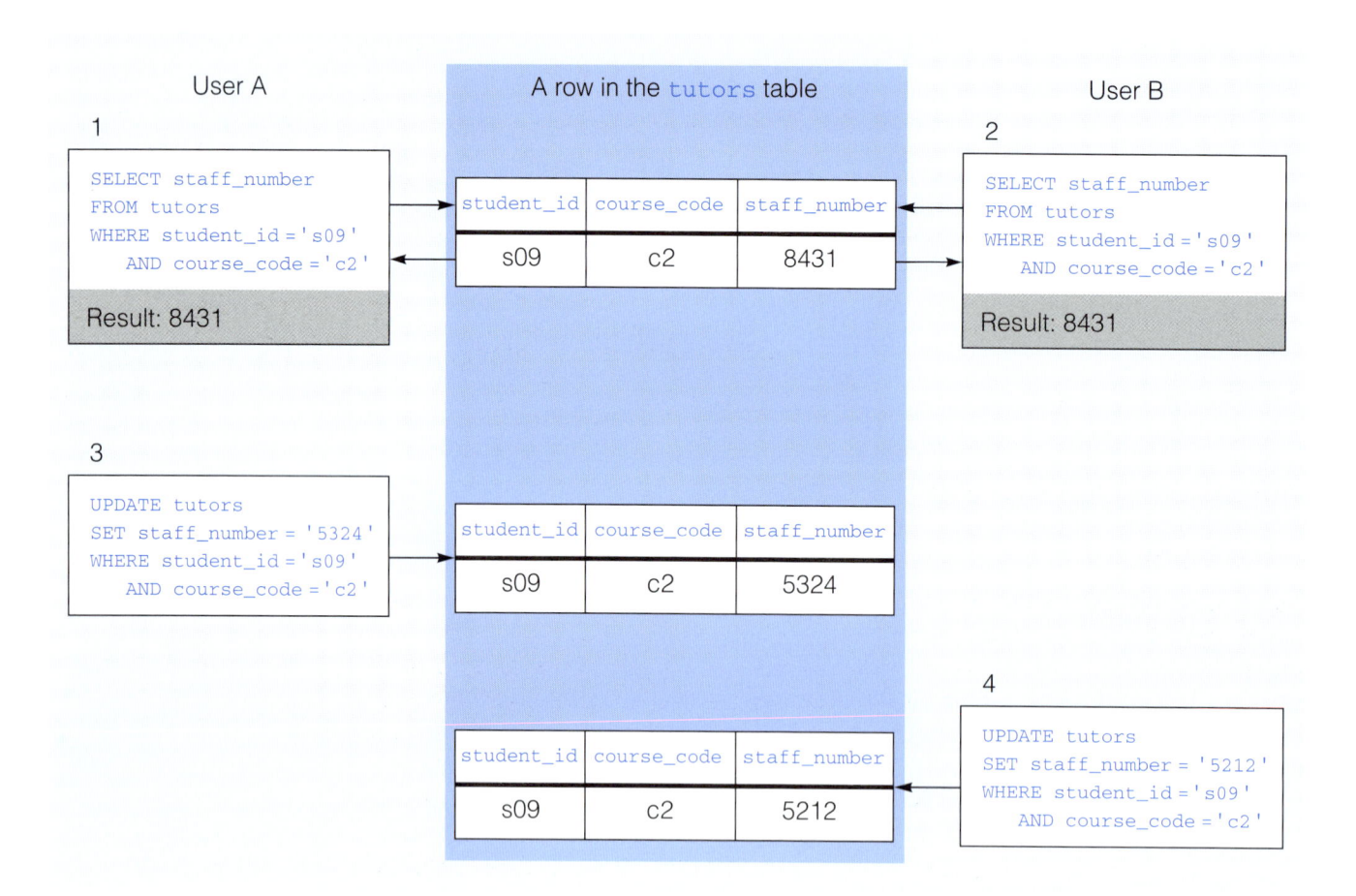

Figure 7.2 The lost update problem

Uncommitted data (or dirty read) problem

User A queries the database to discover that student s09 has been allocated tutor 8431 for course c2. User A then begins a transaction to update the table to allocate tutor 5324 to student s09 on c2. While the transaction is in progress, User B views the database and sees that student s09 has been allocated tutor 5324. However, User A's transaction then fails to complete successfully (perhaps because of a constraint violation or system failure) and, as a consequence, the work in that transaction is rolled back. The result is that User B thinks that student s09 is tutored by staff member 5324, whereas the database shows that the tutor is 8431. This sequence is illustrated in Figure 7.3. It is known as the **uncommitted data** or **dirty read** problem, and is caused by the DBMS allowing users to read data before it is committed.

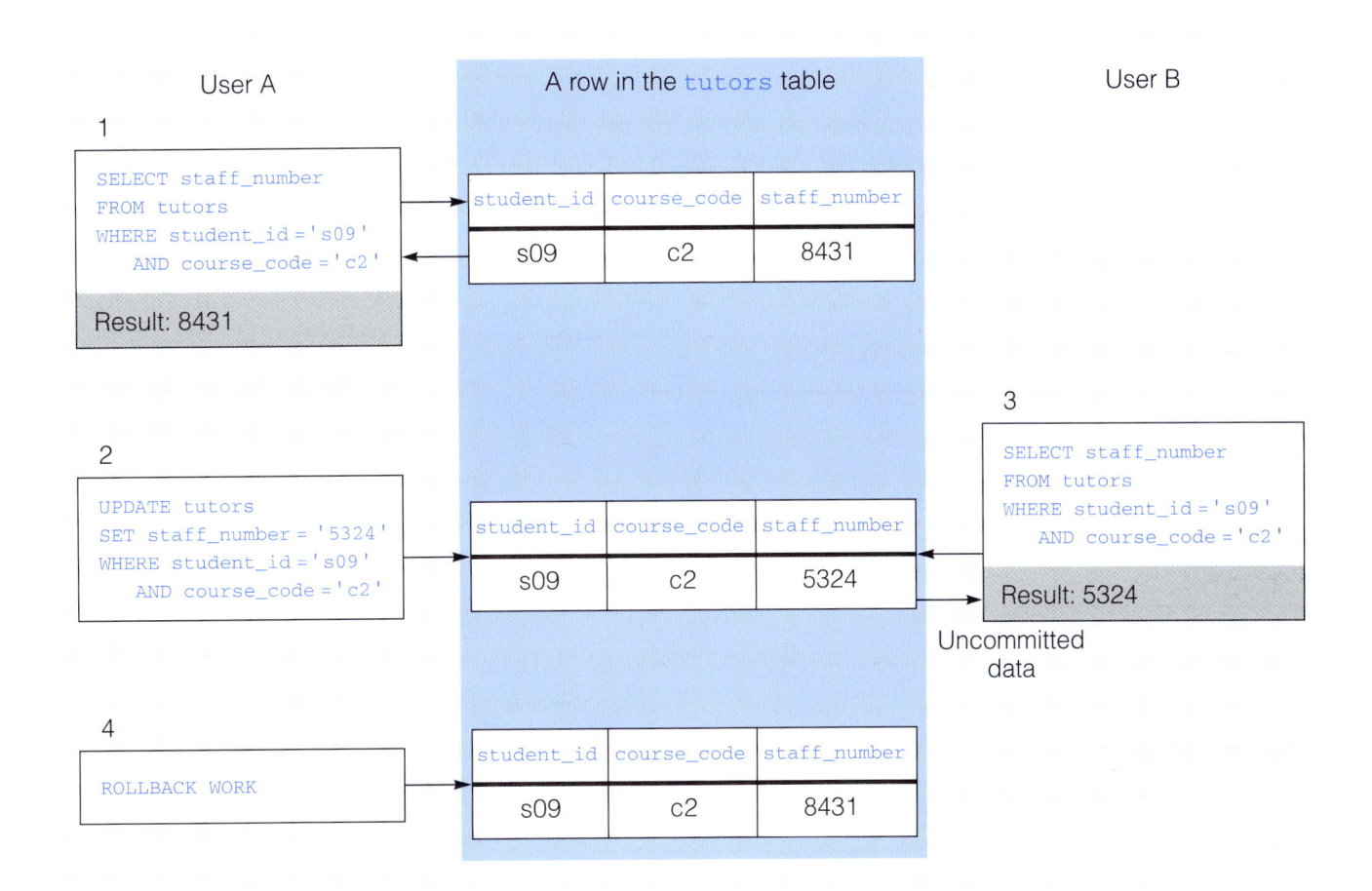

Figure 7.3 The dirty read problem

Non-repeatable read

User A queries the database to discover that student s09 has been allocated tutor 8431 for course c2. Meanwhile, User B executes a process that queries the database, and obtains the same result, that tutor 8431 tutors student s09 on course c2. While User B executes other processes, User A updates the `tutors` table to allocate tutor 5324 to student s09 on course c2. After User A's update, User B executes a second process that also queries the database, but this time finds that the student has been allocated tutor 5324. Unlike the first two problems, the data in the database is always consistent. However, the processes that User B uses to query the database return different results for the same query because the database has been updated in the meantime. This is illustrated in Figure 7.4 (overleaf), and is known as the **non-repeatable read** problem.

Phantom rows

The fourth problem is similar to the 'non-repeatable read' problem in that it involves the same query giving different results at different times but, in this case, involving multiple-row queries. In Figure 7.5, user A executes a query to count the number of enrolments which are not tutored by staff number 8431. The result is 16. Then user B updates the database to allocate tutor 5324 to student s09 on course c2. Now if user A executes the same query again, this time the result is 17, indicating that a row has appeared that was not present before. This is known as the **phantom row** or **phantom insert** problem.

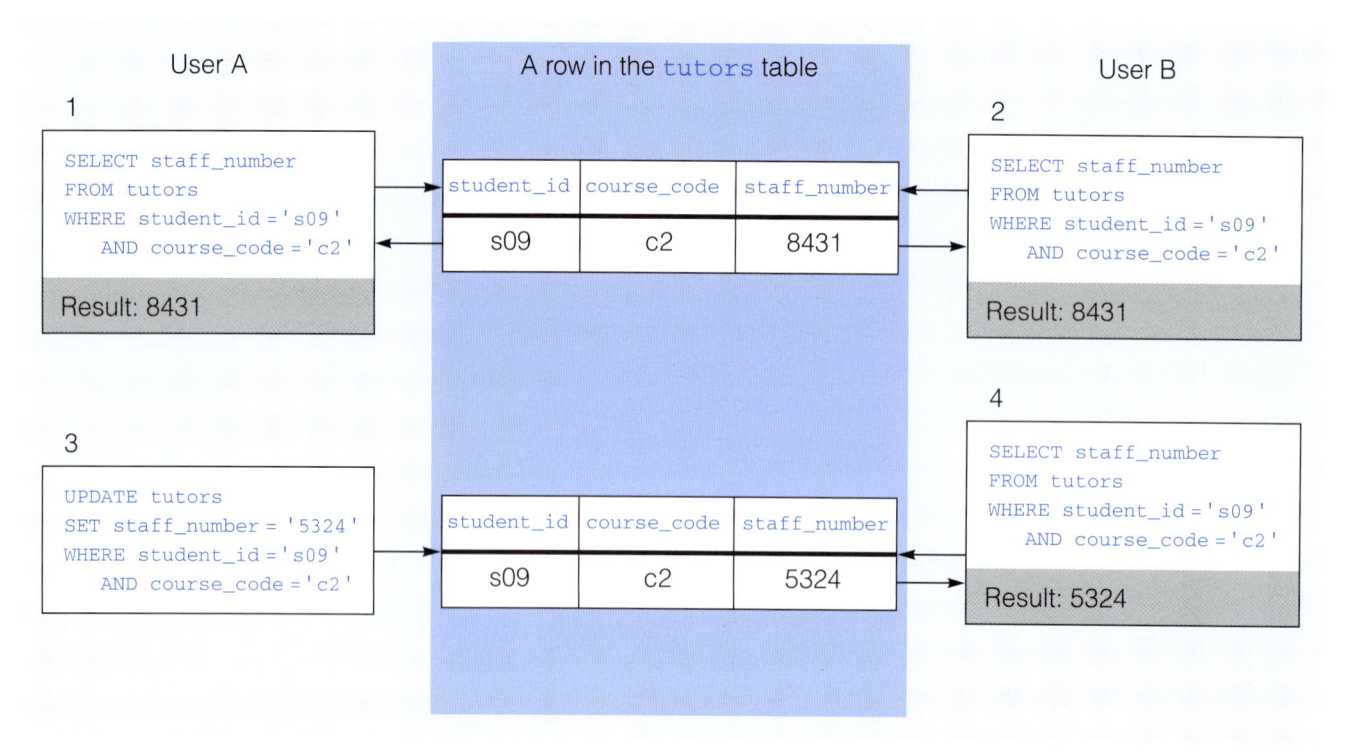

Figure 7.4 The non-repeatable read problem

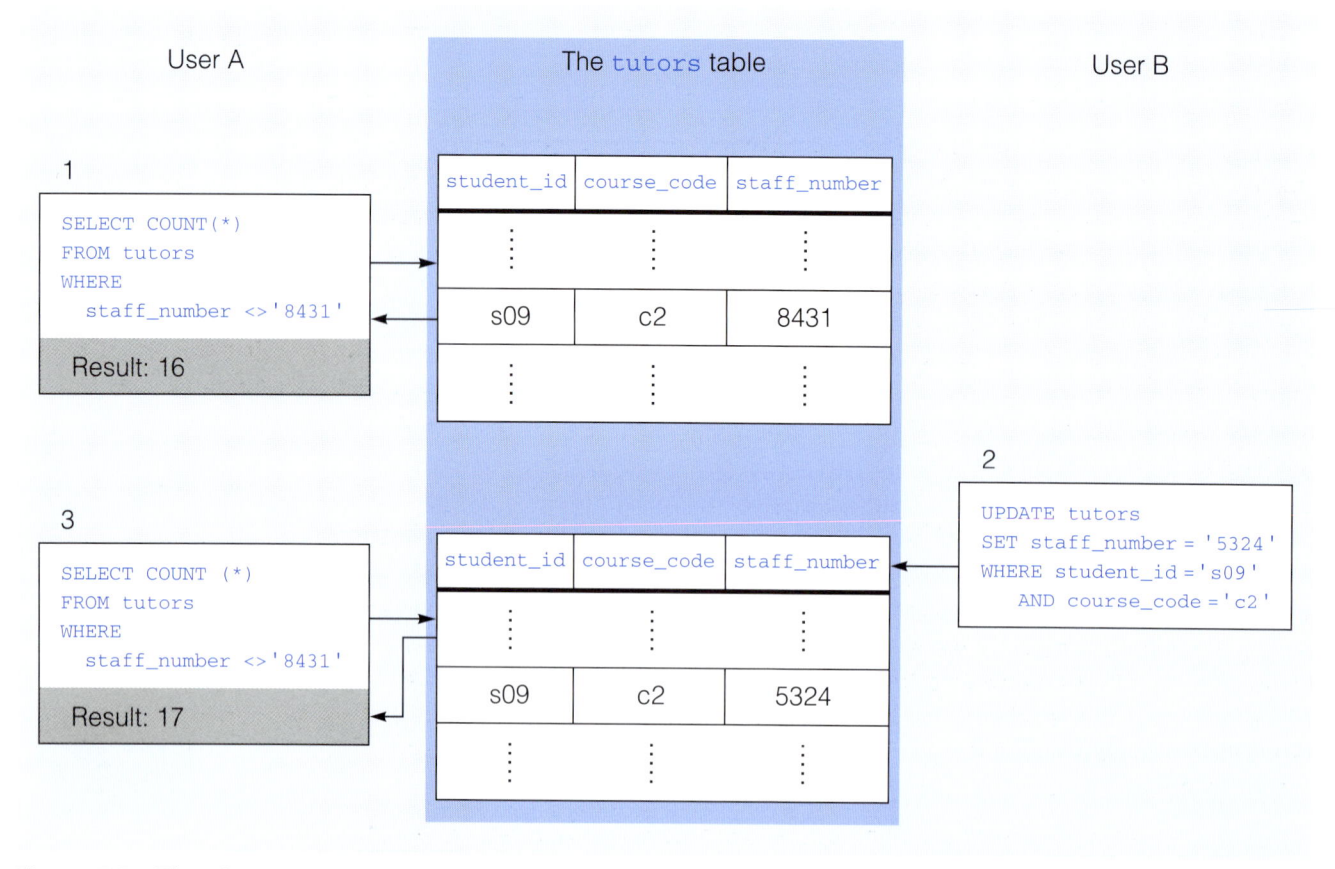

Figure 7.5 The phantom row problem

Serializable execution

Some of these problems can be partially addressed by restricting which transactions are allowed to run at the same time. The aim is to enable all transactions to be effectively isolated from other transactions, so that the effect of one transaction does not affect any others. Of course, this can only partially address the concurrent transaction problems, as once a transaction is complete, then another user may subsequently change or query the database. Users who share a database cannot expect the data to remain unchanged by other users if that is the way that they have decided to work. Isolation from other users' processes is possible only *within* a transaction.

A simplistic way for a DBMS to provide this isolation is to allow only one user to execute a transaction at a time. Only when one user's transaction has finished may another user's transaction start. This is known as **serialized execution** of transactions. However, this is not a practical solution for sharing a database because one long transaction would prevent all other users from accessing the data.

What is needed is for a DBMS to provide the isolation *equivalent* to serialized execution while executing the transactions concurrently. If this degree of isolation can be achieved, we say that the execution of the concurrent transactions is **serializable**. In a serializable execution, each transaction can execute to completion as if it were the only transaction executing in the database. This does not mean that the DBMS actually processes the transactions sequentially, rather that the result of the processing is the same *as if* the transactions had been processed sequentially. There may be several ways of achieving such a result.

EXERCISE 7.13

Explain why it is possible for two DBMSs to give different results for the serializable execution of the same set of transactions.

As an example of what is explained in the solution to Exercise 7.13, consider the situation described for the lost update problem illustrated in Figure 7.2. We could avoid the problem by making user A's statements transaction T1 and user B's statements transaction T2. Then either T1 would run to completion and then T2 would run to completion, or T2 would run to completion and then T1 would run to completion. Crucially, the update that the user expected is made at the end of each transaction (although the subsequent transaction may then make further changes). A serializable execution of these two transactions is free to choose the order as either T1 followed by T2 or T2 followed by T1. The end result, as far as the content of the database is concerned, is different in each case.

Locking and isolation levels

Implementing serializable execution of transactions involves **locking**. A DBMS processes a concurrent transaction by marking any data involved in the transaction as locked. If another transaction needs access to data that is locked (even just to read it), it is forced to wait until the locking transaction is completed and the data is released – that is, unlocked. This enables a DBMS to provide complete isolation for each transaction, and so, within a transaction, to overcome the concurrency problems described above.

However, this locking is very strict in the sense that once data is locked it cannot be accessed by another concurrent transaction in any way. Therefore, locking introduces a problem: a transaction may have to wait for some time before locked data is released and execution can continue. This problem can be alleviated to a certain extent by considering how the four problems of concurrency may affect transactions – some are not as serious as others. For some transactions, it is possible to relax the locking and allow a certain level of concurrent access to locked data and therefore avoid transactions having to wait unnecessarily.

The level of concurrent access for a transaction is determined by its **isolation level**. The highest level of isolation is known as **serializable isolation**, which guarantees serializable execution of a transaction. Lower isolation levels may result in one of the concurrency problems occurring, but generally allow quicker execution. The choice of isolation is a trade-off between accuracy of data and speed of execution. Note that none of the isolation levels allows a lost update to occur within a transaction. The table in Figure 7.6 gives the SQL isolation levels and the possible concurrency problems within transactions for each level.

Isolation level	Lost update	Reading uncommitted data	Non-repeatable read	Phantom rows
`SERIALIZABLE`	Not possible	Not possible	Not possible	Not possible
`REPEATABLE READ`	Not possible	Not possible	Not possible	Possible
`READ COMMITTED`	Not possible	Not possible	Possible	Possible
`READ UNCOMMITTED`	Not possible	Possible	Possible	Possible

Figure 7.6 Isolation levels and concurrency problems in SQL within transactions

The isolation level can be set for each transaction, and the SQL statement for this purpose has the format:

`SET TRANSACTION ISOLATION LEVEL <level>`

Note that the SQL Standard defines the behaviour of the different isolation levels, but different SQL implementations may implement the isolation levels differently.

EXERCISE 7.14

The default setting for the isolation level is 'serializable', which is what you get without using the `SET TRANSACTION ISOLATION LEVEL` statement. Explain the reason for using this statement at all, since all other levels give less isolation.

To conclude, transactions are an essential part of database management, and SQL provides `COMMIT` and `ROLLBACK` statements that allow transactions to be defined as atomic units of work. Furthermore, a DBMS must ensure that transactions are supported for both recovery (to guarantee the persistence of committed transactions) and concurrency (to guarantee appropriate levels of isolation for concurrent transactions).

7.6 Summary

In this section, you have seen how SQL can be used in various ways that are different from the direct, interactive execution of individual statements which you have used in previous sections of this block.

An SQL routine, either a function or a procedure, can be defined by a user to be stored as part of a database and executed as required. A routine can declare its own variables and, with SQL control statements, can express complex processing for a database. An **EXECUTE** privilege can be granted by the owner of a routine to other users, enabling them to use the routine to access data without having to be granted any privileges on the data itself. Cursors can be defined that allow a table to be processed one row at a time.

A trigger can be defined for a table, specifying an action which is fired whenever a specified updating event takes place. The trigger is owned by the owner of the table, who must have the appropriate privileges for that table, and any other tables used in the action. Triggers are used to maintain consistency in a database and to enforce dynamic constraints.

Transaction management involves the definition of a logical unit of work, a transaction, which is designed to ensure a database is left in a consistent state should an update fail for any reason. There are SQL statements for requesting DBMS action on either completing a successful transaction or recovering from a failed transaction. We have also discussed four problems that may arise in executing transactions concurrently, and examined how the notion of serializable execution prevents these problems within a transaction.

LEARNING OUTCOMES

Having completed this section, you should now be able to do the following:

▶ Describe the features of SQL routines in terms of how procedures and functions are defined, and how they are used.
▶ Explain the processing of an SQL routine.
▶ Define a procedure or function for simple requirements, and give appropriate test statements.
▶ Describe the role of cursors, and explain the way statements associated with their use are organised within an application program.
▶ Describe the features of triggers in terms of how they are defined and how they are used.
▶ Write SQL triggers to fire when tables are updated, and explain the processing of a trigger.
▶ Describe the notion of a transaction, explain how the statements **COMMIT** and **ROLLBACK** are used to define an SQL transaction, and use savepoints to control a transaction.
▶ Describe the potential problems of concurrent transactions, and explain how serializable execution and isolation levels at least partially resolve these problems.

Block summary

In this block, you have seen and used the SQL that you will need in the remainder of the course. Section 1 gave a brief overview and history of SQL. Sections 2 and 3 described the SQL necessary to extract data from an existing database, and Section 4 described the use of NULL to represent unknown data. Section 5 described the mechanisms for defining and populating tables, and Section 6 described the administrative mechanisms that allow a database to be used securely by multiple users. Finally, Section 7 described the control structures available in SQL that enable users to define their own functions and procedures, and to allow SQL to be embedded in external applications.

Solutions to Exercises

SOLUTION 1.1

(a) The different Standards are SQL:1987, SQL:1989, SQL:1992 (also known as SQL2), SQL:1999 and SQL:2003.

(b) One SQL implementation is SQL Anywhere. Another is Microsoft's Transact-SQL. The implementation of SQL used in Oracle's DBMS is just known as 'Oracle SQL'.

SOLUTION 2.1

This is a query expressed in English; the sentence states which table should be used to find the information that we are interested in.

SOLUTION 2.2

(a) `SELECT *`
    `FROM staff`

(b) `SELECT name, staff_number`
    `FROM staff`

(c) `SELECT DISTINCT staff_number, student_id`
    `FROM tutors`

For the logical processing model:

1. Processing the `FROM` clause results in an intermediate table which is the same as the `tutors` table.
2. Processing the `SELECT DISTINCT` clause copies the values from `staff_number` and `student_id` from each row in the intermediate table into a final table, excluding those rows that contain duplicate values.

Without `DISTINCT` there would be duplication of some values of `student_id` because a given student may have the same tutor for more than one course.

SOLUTION 2.3

```
SELECT patient_id, height/2.54 AS height_in,
       weight/6.35 AS weight_stone
FROM patient
```

SOLUTION 2.4

Find the average height-to-weight ratio of the patients in the `patient` table, in inches per pound.

SOLUTION 2.5

(a) The answer to the first query is 9.2, whereas the second query gives 9.5. This is because the second query ignores the duplicates in the `number_of_beds` column when the average is calculated.

To determine the average number of beds in the hospital wards we would, of course, use the first query. For this calculation, it makes no sense to exclude duplicate values in the `number_of_beds` column.

(b) The two value expressions in the `SELECT` clause do not return the same number of rows: `type`, a column name, results in the same number of rows as there are in `drug`, whereas `AVG(price)`, an aggregate function, results in a single value in a single row. (You are not yet expected to understand the details of the error message that this query generates.)

7 Solutions to Exercises

SOLUTION 2.6

The first query gives the answer 18 which, as you can see from the *Hospital Database Card* (or from the table in the database), is the number of names in the `patient_name` column of the `patient` table. The second query, however, results in the value 16, because only the number of distinct values is calculated. The repeated names, 'Boswell' and 'Harris', are each counted only once.

SOLUTION 2.7

(a) It would produce a table containing a single column, displayed as `MAX(drug.price)`, containing the single value 1.05.

(b) The result would be a table containing a single column, displayed as `MIN(drug.price)`, containing the single value 0.01.

Of course, we would generally rename the columns to, for example, `max_price` and `min_price`.

SOLUTION 2.8

Aggregate functions apply a function to all the values in a column and produce a single result. Other (non-aggregating) functions apply that function to every value in a column and produce a result for every applicable row.

SOLUTION 2.9

The `name` column used in the condition of the `WHERE` clause in the **where_Jennings** query is not specified in the `SELECT` clause. If the `SELECT` clause were processed before the `WHERE` clause, the column needed to determine which rows are required would not be available in the intermediate table. The data required by the condition in the `WHERE` clause would not then be available.

SOLUTION 2.10

(a) It is not a well-formed query because an aggregate function cannot be used in a `WHERE` clause. Note that if you attempt to run the filed statement **above_avg**, the displayed message indicates that the error could have occurred in one of two possible situations: one is the `WHERE` clause in this query, the other is an `UPDATE` statement.

(b) Given your present knowledge of SQL, you will need to formulate two queries to obtain the required answer. First, find the average mark as follows:

`SELECT AVG(mark) AS average_mark`
`FROM assignment`

average_mark

Then, use the answer obtained in a second query based on **above_avg**, replacing `AVG(mark)` in the `WHERE` clause with the actual value, which is the result of the first query.

SOLUTION 2.11

`SELECT AVG(height/weight) AS avg_hw_ratio`
`FROM patient`
`WHERE gender = 'M'`

SOLUTION 2.12

Using the same reasoning:

p89: Condition (1) is TRUE because `gender` is equal to 'F'.

Condition (2) is FALSE because `height` is not less than 160 and `weight` is not greater than 60.

So without checking the third condition, we know that the search condition evaluates to FALSE and this patient's data should not appear in the intermediate table that is produced after the **WHERE** clause is processed. Therefore this row will not appear in the final table.

SOLUTION 2.13

(a) `SELECT name, address, email_address, registration_date`
   `FROM student`
   `WHERE name = 'ellis' OR name = 'reeves'`

Remember that the databases that you are using are not case sensitive; for example, you could also use 'Ellis'.

(b) `SELECT DISTINCT student_id, course_code`
   `FROM assignment`
   `WHERE mark >= 70 AND course_code <> 'c4'`

An alternative way of expressing the second part of the search condition in the **WHERE** clause would be **NOT** `course_code = 'c4'`. Also note that students could have more than one mark for each course, so duplicate rows in the final table should be prevented by including **DISTINCT**.

SOLUTION 2.14

(a) `WHERE quantity >= 50 AND quantity <= 100`

(b) `SELECT staff_no, nurse_name`
   `FROM nurse`
   `WHERE nurse_name BETWEEN 'Descartes' AND 'Sesonske'`

(c) `WHERE patient_id NOT IN ('p37', 'p78', 'p87')`

(d) `SELECT student_id, course_code`
   `FROM examination`
   `WHERE examination_location IN ('Bedford', 'Taunton', 'Bath')`

(e) The most directly comparable form of the clause is:
   `WHERE examination_location = 'Bedford'`
   `   OR examination_location = 'Taunton'`
   `   OR examination_location = 'Bath'`

SOLUTION 2.15

(a) Maher and Monroe.

(b) The character string 't' does not match with **LIKE** `'s%'`, otherwise the same set of strings satisfy both conditions.

SOLUTION 2.16

(a) `SELECT drug_name`
   `FROM drug`
   `WHERE drug_code LIKE 'P%'`

(b) `SELECT ward_no, ward_name`
   `FROM ward`
   `WHERE ward_name LIKE '%a%'`

SOLUTION 2.17

(a) `small_ward.ward_no` and `small_occupied_by.ward_no`.

(b) `small_ward.ward_no = small_occupied_by.ward_no`

(c) `SELECT patient_id, small_ward.ward_no, ward_name`
   `FROM small_occupied_by, small_ward`
   `WHERE small_occupied_by.ward_no = small_ward.ward_no`

Note that only the potentially ambiguous column names have been qualified.

7 Solutions to Exercises

SOLUTION 2.18

(a) One possible solution is as follows, but you may have expressed the **WHERE** clause differently.

```
SELECT student_id, course_code
FROM tutors
WHERE staff_number IN ('3158', '8431')
```

(b) Using our answer from part (a) as the basis, the query can be modified as follows:

```
SELECT student.student_id, name, course_code
FROM student, tutors
WHERE student.student_id = tutors.student_id
  AND staff_number IN ('3158', '8431')
```

The join condition is:

```
student.student_id = tutors.student_id
```

Note that there is a column named **student_id** in both the **student** and **tutors** tables; so we need to use the qualified column name **student.student_id** in the **SELECT** clause.

SOLUTION 2.19

(a) $10 \times 20 = 200$.

(b) A join condition imposes a condition on those columns which represent a relationship between the tables being joined so that only those rows satisfying the condition appear in the final table.

SOLUTION 2.20

(a)
```
SELECT student.name, student.address, staff.name, staff.address
FROM student, staff, tutors
WHERE student.student_id = tutors.student_id
  AND staff.staff_number = tutors.staff_number
```

(b)
```
SELECT s1.name, s1.address, s2.name, s2.address
FROM student s1, staff s2, tutors t
WHERE s1.student_id = t.student_id
  AND s2.staff_number = t.staff_number
```

Your aliases may, of course, be different from ours.

SOLUTION 2.21

(a) Staff members 153 and 424 both have the name 'Cooke'.

(b) You probably scanned down the printed page and compared the name in each row with every other row.

SOLUTION 2.22

```
SELECT f1.name
FROM floor_staff f1, floor_staff f2
WHERE f1.staff_no = f2.supervisor_no
  AND f2.staff_no = '345'
```

SOLUTION 2.23

```
SELECT f1.name
FROM floor_staff f1 INNER JOIN floor_staff f2
  ON f1.staff_no = f2.supervisor_no
WHERE f2.staff_no = '345'
```

SOLUTION 2.24

```
SELECT prescription_no, reason
FROM treatment NATURAL JOIN prescription
```

Note that all three of the columns `staff_no`, `patient_id` and `start_date` are matched.

SOLUTION 2.25

It is not possible, given what you have learned so far, to answer this request using one query. Because the University database currently contains information about five regions, five queries are necessary, one for each region. For example, for region 1 you would use the query:

```
SELECT COUNT(*) AS students_in_region_1
FROM student
WHERE region_number = '1'
```

Similar queries would be required for each of the other regions, replacing '1' with '2', '3', '4' and '12'.

SOUTION 2.26

(a) **group1** is well formed because every column in the `SELECT` clause either appears in the `GROUP BY` clause or has an aggregate function applied to it.

(b) **group2** is not well formed because a column, `drug_name`, appears in the `SELECT` clause which neither has an aggregate function applied to it nor appears in the `GROUP BY` clause.

(c) **group3** is well formed, because every column in the `SELECT` clause either appears in the `GROUP BY` clause or has an aggregate function applied to it.

An error message is produced if you run **group2**.

SOLUTION 2.27

Sequence of clauses as written:	Sequence of clauses as logically processed:
1 SELECT	1 FROM
2 FROM	2 WHERE
3 WHERE	3 GROUP BY
4 GROUP BY	4 SELECT

SOLUTION 2.28

(a) You should check your own answer by running **group_prod**.

(b)
```
SELECT ward_no, COUNT(patient_id) AS occupying
FROM patient
WHERE ward_no NOT IN ('w5', 'w7')
GROUP BY ward_no
```

SOLUTION 2.29

```
SELECT course_code, COUNT(student_id) AS number
FROM enrolment
GROUP BY course_code
HAVING course_code IN ('c2', 'c4')
```

7 Solutions to Exercises

SOLUTION 2.30

Columns referenced in the search condition must either be grouping columns or have an aggregate function applied to them.

SOLUTION 2.31

(a) **having1** is not well formed because the `HAVING` clause refers to a column, `drug_code`, which neither has an aggregate function applied to it nor is a grouping column.

(b) **having2** is not well formed because the `WHERE` clause contains an aggregate function, `MAX(drug_name)`. Such functions cannot be used at the row level.

(c) **having3** is not well formed because the `WHERE` and `GROUP BY` clauses have been written in the wrong order. Otherwise, all the individual clauses are well formed (as you could confirm by correcting the order and running the amended query).

SOLUTION 2.32

(a) `SELECT patient_id, COUNT(prescription_no) AS prescription_count,`
`        MIN(start_date) AS earliest_prescription`
`FROM prescription`
`GROUP BY patient_id`
`HAVING COUNT(prescription_no) > 1`

An alternative version of the last line is:

`HAVING NOT (COUNT(prescription_no) <= 1)`

(b) Add the following clause between the `FROM` clause and the `GROUP BY` clause in part (a):

`WHERE staff_no <> '462'`

It is incorrect to place this condition in the `HAVING` clause because the column `staff_no` neither is referred to in the `GROUP BY` clause, nor has an aggregate function applied to it.

(c) One way is to amend the following clause between the `FROM` clause and the `GROUP BY` clause in part (a):

`WHERE patient_id <> 'p39'`

Another way is to amend the `HAVING` clause to:

`HAVING COUNT(prescription_no) > 1`
`   AND patient_id <> 'p39'`

This is possible because `patient_id` is a grouping column.

SOLUTION 2.33

Give the **drug** table, excluding the data for the drug named 'Placebo', sorted according to **type**, in *ascending* order, and then **price**, in *descending* order.

Note that the parameter `DESC` applies only to the column name that it immediately follows (in this case, **price**); the column **type** is sorted in the default, ascending order.

SOLUTION 2.34

If several different drugs have the same type and price, then declaring an order on **drug_name** may affect the presentation of the table, because without the appearance of **drug_name** in the `ORDER BY` clause, the order in which the data is returned is not defined.

SOLUTION 2.35

(a) `FROM assignment`

(b) The whole of the `assignment` table.

SOLUTION 2.36

```
WHERE course_code NOT IN ('c4', 'c7')
   AND assignment_number <> '3'
```

Note that `assignment_number` is implemented as `VARCHAR`, so single quotes are used in the `WHERE` condition.

SOLUTION 2.37

```
SELECT *
FROM assignment
WHERE course_code NOT IN ('c4', 'c7')
   AND assignment_number <> '3'
```

SOLUTION 2.38

(a) It needs to be divided into *groups* based on the values of `course_code`, as shown in Figure 2.17.

(b) `GROUP BY course_code`

SOLUTION 2.39

(a) The rows of each group need to be grouped according to student identification numbers.

(b) `GROUP BY course_code, student_id`

SOLUTION 2.40

(a) `HAVING AVG(mark) > 70`

(b) It will eliminate all groups having an average mark less than or equal to 70, as shown in Figure 2.19.

SOLUTION 2.41

(a) The request asks: 'For each course ..., list those students whose average mark .... Also, list the average marks for these students.' So we need three columns: one for the course code, one for each student who satisfies the average mark requirement, and one for each student's average mark.

`SELECT course_code, student_id, AVG(mark) AS avg_mark`

construct1

(b) The processing of the `SELECT` clause will condense the intermediate table to that shown in Figure 2.20, by eliminating the column `assignment_number` and combining the individual marks within each group to give an average mark.

SOLUTION 2.42

```
SELECT course_code, student_id, AVG(mark) AS avg_mark
FROM assignment
WHERE course_code NOT IN ('c4', 'c7')
   AND assignment_number <> '3'
GROUP BY course_code, student_id
HAVING AVG(mark) > 70
```

construct

7 Solutions to Exercises

SOLUTION 2.43

```
SELECT course_code, staff_number,
       COUNT(student_id) AS number_tutored
FROM tutors
WHERE staff_number IN ('5324', '8431')
GROUP BY course_code, staff_number
HAVING COUNT(student_id) >= 2
```

SOLUTION 3.1

(a) Because **height** in the **patient** table is a DECIMAL(4, 1), and 'Unknown' is a string constant, the tables generated by the two query specifications are not union compatible.

(b) Use a cast to convert the values in **height** to strings:

```
SELECT patient_name, CAST(height AS VARCHAR(4))
FROM patient
UNION
SELECT nurse_name, 'Unknown'
FROM nurse
```

SOLUTION 3.2

(a) **except2** is well formed. This query could be used to answer the request:

> What are the staff numbers of the nurses who do not supervise other nurses in the hospital?

union4 is well formed because **prescription_no** and **ward_name** are both string types (implemented in SQL as VARCHAR), and **quantity** and **number_of_beds** are both of type INTEGER, so the results of the query specifications are union compatible. However, the columns of the tables are meaningless; it makes no sense to combine the number of beds in a ward with the quantity of dosages on a prescription.

(b)
```
SELECT *
FROM drug
WHERE type IN ('Painkiller', 'Antibiotic', 'Sedative')
```

(c)
```
SELECT student_id, assignment_number AS assessment_number, mark
FROM assignment
WHERE course_code = 'c4'
UNION
SELECT student_id, '99', mark
FROM examination
WHERE course_code = 'c4'
```

Note the use of the constant **99** in the above SELECT clause, which is a valid string expression. The term AS assessment_number has been included to provide a column heading that is not specific either to an assignment or to the examination.

(d)
```
SELECT a.student_id, name,
       assignment_number AS assessment_number, mark
FROM assignment a, student s
WHERE a.student_id = s.student_id
  AND course_code = 'c4'
UNION
SELECT e.student_id, name, '99', mark
FROM examination e, student s
WHERE e.student_id = s.student_id
  AND course_code = 'c4'
```

SOLUTION 3.3

`INTERSECT` is commutative. Because the table generated by `INTERSECT` contains the rows that are common to both tables, the order in which the tables are presented to `INTERSECT` does not matter.

`EXCEPT` is not commutative. For example, consider the following two tables, `t1` and `t2`:

t1

a
1
2
3

t2

a
2
3
4

If these two tables were in the database, then the query

```
SELECT a
FROM t1
EXCEPT
SELECT a
FROM t2
```

would return

a
1

and the query

```
SELECT a
FROM t2
EXCEPT
SELECT a
FROM t1
```

would return a different table:

a
4

SOLUTION 3.4

It does not answer the request because it is not well formed – an aggregate function is not allowed in the search condition of a `WHERE` clause.

SOLUTION 3.5

First, a query is needed to find the average weight of the male patients.

```
SELECT AVG(weight) AS avg_weight
FROM patient
WHERE gender = 'M'
```

weight1

7 Solutions to Exercises

This produces a table which has just one row and one column, containing the value 75.95. This value can now be used in the second query as follows.

```
SELECT patient_id, patient_name
FROM patient
WHERE gender = 'M' AND weight < 75.95
```

weight2

The final table has five rows, which contain the identifiers and names of those male patients whose weight is lower than 75.95 kg.

SOLUTION 3.6

(a) A correlated subquery has a search condition containing one or more references to a column or columns in its outer, main query.

(b) A correlated subquery has to be evaluated for every row of the appropriate intermediate table in the main query, whereas an ordinary subquery is evaluated only once – at the start of the processing.

SOLUTION 3.7

(a)
```
SELECT drug_name, type, price
FROM drug p
WHERE price = (SELECT MIN(price)
               FROM drug q
               WHERE p.type = q.type)
```

(b) The subquery is evaluated 12 times because the **drug** table has 12 rows and the subquery is evaluated for every row in the main query. There are five different types of drug in the **drug** table, so the subquery processes a different product on only five occasions, with some evaluations being repeated.

SOLUTION 3.8

The subquery results in the set consisting of all four distinct values in the **number_of_beds** column.

SOLUTION 3.9

The only value in the **ward** table that satisfies this condition is the value 6, that is, the smallest of the values in the **number_of_beds** column, since it is equal to the smallest and less than all the rest.

SOLUTION 3.10

From Exercise 3.9, it is clear that the query returns a table which contains those rows that have the smallest number of beds. In other words, it *lists the names of wards which contain the smallest number of beds*. Even though the name of just one ward is displayed, in principle there could be many names resulting from this query.

SOLUTION 3.11

Another way is as follows.

```
SELECT ward_name
FROM ward
WHERE number_of_beds = (SELECT MIN(number_of_beds)
                        FROM ward)
```

SOLUTION 3.12

(a) From the *University Database Card*, it can be seen that the `enrolment` table contains all the information required, so this is the only table that will be used in the query.

(b) The `FROM` clause is:

```
FROM enrolment
```

(c) In the request, there are no apparent exclusions as far as the individual rows of the table are concerned. Therefore, there is no need for a `WHERE` clause.

(d) `GROUP BY course_code`

The phrase 'number of' in the request should alert you to the need for a `GROUP BY` clause. The fact that the request specifies that a course code is required should indicate to you that `course_code` should be the grouping column.

(e) The word 'largest', in association with 'number of students', points to a comparison based on an aggregate function applied to the groups, and therefore the need for a `HAVING` clause. In its simplest form, the search condition must express the condition that the count of the students in the required course group is the largest of this count for each of the course groups, that is, the group to be chosen has a count that is larger than or equal to all of the other counts.

(f)
```
SELECT COUNT(student_id)
FROM enrolment
GROUP BY course_code
```

(g) An appropriate `HAVING` clause can be written as follows.

```
HAVING COUNT(student_id) >= ALL (SELECT COUNT(student_id)
                                 FROM enrolment
                                 GROUP BY course_code)
```

In this clause, we again use the quantifier `ALL` to express the condition that the value of the left-hand expression must be greater than or equal to *every* value in the list returned by the subquery.

(h) The query states that we require the course code and the number of students, so the `SELECT` clause should be (using the `AS` keyword to give the columns meaningful names):

```
SELECT course_code, COUNT(student_id) AS num_students
```

(i)
```
SELECT course_code, COUNT(student_id) AS num_students
FROM enrolment
GROUP BY course_code
HAVING COUNT(student_id) >= ALL (SELECT COUNT(student_id)
                                 FROM enrolment
                                 GROUP BY course_code)
```

all2

SOLUTION 3.13

(a) **any1** is not well formed because the subquery results in two columns of data.

(b) **any2** is well formed, and answers the request to find the staff numbers of all the doctors whose name is the same as their `position` in the `doctor` table. When you run this query you will find there are no doctors that satisfy this condition.

SOLUTION 3.14

A query that could be used is:

```
SELECT patient_id, patient_name
FROM patient
WHERE ward_no IN (SELECT ward_no
                  FROM nurse
                  WHERE nurse_name = patient_name)
```

SOLUTION 3.15

What are the student identification numbers and names of all the students who are registered, but have not enrolled on any course.

SOLUTION 3.16

(a) List the student identification numbers and the names of all the students who are enrolled on at least one course.

(b) The following query uses a join:

```
SELECT DISTINCT s.student_id, name
FROM student s, enrolment e
WHERE s.student_id = e.student_id
```

Another possibility is to use a subquery:

```
SELECT student_id, name
FROM student
WHERE student_id IN (SELECT student_id
                     FROM enrolment)
```

(c) One possible solution is:

```
SELECT staff_number, region_number
FROM staff s
WHERE EXISTS (SELECT *
              FROM tutors t
              WHERE t.staff_number = s.staff_number)
```

SOLUTION 3.17

(a) Using a join, the query is:

```
SELECT DISTINCT title, credit
FROM course c, enrolment e
WHERE c.course_code = e.course_code
  AND student_id = 's05'
```

Aliases have been used to save typing. Using NATURAL JOIN, the query is:

```
SELECT DISTINCT title, credit
FROM course NATURAL JOIN enrolment
WHERE student_id = 's05'
```

(b) Using a subquery, the query is:

```
SELECT DISTINCT title, credit
FROM course
WHERE course_code = ANY (SELECT course_code
                         FROM enrolment
                         WHERE student_id = 's05')
```

In these cases, DISTINCT is not essential because the rows of the final table come from the course table which does not contain duplicates. However, it is good practice to include DISTINCT because duplication may occur with different base tables.

SOLUTION 3.18

```
SELECT student_id, course_code, mark
FROM assignment
WHERE mark > (SELECT AVG(mark) AS average_mark
              FROM assignment)
```

SOLUTION 3.19

The only difference between the processing of **nested_above_avg** and the previous examples is that the nested query must be processed first, and the result is then used as the input to the main `FROM` clause. The processing steps are as follows.

▶ First, the nested query

```
SELECT AVG(mark) AS average_mark
FROM assignment
```

is processed according to the model in Section 2, Figure 2.7. Processing the `FROM` clause copies the `assignment` table into an intermediate table. Then processing the `SELECT` clause evaluates the `AVG` function to produce a final table with a single value in a column named `average_mark`. This table is named `a1`.

▶ Next, the main query

```
SELECT student_id, course_code, mark
FROM a1, assignment
WHERE mark > average_mark
```

is processed according to the model in Section 2, Figure 2.12. The initial specified tables are `a1` and `assignment`. Processing the `FROM` clause creates an intermediate table containing the Cartesian product of `a1` and `assignment`. Next, processing the `WHERE` clause copies all those rows for which `mark` is greater than `average_mark` into a further intermediate table. Finally, the `SELECT` clause copies the `student_id`, `course_code` and `mark` columns of this intermediate table into the final table.

SOLUTION 3.20

(a) **nested1** is not well formed; there is an aggregate function (`MAX(mark)`) in a `WHERE` clause. Aggregate functions cannot be used in conditions that are applied to rows.

(b) **nested2** is not well formed because the table returned by the nested query has not been named with `AS`. This naming is necessary, even if the name of the table is not used in the rest of the query.

(c) **nested3** is well formed, and answers the request:

What are the staff numbers and names of the members of staff who tutor, and how many courses do they tutor?

(d) **nested4** is not well formed because the outer `SELECT` clause makes reference to the `course_code` column in `c1`. However, the table returned by the nested query has columns named `code` and `title`, and therefore the expression `c1.course_code` does not refer to an existing column.

SOLUTION 3.21

(a)
```
SELECT staff_no, COUNT(*) AS patient_numbers
FROM patient
GROUP BY staff_no
```

(b) ```
SELECT d.staff_no, doctor_name, patient_numbers
FROM (SELECT staff_no, COUNT(*) AS patient_numbers
      FROM patient
      GROUP BY staff_no) AS p, doctor d
WHERE p.staff_no = d.staff_no
  AND patient_numbers >= 6
```
number_of_patients

## SOLUTION 3.22

The following query returns a table that lists each patient's identifier, the number of prescriptions written for him/her, and the date of the earliest of those prescriptions.

```
SELECT patient_id, COUNT(prescription_no) AS prescription_count,
       MIN(start_date) AS earliest_prescription
FROM prescription
GROUP BY patient_id
```

To obtain the rows of this table for which the column **prescription_count** has a value greater than 1, use the above query as a subquery, and put the appropriate condition in the **WHERE** clause.

```
SELECT *
FROM (SELECT patient_id,
             COUNT(prescription_no) AS prescription_count,
             MIN(start_date) AS earliest_prescription
      FROM prescription
      GROUP BY patient_id) AS t
WHERE prescription_count > 1
```

SOLUTION 3.23

(a) ```
SELECT gender, AVG(weight) AS avg_weight
FROM patient
GROUP BY gender
```

(b) ```
SELECT patient_id, patient.gender, weight
FROM (SELECT gender, AVG(weight) AS avg_weight
      FROM patient
      GROUP BY gender) AS p, patient
WHERE patient.gender = p.gender
  AND weight > 1.1 * avg_weight
```

Note that in this case, the join condition (**patient.gender = p.gender**) requires that **gender** be qualified for both tables, **p** and **patient**.

## SOLUTION 4.1

The first query returns a table containing the row <c2, 3> which shows the number of students who took an examination for the course c2. However, the second query contains the row <c2, 2> because the **mark** column is NULL for the student s22. As described in the definitions of the aggregate functions, the NULL is not counted by the **COUNT** function.

## SOLUTION 4.2

(a) The numerical expression **(sell – buy)** evaluates to NULL for the row in which the value of **sell** is NULL. Therefore, the entry for **buy** in that row (i.e. 1.85) is not included in the final summation for the first query. However, because the values of **buy** and **sell** are summed separately in the second query, this value *is* included in the calculation for the second query.
```

(b) Remember that any `AND` clause containing a FALSE subexpression evaluates to FALSE, even if the other subexpression evaluates to UNKNOWN. The final table generated is:

transaction	buy	sell	manufacturer
00210	2.50	4.00	(NULL)
00402	2.15	3.50	misto

(c) In the first case, the table returned by the query is the same as the `stock` table and contains four rows of data. In the second case, the table contains only those rows for which the `WHERE` condition evaluates to TRUE. These are the rows for which `manufacturer = 'misto'` is TRUE, or for which `manufacturer <> 'misto'` is TRUE. However, when an entry for `manufacturer` is NULL, both the expressions `manufacturer = 'misto'` and `manufacturer <> 'misto'` evaluate to UNKNOWN, and so the `OR` clause also evaluates to UNKNOWN. Therefore, the row with transaction code 00210 does not appear in the table generated by the second query.

SOLUTION 4.3

There are several ways of solving this problem, but a reasonably tidy solution is to perform a union between the non-NULL values and a table where the column containing NULL is replaced with the required default.

```
SELECT *
FROM student
WHERE address IS NOT NULL
UNION
SELECT student_id, name, 'Unavailable', email_address,
       registration_date, region_number
FROM student
WHERE address IS NULL
```

SOLUTION 4.4

```
SELECT e1.student_id, e1.course_code, mark
FROM enrolment e1 LEFT OUTER JOIN examination e2
  ON e1.student_id = e2.student_id
    AND e1.course_code = e2.course_code
```

SOLUTION 4.5

While we have stated that primary keys may not contain NULL, we have not discussed whether alternate keys may or may not contain NULL. Clearly, one or more columns in a table that is/are defined as an alternate key must have distinct values otherwise the key would not distinguish different rows. In this situation, a NULL could be assumed to mean 'an unknown value, that is different from any of the existing values', and the values of that column constrained to either all be different or be NULL.

However, such an understanding of NULL in an alternate key would make it difficult to decide whether referential integrity was being maintained. In these circumstances, referential integrity is maintained by insisting that values in the foreign key must also exist explicitly in the referenced table's key.

Some experts think that a better policy is not to allow values in an alternate key to be NULL either. Then the values of the alternate key genuinely identify distinct rows of the table.

7 Solutions to Exercises

SOLUTION 5.1

The existing table could have some data stored in it, and the data would be lost if the new definition replaced the existing one because the existing data cannot be expected to be compatible with the new definition.

SOLUTION 5.2

We would probably represent a telephone number using **CHAR(12)**. As with the book codes, applying mathematical functions to telephone numbers does not yield meaningful results, and so we would probably not use a numerical data type. Furthermore, using **CHAR(12)** allows leading zeros to be represented. (When SQL displays values of type **INTEGER**, any leading zeros are not shown.) However, as with any design decision, the final choice rests with the database designer.

SOLUTION 5.3

(a) A row is added with **bookcode** = '93881', **title** = 'Farmer, S.J.', **author_name** = 'Advances in Pragmati', **no_pages** = NULL, **course_code** = 'c7'.

Although the values of **author_name** and **title** are given in the incorrect order, no error is generated as they are both **VARCHAR**s, and so can be any string value. However, the title is truncated to 20 characters, which is the maximum allowed for entries in the **author_name** column.

(b) The statement generates an error: **no_pages** is defined as an **INTEGER**, and the string 'Jane Hanley' cannot be converted to an integer.

(c) The statement generates an error. No value has been provided for the column **title**, and so the default value is NULL (as no other is specified in the definition of **textbook**). However, as the definition of **textbook** states that **title** is NOT NULL, an error is generated.

SOLUTION 5.4

An **INSERT** statement for a table must include all columns of the table which are either defined as **NOT NULL** or declared as part of the primary key.

SOLUTION 5.5

The rows to be deleted are specified by means of a **WHERE** clause, which specifies the conditions that a row must satisfy before it is deleted. However, if there is no **WHERE** clause, then *all* the rows in the table are deleted.

SOLUTION 5.6

(a) **DELETE FROM textbook**
    WHERE no_pages < 250

(b) **DELETE FROM textbook**

SOLUTION 5.7

(a) (i) The **INSERT** succeeds by putting a copy of the drug name into the **patient_id** column and the price into the **name** column and **height** column. The name of the drug is truncated to three characters; note that if two drugs were to start with the same three letters, this would violate the uniqueness of the primary key.

(ii) The **INSERT** fails; because several nurses work on each ward, the primary key uniqueness constraint is violated. The presence of NULL does not affect the answer; this column has not been defined as **NOT NULL**.

Both these statements illustrate that data may be copied between tables although the resulting tables do not necessarily contain meaningful values.

(b) ```
INSERT INTO tmp_patient
    SELECT patient_id, patient_name, height
    FROM patient
    WHERE ward_no IN (SELECT ward_no
                      FROM ward
                      WHERE number_of_beds >= 10)
```

## SOLUTION 5.8

```
UPDATE textbook
  SET no_pages = no_pages + 5
  WHERE course_code = 'c2'
```

SOLUTION 5.9

INSERT or **UPDATE** statements may be prevented for certain values if the constraint which has been defined is violated. **DELETE** statements will not be affected, as deleting a row cannot introduce a violation of a unique constraint.

SOLUTION 5.10

(a) This statement will succeed as there exists a row in **course** for which **course_code** is c5.

(b) This statement will fail, as there is no row in **course** for which **course_code** is c3.

(c) This statement will fail. Although foreign keys may be NULL in general, in this case, the table explicitly defines this column as not NULL.

SOLUTION 5.11

SET NULL is not appropriate because the textbooks are associated with specific courses. In fact, using **SET NULL** would be incorrect according to the conceptual model, because only textbooks that are used on a course are recorded. The **NOT NULL** is used to enforce the mandatory participation condition of **textbook** in the relationship.

CASCADE would be appropriate because removing a course would mean that the textbooks associated with that course should also be removed.

SET DEFAULT would not be appropriate. The participation conditions state that each textbook must be associated with just one course, and there is no 'default' course with which an arbitrary textbook could be associated.

RESTRICT could be an appropriate choice if we needed to retain textbooks in the database for reasons other than their association with courses. As we do not currently have any such reasons, using **CASCADE** provides a neater solution.

Note that as this is a question about the most *appropriate* solution, these arguments are not necessarily hard and fast. As with the development of any complex software system, where there is no clear answer, the developer may need to take any decisions (such as whether to use **CASCADE** or **RESTRICT**) back to the customer.

SOLUTION 5.12

One solution is:

```
CREATE TABLE textbook (
  ...
  title VARCHAR(40),
  ...
  CONSTRAINT title_is_not_null
    CHECK (title IS NOT NULL) )
```
```

7 Solutions to Exercises

SOLUTION 5.13

One solution is:

```
CONSTRAINT max_5_textbooks
   CHECK (5 >= ALL (SELECT COUNT(*)
                    FROM textbook
                    GROUP BY course_code) )
```

SOLUTION 5.14

A possible solution is:

```
CREATE DOMAIN bookcodes AS CHAR(5)
   CHECK (CAST(VALUE AS INTEGER) BETWEEN 0 AND 99999)

CREATE DOMAIN book_titles AS VARCHAR(40)

CREATE DOMAIN author_names AS VARCHAR(20)

CREATE DOMAIN book_length AS INTEGER
   CHECK (VALUE BETWEEN 0 and 400)
```

We can then rewrite **table_creation** as:

```
CREATE TABLE textbook (
   bookcode bookcodes,
   title book_titles NOT NULL,
   author_name author_names DEFAULT 'None',
   no_pages book_length,
   course_code course_codes NOT NULL,
   PRIMARY KEY (bookcode),
   CONSTRAINT textbook_in_used_on
      FOREIGN KEY (course_code) REFERENCES course )
```

domain_table_creation

There are certain design decisions we have taken here. The **NOT NULL** and **DEFAULT** declarations have been left in the **CREATE TABLE** statement, rather than moved into the **CREATE DOMAIN** statements. This allows us, for example, to have book titles in different tables that are NULL, or tables that give a different default value for an author's name.

We have also defined a new domain **author_names**. In fact, the database already contains an existing domain **person_names**, which you were probably not aware of. We have used **person_names** to define the **student** and **staff** tables; in practice, we would probably choose to use this for the authors as well. You can find the definition of **person_names** (and the definitions of the **student** and **staff** tables) in the SQL script for the University database.

SOLUTION 5.15

▶ Change the name of a column; there is no need to change any data.

▶ Change the data type of a column; the representation of the data in that column must be changed to the new data type.

▶ Add a new column; there is no need to change any existing data but the new column must be assigned some value for each row (perhaps by default).

▶ Remove an existing column; the values in that column will be deleted.

You may also have included adding or removing constraints, such as **NOT NULL**, and setting default values.

SOLUTION 5.16

If a table is not empty, executing the **ALTER TABLE** statement requires the assignment of some value to the new column for each row. In the absence of a specified default value, the default is NULL, and so the not null constraint on the column will immediately cause the statement to fail.

SOLUTION 5.17

The **textbook** table is defined with a **printed_by** column referencing **printer**, as though **Textbook** had mandatory participation in **Prints**. Then any rows of the table that represent books that do not participate in the **Prints** relationship have NULL in the **printed_by** column.

SOLUTION 5.18

The foreign key column would also need to have a unique constraint defined on it. Then no two printers could print the same book.

SOLUTION 5.19

The definition of the printer business codes states that the first two characters are **PX**, followed by four digits. We will define a domain **printer_business_codes** for the business codes of printing companies as follows:

```
CREATE DOMAIN printer_business_codes AS CHAR(6)
   CHECK (SUBSTR(VALUE, 1, 2) = 'PX'
     AND (CAST(SUBSTR(VALUE, 3, 4) AS INT) BETWEEN 0 AND 9999))
```
codes_domain

Remember that in SQL Anywhere you need to use **@VALUE** rather than **VALUE**.

Although the domain **names** already exists in the SQL implementation of the model (for student names and staff names) we will use a different domain for business_names, to distinguish them from individuals' names. This is good practice in general, as it would not usually be sensible to compare the name of a person with the name of a business. The domain **business_names** is defined with the statement:

```
CREATE DOMAIN business_names AS VARCHAR(40)
```
business_name_domain

The selected length of 40 characters is an estimate; you may want a higher number if business names exceed this length.

SOLUTION 5.20

This solution uses the domain names that we proposed in the solution to Exercise 5.19; your answer may differ.

```
CREATE TABLE printer (
   business_code printer_business_codes,
   name business_names NOT NULL,
   address addresses,
   telephone_number telephone_numbers,
   PRIMARY KEY (business_code) )
```
create_printer_table

Our decision not to allow the name to be NULL reflects that UK businesses are required to register with a name, and so the name of a printing business should never be unknown. For this reason, we could equally well have chosen to add a not null constraint to the domain definition of **business_names**, rather than putting the constraint here. It is possible (though unlikely) that either the telephone number or the address of a printing business may be unknown (if, for example, the business is moving premises at some time), and we have allowed these fields to be NULL.

SOLUTION 5.21

```
INSERT INTO printer
  VALUES ('PX0348', 'Trent Press',
          '17 Ash Street, Nottingham, NG3 2XX ', '0115 586423')

INSERT INTO printer
  VALUES ('PX8453', 'Vaughn and sons',
          'Flintoff House, Manchester, M23 4QY ', '0186 646842')

INSERT INTO printer
  VALUES ('PX7129', 'Iliad Binding',
          '158 Pietersen Row, Vauxhall, London, SE11', '0178 352154')
```
printer_data

SOLUTION 5.22

We first define the new column:

```
ALTER TABLE textbook
  ADD printed_by printer_business_codes
```
printer_referring_column

We then add a constraint to the **textbook** table so that the **printed_by** column references (the primary key of) the **printer** table:

```
ALTER TABLE textbook
  ADD CONSTRAINT textbook_in_prints
    FOREIGN KEY (printed_by) REFERENCES printer
      ON DELETE SET NULL
```
printer_referring_constraint

We have chosen **SET NULL** as the referential action on deletion; this might be appropriate if NULL in this column is taken to show that the textbook was written for a course that no longer exists. However, other possibilities are plausible. We might decide that courses should not be removed from the database until any outstanding orders with external printers have been resolved, in which case **RESTRICT** might be a more appropriate referential action. In practice, a decision should be made in consultation with users of the database.

SOLUTION 5.23

(a) Use the two statements:

```
UPDATE textbook
  SET printed_by = 'PX0348'
  WHERE course_code = 'c2' OR course_code = 'c4'

UPDATE textbook
  SET printed_by = 'PX7129'
  WHERE course_code = 'c7'
```
update_printers

(b) For those rows in which the value of **course_code** is 'c5', the value of **printed_by** is NULL. We interpret this as meaning that an external printer is not used to print these textbooks, and therefore the University prints the textbooks for the logic course internally.

SOLUTION 5.24

There is a subtlety to this constraint; the requirement that the same printer prints all the textbooks for a course is violated if there are two rows in **textbook** which have the same value for **course_code**, but in the column **printed_by**:

▸ there are different values,

▸ or there is a value in one row, and NULL in another.

One possible solution is to use a quantifier (as you saw in Section 3.4):

```
ALTER TABLE textbook
  ADD CONSTRAINT same_printer
    CHECK (NOT EXISTS (SELECT *
                       FROM textbook a, textbook b
                       WHERE a.course_code = b.course_code
                         AND (a.printed_by <> b.printed_by
                          OR (a.printed_by IS NULL
                              AND b.printed_by IS NOT NULL) )))
```

same_printer_constraint

In this case (and for any complicated constraint), you should write down the logic of the constraint before trying to implement the SQL. When writing this constraint, it is easy to focus on the first condition (that there must not be different values in **printed_by** for books on the same course) while missing the second (that for any textbook, either all or none of the values for **printed_by** can be NULL).

SOLUTION 5.25

```
CREATE INDEX name_index ON student (name)
```

SOLUTION 5.26

If a column has a unique index, an **INSERT** or **UPDATE** statement that attempts to duplicate a value in that column will be unsuccessful, whereas the statement will be successful without the index. Therefore the result of processing such a statement is affected by the presence of the index (which is regarded as part of the storage schema), and so physical data independence is violated.

SOLUTION 6.1

(a) The tables **patient** and **ward**

(b) ```
SELECT patient_id, patient_name, ward_name
FROM patient p, ward w
WHERE p.ward_no = w.ward_no
```

**occupying2**

## SOLUTION 6.2

We write a query in the same way as if **occupying** were a base table:

```
SELECT ward_name, COUNT(*) AS occupancy
FROM occupying
GROUP BY ward_name
```

SOLUTION 6.3

The mapping from the view to the base tables is as follows.

▸ occupying.patient_id ↦ patient.patient_id

▸ occupying.patient_name ↦ patient.patient_name

▸ occupying.ward_name ↦ ward.ward_name
```

SOLUTION 6.4

```
SELECT s.student_id, s.name, c.name, course_code
FROM student s, staff c, tutors t
WHERE t.student_id = s.student_id
   AND t.staff_number = c.staff_number
```

SOLUTION 6.5

The view inherits all the column names of the **course** table, namely **course_code**, **title** and **credit** in that order.

Since no column list is specified for the view, its column names are inherited from the **SELECT** clause of the query specification. The asterisk in the **SELECT** clause includes all the columns in the table on which the view is based. Therefore, the view has the same column names as the table from which it is derived.

SOLUTION 6.6

(a)
```
SELECT course_code AS course, COUNT(*) AS students_per_course
FROM tutoring
GROUP BY course_code
```

(b)
```
CREATE VIEW course_numbers AS
    SELECT course_code AS course, COUNT(*) AS students_per_course
    FROM tutoring
    GROUP BY course_code
```

Note that, in defining this view (and any view), we must ensure that we have provided names for all the columns in the view. In this case, the default behaviour is that the view will inherit the names given in the **SELECT** clause of the query specification. So we have given a name to the column derived from **COUNT(*)** by using the **AS** keyword in the **SELECT** clause.

SOLUTION 6.7

There is no possible primary key in the table. We cannot use **student_id** as the primary key because there are rows which have the same entry in the **student_id** column (for example, the rows with value s02 in this column). However, while the values in the pair of columns (**student_id**, **course_code**) are unique, some rows contain NULL in the **course_code** column and so violate the entity integrity rule. This illustrates that a view is for displaying information rather than storing it.

SOLUTION 6.8

The insertion would fail. We might expect the **INSERT** statement to insert a row into **textbook**, the underlying base table. However, we have already seen that where values are missing (such as **course_code** here), they are replaced with NULL (or the default value, if one has been defined). But the definition of **textbook** defines **course_code** as **NOT NULL** and does not specify a default, and so this insertion will fail.

In fact, any **INSERT** of this type will fail if integrity constraints are violated. We cannot, for example, insert a row into a base table via a view that does not have a value for the table's primary key, or a row that leads to the table's primary key column containing duplicate values.

SOLUTION 6.9

The purpose of **DISTINCT** in a query is to ensure that there are no duplicate rows in the result, but in general, each row of the final table resulting from this process may correspond to many rows in some base table. In these circumstances, the requirement for updating cannot in general be satisfied. (Of course, some queries will not contain any duplicate rows, even if `DISTINCT` is not specified. For example, a query containing a primary key will have distinct rows whether or not `DISTINCT` is given in the `SELECT` clause.)

SOLUTION 6.10

First, a database administrator has to create an authorisation identifier for the user. Second, when the user wishes to access data in the database, he or she must provide the necessary authorisation identifier and authentication (for example, by means of a password).

SOLUTION 6.11

You are not allowed to create a table with the same name as an existing table, so the statement **create_student** would not succeed. Note that this is because a table called `student` already exists for user `m359`. A database can contain two tables such as `m359.student` and `admin.student`, where different users have created the tables.

SOLUTION 6.12

(a) `m359.student.name` and `m359.staff.name`.

(b) In the same way, except that the prefix `m359` may be omitted.

SOLUTION 6.13

Qualification of a column name by a table name (or alias) is necessary only when the column name is not unique among the tables included in the SQL statement. Qualification of a table name by a schema name is necessary only when the table is owned by another user. If these conditions do not apply, the use of the qualifications is optional.

SOLUTION 6.14

The base table would be referred to as `m359.student` and the view as `admin.student`.

SOLUTION 6.15

The constraint prevents the table `bill.t_bill` containing more rows than the table `fred.t_fred`. So `bill` cannot insert rows to his own table `t_bill` if that insertion would result in the table `bill.t_bill` containing more rows than the table `fred.t_fred`. Of course, `fred` is also prevented from deleting rows from his table `fred.t_fred` if that would result in the table containing fewer rows than the table `bill.t_bill`.

SOLUTION 6.16

    GRANT SELECT ON enrolment TO admin
    GRANT SELECT ON quota TO admin

These privileges must be granted by the owner of the tables, namely user `m359` in this example.

SOLUTION 6.17

    GRANT ALL PRIVILEGES ON textbook TO admin, clerk, faculty
    REVOKE DELETE ON textbook FROM clerk

There is an alternative approach which grants all privileges to users `admin` and `faculty`, and separately grants the three required privileges to user `clerk`. This solution demonstrates that a single privilege granted to a user for a given table can be granted or revoked separately from other privileges. However, it is not possible to grant a privilege to `PUBLIC` and then revoke this privilege from particular users.

SOLUTION 6.18

▶ Tables which are owned by the user, who is automatically granted all privileges.
▶ Tables where privileges have been granted to **PUBLIC**.
▶ Tables where privileges have been explicitly granted to the user.

SOLUTION 6.19

User `m359` is the owner and is the grantor of the privilege to user `admin`.

User `admin` is the grantee who is granted the privilege by user `m359` and, in turn, is the grantor of the privilege to `faculty`.

`faculty` is the grantee who is finally granted the privilege by user `admin`.

SOLUTION 6.20

First, the view is created by the owner of the `patient` table with:

```
CREATE VIEW patient2 AS
  SELECT *
  FROM patient
  WHERE ward_no = 'w2'
```

Second, the owner grants privileges to user `n113` by using:

```
GRANT SELECT, INSERT, DELETE ON patient2 TO n113
```

SOLUTION 6.21

User `admin` would find the view empty as the **WHERE** clause in the subquery would be false, and so no ward would be chosen. In fact, any user whose authorisation identifier did not end in a nurse's staff number would find the view empty.

SOLUTION 6.22

```
CREATE VIEW my_treatments AS
  SELECT *
  FROM treatment
  WHERE patient_id = USER
```

SOLUTION 6.23

By using `nurse_role`, maintenance is simplified; when identifiers are created for new nurses or destroyed for nurses who are no longer employed by the hospital, only `nurse_role` needs to be updated. If `nurse_role` and `medical_staff_role` were both granted to nurses on an individual basis, then both would need to be changed whenever the list of nurses was altered (and so on, for each role of which the nurses are a part). This would lead to a significant danger of the roles becoming inconsistent.

SOLUTION 7.1

One possible solution is:

```
CREATE FUNCTION hw_fun (p_id CHAR(3))
             RETURNS DECIMAL(4, 1)
  BEGIN
    DECLARE hw_ratio DECIMAL(4, 1);
    SELECT height/weight
      INTO hw_ratio
    FROM patient
    WHERE patient_id = p_id;
    RETURN hw_ratio;
  END
```

create_hw_fun

Alternatively, the body could be expressed as:

```
BEGIN
  DECLARE h DECIMAL(4, 1);
  DECLARE w DECIMAL(4, 1);
  SELECT height, weight
    INTO h, w
  FROM patient
  WHERE patient_id = p_id;
  RETURN h/w;
END
```

SOLUTION 7.2

```
CREATE PROCEDURE hw_proc2 (IN p_id CHAR(3),
                           OUT hw_var DECIMAL(4,1))
  BEGIN
    CALL hw_proc (p_id, hw_var);
    SET hw_var = hw_var * 0.179;
  END
```

SOLUTION 7.3

The value of **SQLSTATE** is updated after each statement, whereas the condition of the **WHILE** statement is evaluated at the beginning of each loop. If the **INSERT** statement executes successfully, then the value of **SQLSTATE** is once again set to 00000 and so cannot itself be used in the loop condition.

SOLUTION 7.4

```
DECLARE tutor CURSOR FOR
  SELECT staff_number, name
  FROM staff, tutors
  WHERE staff.staff_number = tutors.staff_number
    AND student_id = StudentId
```

SOLUTION 7.5

A cursor has a position from when it is open (i.e. a cursor table exists) until it is closed. A cursor position is used indirectly by a routine, in an **OPEN** statement, which sets its initial position, and in a **FETCH** statement, which moves it to the next row.

SOLUTION 7.6

```
DELETE FROM assignment
  WHERE CURRENT OF failed
```

SOLUTION 7.7

The variables within an SQL procedure may be:

▶ declared in the parameter list for a procedure,

▶ declared by a **DECLARE** statement inside the body of the procedure,

▶ a column of a cursor table in a **FOR** statement, defined either in the table to which it belongs or in the cursor definition.

SOLUTION 7.8

Two triggers are required, first for the deletion of a row:

```
CREATE TRIGGER remove_textbook
    AFTER DELETE ON textbook
    REFERENCING OLD AS old_textbook
    FOR EACH ROW
        BEGIN ATOMIC
            UPDATE books_per_course
                SET book_count = book_count - 1
                WHERE books_per_course.course_code = old_textbook.course_code;
        END
```

When a row in the `textbook` table is altered with an `UPDATE` statement, the `book_count` value in `books_per_course` must be decreased for the row containing the book's original `course_code`, and increased for the row containing the book's updated `course_code`.

```
CREATE TRIGGER update_textbook
    AFTER UPDATE ON textbook
    REFERENCING OLD AS old_textbook
               NEW AS new_textbook
    FOR EACH ROW
        BEGIN ATOMIC
            UPDATE books_per_course
                SET book_count = book_count - 1
                WHERE books_per_course.course_code = old_textbook.course_code;
            UPDATE books_per_course
                SET book_count = book_count + 1
                WHERE books_per_course.course_code = new_textbook.course_code;
        END
```

SOLUTION 7.9

The trigger is probably the better solution because it always fires for any change to the `mark` column, irrespective of how it might be changed and by whom.

For the procedure, it is often possible to update the `mark` column in some other way – the owner of the `assignment` table is not restricted at all, and there may be other procedures that update `mark` without the associated change to the `audit_percentage` table.

SOLUTION 7.10

The designers of an application program determine what constitutes a transaction, that is, the statements which together form the unit of work, and the application program requests appropriate action according to whether a transaction succeeds or fails.

A DBMS supports transactions by ensuring that a request for commit makes all changes permanent, and that a request for rollback (which may be implicit if there is a system failure) undoes all the processing that was part of the transaction.

SOLUTION 7.11

The first statements declare the `max_length` variable and update the table `textbook`. Next, the query uses the expression containing the aggregate function `MAX(no_pages)` to set the variable `max_length` to the maximum value of `no_pages` in the updated table (in this case, 380, for the book with code 38572). The `IF` condition checks whether `max_length` is greater than 360. Because `max_length` is greater than 360, the `ROLLBACK` statement is executed, causing the update to be undone.

The transaction fails and the table does not change.

SOLUTION 7.12

1. Retrieve the old value in the **mark** column for the row that is to be updated.
2. Update that value in the **mark** column of the **assignment** table.
3. If the update is satisfactory according to **SQLSTATE**:
   (a) Insert a row into the **audit_percentage** table to record the old value.
   (b) Commit changes.
4. Otherwise, rollback changes.

Note that the possibility of an unsatisfactory update of the **assignment** table is allowed for (whether due to a constraint or to a test as in the activity) but the insertion of a row in the **audit_percentage** table is not expected to fail. However, if there is any system failure, the DBMS will automatically rollback all changes.

SOLUTION 7.13

A serializable execution is valid if it is equivalent to *some* serialized execution of transactions, but two DBMSs may each choose a different ordering and so give different results.

SOLUTION 7.14

An isolation level of 'serializable' means that there is no sharing of data at all with other transactions. Waiting for other transactions to release data may cause unnecessary delays in processing the transaction. Setting a lower isolation level may avoid delays in processing, and the concurrency problems may be acceptable in many circumstances.

Index

A
access control 143, 154
access method 128
ADD 122
aggregate function 24, 47, 83, 91
alias 40, 147
ALL PRIVILEGES 149, 154
ALTER 123
ALTER TABLE 121
alternate key 110
American National Standards Institute (ANSI) 7
AND 31
ANY 71
application programs 171
arithmetic operators (+, −, *, /) 20
AS 20, 76
ASC 53, 129
ATOMIC 161
atomic compound statement 161
attribute 121
authorisation identifier 143
AVG 25, 84

B
base table 9, 132
BEFORE 179
BEGIN 160
BETWEEN 33
BIGINT 17
BINARY LARGE OBJECT 18
BIT 18
BIT VARYING 18
BIT_LENGTH 23
BLOB 18
body (of function) 162

C
CALL (procedure) 165
candidate key 110, 113
Cartesian product 35
CASCADE 114, 121, 138
case sensitivity 11
cast 23–24
CHAR 17
CHARACTER 17
CHAR_LENGTH 23
CHECK 115
classical logic 32, 88
clause 10
CLOB 18
CLOSE 173
column constraint 109, 117
commit 184
COMMIT WORK 185
commutative 64
compare (attributes) 121
comparison operators (=, <, >, <=, >=, <>) 29
composite query 9
compound statement 160, 163
concatenation 20
conceptual data model 118
concurrency 192
concurrent transaction 184, 187, 191
conditional expression 29
conformance 8
connection 146
consistency 183
constraint 110, 118
    check 109, 115–116, 124, 149
    column 109, 117
    dynamic 181
    not null 109–110, 117
    static 181
    table 109, 111
    unique 109, 123
control flow 175
control statement 163
core SQL 8
correlated subquery 116
COUNT 27, 84
CREATE
    domain 119
    function 162
    index 129
    procedure 166
    role 157
    table 96
    trigger 180
    view 133–134
CURRENT DATE 23
CURRENT TIME 23
CURRENT_DATE 23
CURRENT_TIME 23
CURRENT_TIMESTAMP 23
cursor 173
cursor table 176

D
data definition language 95
data independence 129
data manipulation 118
data manipulation language 10
data storage 128
data type 17
    predefined 17, 119
    underlying 119
    user-defined 17
database administrator 143
database connection 143
database procedure 164
DATE 18

DAY 23
dba 150
DECIMAL 17
default value 93, 123
DELETE 103, 177, 179
DELETE privilege 148
dependent row 114, 138
derived table 76, 132
DESC 53, 129
design decisions 98
dialect of SQL 7
direct access 128
dirty read 188
DISTINCT 14
domain (SQL)
    creating 119
    dropping 121
dot notation 147
DOUBLE PRECISION 18
DROP 122
    constraint 123
    domain 121
    function 168
    index 129
    procedure 168
    role 157
    table 99, 105
    trigger 181
    view 137
dynamic constraint 181

E
efficiency 170
END 160
END LOOP 175
entity integrity 92
entry level SQL 8
EXCEPT 62
EXECUTE 170
EXISTS 73
expression 106, 140
extensions to SQL 7

EXTRACT 23
F
FETCH 173
file organisation 128
FLOAT 18
FOR loop 175
foreign key 92, 112, 152
foreign key constraint 149
FROM 11
full outer join 90
function 22, 106, 161
    body 162
    creating 162
    dropping 168

G
grant (privilege) 148, 154
GRANT EXECUTE 170
GRANT ROLE 157
grantee 153
grantor 153
GROUP BY 140
grouping 106
grouping column 47

H
HAVING 49
HOUR 23

I
IBM 7
IF 163
IN 33, 66, 166
inapplicable entry 82
inclusive OR 32
inconsistent data 109
incorrect data 109
index
    creating 129
    dropping 129
inner join 35, 42
INOUT 166

INSERT 100, 179
INSERT privilege 148
INT 17
INTEGER 17, 163
integrity 109
International Organization for Standardization (ISO) 7
INTERSECT 62
INTERVAL 18
INTO 164, 173
IS NOT NULL 83
IS NULL 83
isolation level 192

J
join 35, 74, 140
join condition 37

K
key
    alternate 110
    candidate 110, 113
    foreign 92, 112, 152
    primary 92, 118

L
left outer join 89
LENGTH 22
LIKE 34
local variable 164
locking 191
logic 88
logical operators (AND, OR, NOT) 31
logical processing model 14
logical schema design 126
loop
    for 175
    while 174–175
lost update 188
LOWER 23

M
MAX 28, 84

Index

MIN 28, 84
MINUTE 23
modifying tables 107, 121
MONTH 23

N
natural join 42
nested roles 158
NEW 180
non-participation 125
non-repeatable read 189
NOT 31, 34
NOT NULL 110
not null constraint 109, 117
NULL 82
null value 82
NUMERIC 18
numeric expression 20

O
OLD 180
ON DELETE 114
OPEN 173
optional participation 124
ordering rows 86, 129, 173
OUT 166
outer join
    full 90
    left 89
    right 90
outer query 66
owner (of table) 146

P
parameter 162, 166
password 143
pattern (matching) 34
phantom rows 189
pointer 172
positioned updates 177
posted foreign key 124
predefined data type 17, 119

primary key 92, 118
    defining 97
privileges 148, 181
    granting 148, 154
    revoking 152
problem statement 11
procedure 164
    calling 165
    creating 166
    dropping 168
PUBLIC 152

Q
qualified name 37
query
    composite 9
    expressed in English 12
    specification 10
    statement 10

R
READ COMMITTED 192
READ UNCOMMITTED 192
REAL 18
recovery 184
recursive relationship 41
REFERENCES 112
REFERENCES privilege 148, 151
REFERENCING 181
referencing/referenced table 93, 112
referential action 124, 149, 213
referential constraint 109, 112, 114, 124, 138
referential integrity 91–92, 138
referential integrity rule 92, 113
relational theory 121
RELEASE SAVEPOINT 187
removing a table 99
REPEATABLE READ 192
request 11
RESTRICT 114, 121, 138
restructuring 171
RETURN 163, 165

RETURNS 162–163, 165
revoke privilege 152
right outer join 90
role 156
    creating 157
    dropping 157
    nested 158
rollback 181
ROLLBACK WORK 185
routine 160
row-by-row processing 173

S
SAVEPOINT 186–187
scrollable 177
search condition 28, 49, 115
SECOND 23
security 170
SELECT 11
SELECT privilege 148
self joins 40
sequel 6
sequential access 128
SERIALIZABLE 192
serializable execution 190
serialized execution 191
SET 108
SET DEFAULT 114
SET NULL 114
signatures 168
simple query 9–10
SMALLINT 17
SQL (Structured Query Language) 6
    history 6
    implementation 6
    SQL Anywhere 6
    SQL2 7
    Standard 7
SQLSTATE 174
statement
    atomic compound 161

compound 160, 163
control 163
query 10

static constraint 181

storage schema 128

stored procedure 164

string matching 34

Structured English Query Language 6

Structured Query Language 6

subject table 178

subquery 65–66
correlated 116

SUBSTR 22, 120

SUBSTRING 23

SUM 28, 84

syntactically correct SQL 47

System R 6

T

table
base 9, 132
constraint 109, 111
creating 96
derived 76, 132
dropping 99, 105
owner 146
referenced 93, 112
referencing 93, 112
target 105–106

underlying 133

table constraint 109, 111

target table 105–106

TIME 18

TIMESTAMP 18

transaction 183

trigger
creating 180
dropping 181

two-valued logic 88

U

uncommitted data 188

underlying
base table 133
data type 119

UNION 60

UNION ALL 61

union compatible 61

UNIQUE 110

unique constraint 109, 123

UNKNOWN 86

unknown data 82–83, 86

updatable (view) 140

UPDATE 107, 177, 179

UPDATE privilege 148

UPPER 23

user 144–145, 155

user ID 143

user-defined data type 17

user-defined functions 162

V

VALUE 120

value expressions 19

VALUES 101

VARCHAR 17

variable 164
declaring 164

view 9, 132, 154
creating 133–134
dropping 137
updatable 140
use of 136

W

well-formed SQL 47

WHEN 180

WHERE 28

WHERE CURRENT OF 177

WHILE loop 175

WITH CHECK OPTION 142

WITH GRANT OPTION 153

Y

YEAR 23